Reading &Writing Chinese

Reading &

Revised Edition

Writing

CHINESE

A Guide to the Chinese Writing System:
The Student's 1,020 List
The Official 2,000 List

Revised Edition

by

William McNaughton

and

Li Ying

TUTTLE PUBLISHING
Boston • Rutland, Vermont • Tokyo

Published by Tuttle Publishing,
an imprint of Periplus Editions (HK) Ltd.

Original edition © 1979 Charles E. Tuttle Co., Inc.
Revised edition© 1999 Tuttle Publishing
All rights reserved.

LCC Card No. 77-77699
ISBN 0-8048-3206-4

Distributed by:

Japan
Tuttle Publishing
Yaekari Building, 3rd Floor
5-4-12 Osaki, Shinagawa-ku
Tokyo 141-0032
Tel: (03) 5437 0171; Fax: (03) 5437 0755
Email: tuttle-sales@gol.com

North America, Latin America & Europe
Tuttle Publishing
Airport Industrial Park
364 Innovation Drive
North Clarendon, VT 05759-9436
Tel: (802) 773 8930; Fax: (802) 773 6993
Email: info@tuttlepublishing.com

Asia Pacific
Berkeley Books Pte. Ltd.
130 Joo Seng Road, #06-01/03
Singapore 368357
Tel: (65) 6280 1330; Fax: (65) 6280 6290
Email: inquiries@periplus.com.sg

08 07 06 05 04
8 7 6 5

TABLE OF CONTENTS

PREFACE TO THE REVISED EDITION (1999)

A great deal has happened in China since 1978, when the first edition of *Reading and Writing Chinese* was prepared, and much has changed regarding China's relationship to the world. A new edition seems in order. Such an edition, of course, should reflect those happenings and changes which have influenced the language and which have affected usage and idiom in the language. A new edition should also incorporate the experience of nineteen years of use of the first edition by classroom students and teachers, and by independent students around the world. The most important revisions to *Reading and Writing Chinese* are as set out below.

The Yale system of romanization has been replaced in this edition by the *Hanyu Pinyin* system of romanization, which is official in the People's Republic of China. As a result, the *Hanyu Pinyin* system is also universally employed in foreign newspapers, magazines and books referring to China; and in almost all textbooks of Chinese, as well as in philological aids like grammars and dictionaries, for foreign students.

While the traditional system of 214 radicals is still presented in full, this presentation is supplemented by the introduction of the set of 226 *modern radicals* which are most likely to be useful to the contemporary foreign student of Chinese. The set of modern radicals chosen for presentation is that used in *Han-Ying Cidian/The Chinese-English Dictionary*, prepared by the English Department of the Beijing Foreign Languages Institute (Commercial Press, various editions since 1978). Sets of "modern radicals" have become necessary with the language reform and the simplification of the writing system which has been carried out by the government of the People's Republic. Familiarity with such a set of modern radicals will be extremely useful to foreign students of Chinese, for it will give them quicker, easier, and better access to contemporary dictionaries, many of which are very good—to both English-Chinese and Chinese-Chinese dictionaries.

Furthermore, the student using *Reading and Writing Chinese* should have little trouble mastering the modern radicals. The logic of modern systems, used as the basis for the organization of modern dictionaries and of indexes to modern dictionaries phonetically arranged, is the same as the logic of the traditional system of 214 radicals. The overlap in actual content between the traditional system and the modern system is about 80%, and modern systems differ in negligible ways from one another.

The basic system of presentation of the contents in *Reading and Writing Chinese* has not been changed, for it has worked well over the last nineteen years. However, the contents have been thoroughly revised to bring the contents up-to-date in idiom and usage, and to more accurately reveal the present state of the language. Over 1,100 new combinations of characters have been introduced to give the user a better picture of the range of functions and meanings of the individual characters and to provide the user with a significantly larger vocabulary. A popular feature of the first edition has been retained, namely, the introduction of new characters only in combination with characters already learned, so as to lessen the burden of learning the new combination and to provide a review of the characters already learned. About 140 combinations have been deleted, as being outmoded or otherwise less likely to help students in their progress towards mastery of contemporary written Chinese. Seventy new notes on usage have been added to enhance students' insight into the contemporary state of the written language, its relation to the spoken language, and its place in the culture of the Chinese-speaking world.

With the 1,100 new combinations, the basic 2,000 characters, and the 1,400 combinations retained from the first edition, the student who works his or her way through *Reading and Writing Chinese* will have a vocabulary of about 4,500 items—an adequate foundation for dealing with most contemporary materials.

PREFACE

Learning to read and write modern Chinese with reasonable fluency has, in recent years, become much less of a chore than it used to be. Any student interested in learning to read and write simple everyday Chinese, or in using a knowledge of everyday Chinese as the foundation for later study, can now reach that goal with less strain on his or her time, attention, and memory. Among American teachers of Chinese, a consensus has been developed as to the 1,020 characters most useful for the student to learn first. In addition, an official list of 2000 characters has been published in mainland China for the purpose of adult education.[1] I have prepared *Reading and Writing Chinese* to help students master both these lists as rapidly and easily as possible.[2]

In selecting and arranging the materials in this book, I have been guided by the following principles:

1. To teach the student the most useful characters, as determined by the "Yale 1,020 List" and the official "2,000 List".
2. To present the characters in the order in which they are likely to be most useful; that is, to begin with the most frequently seen characters and to proceed to the less frequently seen ones.
3. To teach the elements of the writing system — the 214 radicals and the "phonetics" (sound components) students will find most valuable in their study of the lists mentioned above.

---

[1] See George A. Kennedy, ed., *Minimum Vocabularies of Written Chinese* (New Haven: Far Eastern Publications, 1954).

[2] *A Guide to Reading and Writing Japanese*, ed. Florence Sakade (Tokyo and Rutland, Vt.: Charles E. Tuttle Co., revised edition, 1961), has played a similar role in the study of Japanese for years.

4. To break down the subject matter (the characters that make up the two lists) into units of information based on the most recent developments in programmed instruction and to arrange these units in order of growing difficulty.

5. To help students master the problem of "look-alike" characters. Through juxtaposition and cross-reference, I have tried to clarify the three main causes of the problem: look-alike radicals, look-alike characters, and different forms of the same radical.[3]

The characters are presented in two groups. The first group presents the basic characters for adult students of Chinese and the elements of the writing system from which these basic characters are made. These are the characters which students, using almost any elementary textbook, will be expected to learn in the first year, or in some cases the first two years, of study. The Yale guidelines, which have become a standard in teaching Chinese in the United States, are followed here.

The second group of characters contains the rest of the characters on the "Yale 1,020 list" and the rest of the 2,000 characters on the officially published China list. In all, this gives the student the 1,500 characters that George A. Kennedy has described as "a good foundation for the Western student of modern Chinese", plus 500 characters officially designated in China as being of most frequent occurrence. It should be noted that another list of 421 characters has been promulgated in China to cover technical terms used by the workers; this list has not been included in the present volume, however, because it is of only slight value to the foreigner studying modern Chinese.

I used earlier versions of this book side by side with the Yale Mirror Series textbooks to teach my Chinese language classes at Oberlin College. Teachers should find it quite easy to use this book with any of the other textbooks now popular in the United States, however, for the logic of the writing system is always the same and the vocabulary in the various series of elementary and intermediate textbooks is virtually identical.

---

[3] See Henry C. Fenn, ed., *Chinese Characters Easily Confused* (New Haven: Far Eastern Publications, 1953).

When I teach, I assign six or seven characters a night as homework. We spend almost all our class time with the spoken Chinese and grammar text, since the format of this character book enables the students to learn on their own. I generally quiz students every day on new characters to enforce regular study habits. These quizzes do not usually take up more than five minutes of regular class time.

Working steadily at this rate, a class can cover all the material in the first character group in two sixteen-week semesters. The class will then know all the characters through *Read Chinese II* and *Read About China*, as well as the frequently seen component radicals and phonetics. More advanced students who have used this book in their first year of Chinese will have a tremendous advantage when they begin to study the characters in the second group. Quite clearly, their knowledge of basic character components will help speed their acquisition of this group, since the presentation here uses these components in programmed sequences.

It has been my experience that students can be safely given *Reading and Writing Chinese* on their first day of Chinese study. Far from discouraging students, the characters and the writing system seem to stimulate enthusiasm and to increase motivation.

For valuable help I am indebted to various editors of the Charles E. Tuttle Publishing Company. I have incurred innumerable debts to students who used these texts in earlier forms for many years in my Chinese classes at Oberlin College, but Howard Spendelow and John Dove deserve special mention for the amount and quality of their contributions. I am also indebted to colleagues who have suggested changes and improvements in the earlier versions. I should acknowledge the importance to this work of *Minimum Vocabularies of Written Chinese*, edited by George A. Kennedy (New Haven: Far Eastern Publications, 1954), and of *Jianhuazi Zongbiao Jianzi* (Peking: Wenzi Gaige Chubanshe, 1965).

— WILLIAM MCNAUGHTON

STUDENT'S GUIDE

The Writing System

The basis of the traditional Chinese writing system is 214 elements often referred to as "radicals". These radicals are used both independently, or as part of more complex characters. The Chinese also use radicals to organize traditional dictionaries, use them to organize some modern dictionaries, and use the radicals to supplement the phonetic organization of other modern dictionaries. Traditional dictionaries begin with one-stroke radicals and characters classified under one-stroke radicals, and end with a seventeen-stroke radical and characters classified under it. The widely used modern Chinese-English dictionary, *Han-Ying Cidian* (of which more will be said below) begins with one-stroke radicals and characters classified under them and ends, before a special category of eleven "left-over characters", with a fourteen-stroke radical and the characters classified under it. In using the writing system to organize dictionaries or to create supplementary radical indexes for dictionaries, the makers take every character which is not itself a radical, determine which of the radicals within it is logically the most important, and then classify the character under that radical in the dictionary or index.

Every time a new character was created to represent some word of the spoken language, the character was formed according to one of six principles. Classifying Chinese writing according to these six principles, we can say that six—and only six—kinds of characters exist: (1) pictures, (2) symbols, (3) sound-loans, (4) sound-meaning compounds, (5) meaning-meaning compounds, and (6) re-clarified compounds.

If we understand these six principles, we will be able to see *why* every new character we study means what it does. Instead of seeming a capricious aggregation of strokes set down by an equally capricious pen, the character will reflect a logical system for representing words and concepts: each new character will be a combination of familiar elements.

Let us look at each of the six kinds of Chinese characters.

1. *Pictures.* Some Chinese characters are mere pictures of things. The character for "man" is a simple stick drawing of a man 人. The character for "child" or "baby" is a drawing of an infant with an open fontanel 兒. Sometimes, though, the modern character is a very stylized picture of what it represents We then have to look into the history of the character before we can see the resemblance clearly. The character for "moon" 月 used to look like this 𝕯; the character for "eye" 目 like this ⌑.

2. *Symbols.* Some Chinese characters are symbols—some more, some less arbitrary—for the concept to which they refer. Some examples of symbols are: 上 "above", 下 "below", 一 "one", 二 "two", 三 "three".

3. *Sound-loans.* Some Chinese characters stand for a word which is, or once was, pronounced the same as another but with a different meaning, like "feet" and "feat". This type of character, a picture or symbol for one of two homonyms, was borrowed to represent the companion homonym, too; the context was relied on to make the meaning clear. For example, the words for "scorpion" and "10,000" were once homonyms. The character 萬, now used to write "10,000," originally meant "scorpion" but was borrowed for "10,000" since there was little danger of confusing the two meanings in context. You can probably see that it would have been inconvenient to write "10,000" in the same symbolic notation used to write the numbers "one", "two", and "three".

4. *Sound-meaning compounds.* Sometimes one part of a Chinese character gives a hint about the meaning, while another part gives a hint about the pronunciation. For example, the character 包, "to wrap", is pronounced *bāo*. (The pronunciation of the romanization and tone markings used here are explained in the section beginning on page 27). If this character is combined with the character 魚 "fish", the result is a new character 鮑 "salted fish", pronounced *bào*. The "fish" component suggests the meaning, and the "wrap" component (*bāo*) suggests the sound.

5. *Meaning-meaning compounds.* Sometimes two characters are put together to form a new character whose meaning derives from some

13

logic in the juxtaposition of the two component characters. The character 女 "woman" beside the character 子 "child" forms 好, a character that means "to love" or "to be lovable, to be likable, to be good". Although the logic in such a juxtaposition is usually not obvious enough to allow you to figure out the meaning of a new character, it is usually a great help when trying to remember a character you have seen only once.

6. *Reclarified compounds.* At various times in the history of the written language, a scribe has wanted to better "control" the meaning of a character he was using, either because the character—by sound-loan perhaps—had come to stand for a number of different words or because the word the character represented had a number of different meanings. In doing this, the scribe could add to the existing character either to clarify the word to which it referred, or to pinpoint the meaning intended in the particular context. For example, the character for "scorpion" 萬, which we saw above, was later re-clarified when it was used to represent "scorpion" (rather than "10,000") by adding the "bug" radical 虫 to produce the new character 蠆 that always meant "scorpion" and only "scorpion". The character 廷 *tíng* stood for "court"—whether it was the king's court or the court in someone's front yard. Eventually someone added the "lean-to" radical 广, which is a picture of a roof and a wall, to distinguish the king's court (庭 *tíng*) from the ordinary citizen's front yard (廷 *tíng*). Some of these re-clarified compounds will, in their new guise, be simple sound-meaning compounds, and some of them—if the re-clarified character itself was already a sound-meaning compound—will be sound-meaning compounds with one component to suggest the sound and two components to suggest the meaning.[4]

---

[4] Bernhard Karlgren identifies dozens of such characters in *Analytic Dictionary of Chinese and Sino-Japanese* (Paris: Paul Geuthner, 1923). Chao Yuen Ren treats reclarified compounds as a sub-class of sound-meaning compounds: see *Mandarin Primer* (Cambridge: Harvard University Press, 1961), pp. 61–63. Traditionally, the sixth of the six principles was something called *zhuanzhu*, and whether or not this had anything to do with reclarified compounds is uncertain, since there is a great deal of dispute about the correct interpretation and reference of *zhuanzhu*.

Explanatory Notes

Below there appears an annotated character entry. It has been slightly modified from the actual entry in this book to show the full range of information for characters in the first character group.

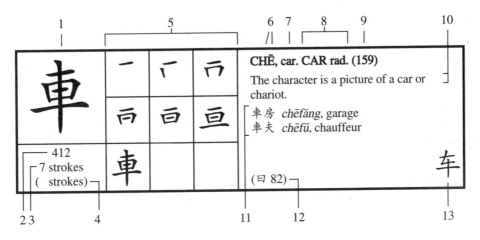

KEY:

1. the character
2. character serial number
3. stroke count
4. if there is a difference between the actual number of strokes as written by hand and the official number of strokes used in traditional dictionaries, the official number will appear in parentheses here. See the discussion of stroke and form discrepancy on pages 16–17.
5. stroke-order diagram
6. pronunciation and tone
7. character definition
8. radical information
9. radical number (an "H" before the radical number means that the character is a "modern radical", used to organise the *Han-Ying Cidian/ The Chinese-English Dictionary*: see below)
10. character explanation
11. character combinations with pronunciation and meaning
12. Since characters may have more than nine strokes, it has sometimes been necessary to add *in toto* to the stroke-order diagram of the main

15

character an element that is itself a character. (The element and serial number shown in this sample are provided only to show how a reference to an element added *in toto* will appear.) If such a reference is missing, either that element's stroke order is obvious or it can be found in one of the preceding two character entries.

13. Simplified character

Understanding the Entries

You should try to keep in mind that a Chinese character is not what we think of as a word in English, and that Chinese words for which the characters stand are often subject to different kinds of syntactic restriction. In fact, what we consider nouns, verbs, adjectives, and adverbs in English are, in classical Chinese, all considered one part of speech—any noun can be a verb, adjective, or adverb. Owing to the unavoidable use in this book of English articles, infinitives, suffixes, and the like, you may be misled into too narrow an interpretation of a character. These explicit definitions are provided for clarity, but you should always be aware that they really represent only the most basic outline of a character's "meaning".

Most of the punctuation marks used in the characters' explanatory blocks are grammatically logical. However, I have also adopted a few rules of my own to help the reader/student. Semicolons are used to distinguish meaning "groups". Semicolons are also used after a character's romanized reading when a character's usage rather than the meaning is given. In addition to their occasional use with slang terms, or for clarity, quotation marks are used around character-compound definitions that are contextually proper in English but which cannot be derived from the characters themselves. For example, the Chinese use a character for "red" 紅 and the character for "tea" 茶 to write what in English is called "black tea". Since the more literal definition "red tea" would be meaningless, I have used quotation marks in the definition of the character compound as follows:

紅茶 *hóngchá*, "black" tea

Stroke and Form Discrepancy

Each character has a traditional stroke count based on the character's placement in traditional dictionaries. Small discrepancies—almost always of one stroke—sometimes exist between this traditional stroke count and

16

the actual count used when the character is handwritten. Such discrepancies are indicated in parentheses throughout the presentation of the first group of characters. The most devastating problem for beginner students, however, is a change in shape and stroke count that occurs when a radical or character is used as an element to form a more complex character. I have therefore treated as entirely separate elements, those characters whose shape changes may pose an identification problem. This treatment reflects more accurately the true nature of the writing system and has resulted in only about 40 characters being added to the text.[5]

For example, the radical 阜 , when used as an element of another character, becomes 阝 , a combined form that appears separately in this text as character 76. Appearing in the small box below the character is "3 strokes (8 strokes)". This means that although this form of the radical is actually written with three strokes, its independent form takes eight strokes; thus, all characters with 阝 as the radical component will appear among the eight-stroke radicals in a traditional Chinese dictionary.

Such anomalies have been eliminated from most modern dictionaries, and what once were different forms of the same radical are now treated as different radicals. The radical system, that is, has been rationalized according to the principle of "what you see is what you get". Dictionaries, therefore, are now easier to use (see below for more on modern dictionaries).

Problems of correct character identification also result from the fact that typeset forms often differ from the handwritten forms that are usually learned first. Always compare a character in a typeset compound with its handwritten counterpart as you work through this book. The typeset list below provides the most common of these variant forms. Numbers

---

[5] Also, twenty-two characters are identified as "heavenly stems" or "earthly branches." These "stems" and "branches" are characters which are sometimes used in Chinese in various special ways of reckoning, calculation, and enumeration. The student who delves into Chinese history will need to know these twenty-two characters, because the traditional way of giving dates makes use of them. They are also used in fortune-telling books and works of astrology in Chinese communities outside of the People's Republic, e.g. Hong Kong.

refer to the serial number of characters in the first group; page numbers are for characters in the second group.

忄	67	令	284	曷	924
八	88	直	301	肖	939
入	152	眞	302	兪	974
辶	171	罒	338	掃	p.263
艹	192	示	480	歡	p.268
靑	198	氵	564	卽	p.283

Simplified Characters

In attempting to deal with the need for adult education and the complexity of the Chinese writing system, the mainland government has simplified many of the characters used for centuries. Traditional principles used for making characters have been retained in making up new short forms. For example, in the short form 牺 "sacrifice", the traditional form 犧 has been shortened by simply replacing the complicated sound-compound 羲 with the simple sound-component 西 . The "cow" radical 牛 appears in both the short and traditional forms because the original meaning of the character was "sacrificial animal." Likewise, the traditional character 廳 *tīng* "room, hall", has been simplified to 厅 mainly by substituting for the complicated sound-component 聽 the simpler sound-component 丁 . Students who understand the logic of the traditional writing system and who have mastered the components of its characters will find that they attain mastery of the short forms much more easily.

In the system of simplified characters, we can find new sound-loans: 里 *lǐ* "village" for 裏 *lǐ* "lining, inside"; 面 *miàn* "face" for 麵 *miàn* "flour;" and 象 *xiàng* "elephant" for 像 *xiàng* "to look like."[6] We can find new sound-meaning compounds: 吓 for 嚇 *xià* "to scare." And we can find new meaning-meaning compounds: 宝 "jade" under "roof" for 寶 "jade", "crock", and "cowrie" under "roof" — standing for the word *bǎo*, "be precious, be valuable." Other techniques of simplification include the

---

[6] The student may notice that the new sound-loan character is often formed, as in the examples given here, simply by removing the meaning element from an old sound-meaning compound.

following. One, the use of simple variant forms which were already widely used in casual and informal writing, such as 头 for 頭, *tóu* "head;" and 个 for 個, *gè*, a measure-word or "enumerator." Two, the use of forms from the so-called "grass script"—a kind of "Chinese shorthand"—such as 马 for 馬 *mǎ* "horse;" and 东 for 東 *dōng* "east." Three, the use of one part of a complex character to stand for the whole character, such as 医 for 醫 *yī* "to heal;" of 离 for 離 *lí* "to depart from;" of 奋 for 奮 *fèn* "to rouse." Four, where the character is composed of several repeated elements, to devise a new character in which the repeated element appears only once, such as 虫 for 蟲 *chóng* "bug, worm" and 断 for 斷 *duàn* "break into segments." Five, the replacement of a complex element with a simple element such as 又 —as in 欢 for 歡 *huān* "be pleased;" as in 难 for 難 *nán* "be difficult;" and as in 对 for 對 *duì* "to face."

We have used the unsimplified forms (most of which are still in use, in mainland China, too) as the basis for this book's presentation. Officially adopted simplified forms have been included since students who want to read what is now published on the mainland will have to learn them sooner or later. To learn only these short forms, however, is a great mistake. In so doing, students effectively cut themselves off from much traditional Chinese literary and historical material (except where such material has been reprinted on the mainland in short-form versions) and have cut themselves off from many of the Chinese books available in Western libraries, which were printed before the process of simplification began. Taiwan and Hong Kong still use the traditional characters.

Modern Dictionaries

After the simplification of many characters, the traditional 214-radical system of organizing dictionaries did not work as well as it had. Furthermore, simplification in one area led to the perception that simplification in another area, like the organization of dictionaries, might be a good thing, too. The modern, classic, encyclopedic dictionary, *Ci Hai* (Shanghai: Shanghai Dictionary Publishers, 1979: 2,216 pages), for example, is organized exactly like a traditional dictionary except that the dictionary's makers have modified the traditional radical system to get a new system of 250 radicals—a system which can be very quickly learned by anyone who knows the traditional system presented in *Reading and Writing Chinese*.

Many modern Chinese-Chinese dictionaries are organized alphabetically, according to the standard spelling (*Hanyu Pinyin*) of the Beijing pronunciation (*Putonghua*, "Mandarin") of the character. The order of entries follows the English alphabetical order, starting with "A" and ending with "Z". Such phonetic organization works fine until you meet a character you don't know how to pronounce—a common experience for foreign students, of course (but it also happens with Chinese readers). So all dictionaries organized phonetically, as just described, also have an index—an index organized according to some modern adaptation of the traditional radical system. There is no universally accepted adaptation, however, so different dictionaries use slightly different radical systems. All such systems, however, are derived from the traditional system of 214 radicals, all of them overlap to a great degree, and all follow quite closely the logic of the traditional system.

For collateral presentation in this book, the authors have chosen the system of 226 radicals plus a supplementary category, which the makers of the *Han-Ying Cidian/The Chinese-English Dictionary* have used to organize their dictionary (prepared by the English Department of the Beijing Foreign Languages Institute, published by Commercial Press in various editions since 1978). That dictionary is probably the most widely-used Chinese-English dictionary in the world and is deemed likely to be the dictionary most often consulted by users of *Reading and Writing Chinese*. The radicals of *Han-Ying Cidian* are identified in *Reading and Writing Chinese* by an "H" plus the serial number in *Han-Ying Cidian's* system of 226 radicals. And on the back endpapers there appears a chart of these 226 "modern radicals" plus a supplementary category, as used to index *Han-Ying Cidian*.

Character Combinations

Individual characters themselves—each of which in general represents a single syllable of the spoken language—may occur in combination with other characters to denote Chinese words and expressions of two or more syllables. For example, a common expression for "woman" in the modern spoken language is the two syllable *nǚrén*, written with the characters for "woman" 女 *nǚ* and "person" 人 *rén*. Many of these common combinations are given in this book so that you will get used to seeing the characters within important expressions and words. Learning the combinations in which a character occurs can be a valuable aid to understanding that character. Moreover, since the characters used in these combinations are restricted to those that have already been presented in the text, these combinations provide review as well as usage examples.

Some examples are also given of a favourite stylistic device in Chinese—four-character set expressions. Learning these four-character set expressions will be useful to the student in the same way as learning two-character combinations, and it will also prepare the student to deal with them when he or she encounters them or similar four-character expressions in discourse, written or spoken. Finally, practice with two-character combinations and four-character set expressions will tend to break down the illusion, which the writing system so insistently encourages, that Chinese is a monosyllabic language. To some extent it may be so, but the disyllable is an extremely important unit in modern Chinese, and the four-character expression is also important in anything above the level of "survival Chinese".

Phonetic Series

When a certain character has been used to give the sound in a number of sound-meaning compounds, a group of characters emerges, each of which has a different meaning but contains the same sound-component. The different meanings are established, of course, by using a different meaning-component in each character. Such a group of characters is called a phonetic series, and students have often found that learning becomes more rapid when they study such character groups. In the second group of characters we have therefore introduced common characters as part of a phonetic series, if the characters belong to an important series. For example, the character "wrap" 包 bāo, mentioned above, is the sound-component for a number of common characters that appear in this book: 飽 , 抱 , 袍 , 泡 , 砲 .

The Chinese Writing System as Cultural Artifact

There are, more or less, thirteen dialects of the Chinese language—spoken languages which differ from one another as much as English, German and Dutch differ from one another, or as French, Spanish, Italian and Portuguese differ. The remarkable thing about the Chinese writing system,

21

including the modern form of it which is studied in this book, is that a literate native-speaker of one dialect can write down anything he might reasonably want to communicate, and a literate native-speaker of any other dialect will immediately understand—although if the two tried to speak in their native dialects, neither would understand the other. That is, with the Chinese writing system, you can simultaneously write down a message in thirteen different languages![7] There has never been anything else like it in human history.

Some foreign students, initially vexed when they see that the Chinese writing system is somewhat more complicated than their own, think that the Chinese should switch to an alphabet. To do so, however, would eliminate that increment of universal intelligibility which exists in China. Furthermore, while it does take some months longer for a Chinese child to master the writing system than it does an American or French child, say, to master their own writing systems, in the long run there is little difference. Japan, where the writing system is based on the Chinese system, has one of the highest literacy rates in the world (illiteracy in Japan is about one-fifth that of the United States). And James Traub notes that only slightly more than four percent of Taiwanese fifth graders and slightly more than ten percent of Japanese scored as low as the average American fifth grader on a battery of reading tests.[8]

The foreign student should also consider that the logic of the Chinese writing system, as sketched on pages 12-14 above, has stimulated a number of outstanding Western thinkers, from Leibniz in his work on the Calculus to Eisenstein on montage. A proposal was floated after World War II to have traffic signs all over the world prepared in Chinese "ideograms". Although derided by Yale's widely respected sinologist, the late George A. Kennedy, who called the suggestion "deranged", something like that has actually happened, with modern pictures, symbols, and especially "meaning-meaning compounds" now to be seen on traffic signs and other public notices around the world: school crossing…men working…slippery

---

[7] True regionalisms and some dialectal slang are not reached by the writing system, but the relative unimportance and the ephemeral nature of slang and regionalisms make this a trivial exception.

[8] James Traub, "It's Elementary," *New Yorker*, 17 July 1995, 78 (74–79).

when wet...steep hill ahead...slow-moving vehicles, keep right...no smoking...no eating or drinking on the subway...do not play boom boxes on the beach...danger of falling rocks...watch out for deer...low-flying aircraft ahead...emergency fire exit, this way... There is a complex ideogram on the bus boats in Venice which clearly says, in just four elements, "sit down or you will block the captain's view and make it difficult for him to navigate the boat safely!" Many computer icons, too are a modern form of ideography, universally intelligible to computer users around the world, whatever their native language. So far, however, these international systems of modern ideograms have not developed sound-loans, sound-meaning compounds, or re-clarified compounds.

Study Methods

Each traditional radical introduced in this book is assigned a number in parentheses (radicals used to organize the modern *Han-Ying Cidian* are identified, as noted, by the letter "H" preceding the number). This number is the radical number and indicates where the radical occurs within the sequence of 214 (or 226) radicals. Every effort you make to memorize the number, at least for radicals having two, three, four, five, or six strokes, will pay off in time saved after you start to use dictionaries. Just as it is a great time-saver with Western-language dictionaries to know approximately where "F" occurs in the alphabet (and whether it occurs before or after "M", for example) these numbers serve the same purpose in Chinese. You or your teacher should make a decision early on about the question of which set of radical numbers you should try and memorize. (All things being equal, the authors feel that the "H" set may be most useful to modern students.) This statement applies only to the radicals' serial numbers: the meaning of all radicals should be learned. The pronunciation should be learned, of course, for radicals which still function in written Chinese as independent characters.

You are also advised, when first learning a character, to be conscious of all the radicals that appear within it. Say aloud the radicals while writing a new character. For example, say "knight-eye-cowrie" while writing 賣 "sell" (character 135), or "grass-mouth-mouth-dove-yawn" while writing 歡 "to be pleased" (character 194). Such incantations may be of considerable help in recalling characters to memory three or four days after first encountering them.

You should read the explanation of the sources of new characters, but you need not formally study these explanations unless (as sometimes happens) you become fascinated by the written Chinese character itself. In that case you may want to learn all the explanations given and even to carry your own studies further afield into the various books which present such explanations in greater (and on occasion even fanciful) detail.

You can easily use *Reading and Writing Chinese* as a programmed textbook. Cover the character with a blank piece of paper placed along the vertical line that separates the character from the box containing its pronunciation and meaning. Then try to write down the character, and immediately after doing so, pull the answer sheet away and compare the character you have written with the character in the book. If you have written the character incorrectly, take note of the error or errors and write the character correctly several times before proceeding to the next one. After working to the bottom of a page in this way, reverse the procedure and try to write down the pronunciation and meaning while looking only at the character. Immediately check your work against the correct pronunciation and meaning that appear in the text.

How to Write the Characters

The Chinese learn to write characters by using an easy and effective method. The essential ingredient of this method is the fixed order in which the strokes of a character are written. Although Chinese people occasionally disagree among themselves about minor details, the method has been developed and perfected through centuries of experience. Follow the stroke-order diagrams presented in this book in order to acquire proper habits early, and remember to keep your characters uniform in size. The rules below explain the method in general.

1. Top to bottom:

三 →	一	二	三	
累 →	冂	田	罗	累
言 →	丶	亠	訁	言

2. Left to right:

川 →	丿	刂	川	
他 →	亻	仃	仳	他
誰 →	言	訁	誰	誰

3. Upper left corner to lower right corner:

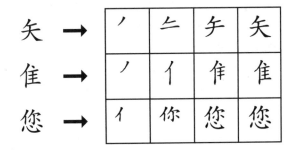

矢 →	丿	느	仁	矢
隹 →	丿	亻	隹	隹
您 →	亻	你	您	您

4. Outside to inside:

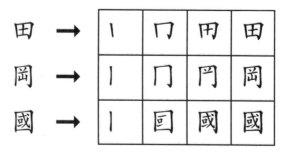

5. When two or more strokes cross, horizontal strokes before perpendicular strokes:

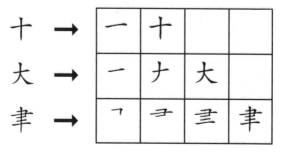

6. Slanting stroke to the left before slanting stroke to the right:

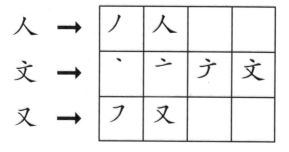

7. Center stroke before symmetrical wings:

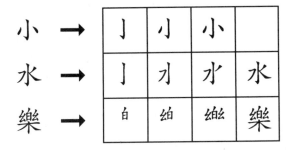

The Pronunciation of Chinese

The system used in this revised edition of *Reading and Writing Chinese* to write Chinese with Roman letters is the *Hanyu Pinyin* system which is standard in mainland China and is now used almost everywhere else in the world, too, in newspapers, magazines, books, textbooks, and so on. The *Hanyu Pinyin* system is as follows:

1. The following letters are pronounced like their English equivalents: *f, k, l, m, n, p, s,* (except in "sh") *t, w,* and *y.*
2. The following letters are pronounced like the English sounds indicated: *a* (except as described in 8, below), as in *father*; *i,* as in *machine* (except when appearing immediately after *u*—see end of this paragraph—or when appearing immediately after *c, r, s, sh, z,* or *zh*: see 9. below); *o* as in *worn*; *ai* as in *aisle*; and *ui,* like *wei* in weight.
3. The following combinations are pronounced like the English sounds indicated: *ao,* like *ow* in *how*; *ou,* like *o* in *so*; and *e* (except *e* after *i* or *y*: see 8, below), like *o* in done.
4. The following letters are pronounced as explained: *b,* like *p in* spy; *d,* like *t* in *sty*; and *g,* like *k sky*; that is, like English *p, t,* and *k* but with less aspiration (cp. 1, above).
5. The following letters are pronounced as described: *h,* with more friction than the English *h*; *u* (but not *ü,* and also not when followed by another vowel or pair of vowels, or when preceded by *j, q,* or by *i* or *y*), like *oo* in *moon* but with the lips rounded and the tongue back; *u* preceded by *i* or *y,* like *o* in *so*; *u* preceded by *j, q,* or *x,* round the

lips to say *oo* as in *moon* but try to pronounce instead *i* as in *machine* (cp. *ü* in 8, below); *z*, like *ds* in *cads*; and *c*, like *ts* in *it's hot*.

6.   The following letters and combinations are pronounced as described: *sh* as in *shred*, tongue very far back; *ch*, tongue flat against roof of mouth, very far back; *zh*, like *ch* just described but with less breath; and *r*, tongue flat against roof of mouth, far back—like a *j* and *r* pronounced together.

7.   The following letters are pronounced as described: *j*, like English *j* but with tongue tip forward where teeth meet; *q*, like *j* just described but with more breath; and *x*, tongue tip against back of lower teeth (like a lisping English *s*).

8.   The following letters are pronounced as described: *e* after *i* or *y*, as in *yet*; *ü*, round the lips to say *oo* as in *moon* but try to pronounce instead *i* as in *machine*; *ü*, plus *e*, like *ü* just described plus English *e* in *yet*; *a* after *i* or *y* and before *n* (but not before *ng*), like *e* in *yet*; and *a* after *ü* and before *n*, like *e* in *yet*.

9.   When *i* comes immediately after *c*, *r*, *s*, or *z*, it indicates that the mouth and tongue are held in place while the consonant is pronounced without a vowel (but with a tone: see next section: we could say that 'the consonant becomes its own vowel'); that is, *si* is just a hiss, *zi* is just a buzz, and *ri* is a kind of purr; when *i* comes immediately after *ch* or *zh*, the resulting syllables *chi* and *zhi* are pronounced as explained in 6, above, but they slide towards the *r* sound and get a tone—rather like the first syllable of *gerbil* and *Churchill*, respectively; and when *i* comes immediately after *sh*, the resulting syllable *shi* sounds like English *shirr* but with the *sh* described above, and with a tone.

10. The letter *u* when followed by another vowel or pair of vowels is pronounced like English *w*; the combination *iu* at the end of syllables is pronounced about like the American greeting *Yo!*; and *yi* is pronounced like the first syllable of *easy*.

To use this system of writing Chinese (*Putonghua*) with Roman letters, the student needs to know about three further features: word-division, the occasional use of apostrophes, and the placement of tone-marks (see below) over vowels when the syllable has more than one vowel-letter (a, e, i, o, u and *ü*) in it. Chinese is written in 'the real world' with Chinese characters, not with Roman letters, so the system of romanization has not been 'worn smooth' by those great creators and molders of language, the folk. Many details, therefore, have not been worked out; the division into words is one of them. For example, should the expression for "overseas Chinese", composed of *Huá* (Chinese) + *qiáo* (person or people living abroad), be written *Huá qiáo* or *Huáqiáo?* I recommend that the student follow the advice I give to my students of translation at City University of Hong Kong: look it up in a good dictionary, like *Han-Ying Cidian*! (It's *Huáqiáo*, one word.) Apostrophes are used, when necessary, to avoid ambiguity. The term *jianai*, for example, could be read as *jia nai* or *jian ai*, so an apostrophe is added to clarify: *jian'ai*. As to the correct placement of tone-marks when a syllable has two or more vowel-letters in it, the situation is fairly simple, and practice and observation will help a great deal. The letters *a* and *e* always get the tone-mark in combinations, and *o* always gets the tone-mark except when the combination is *ao* or *iao*, in which case the *a* gets it. When *i* and *u* appear together—as *iu* or as *ui*—whichever one comes second gets the tone-mark.

Tone

In addition to its vowels and consonants, a word in modern Chinese has a characteristic "tone". The tone of a word is very important because it allows our ears to discriminate among words that have the same vowels and consonants. Tones result from changes in pitch which the speaker produces with the vocal cords while pronouncing the vowels and consonants. The difficulty of learning these tones has been much exaggerated. In fact, the system of tones in *Putonghua* ("Mandarin", the standard, or most commonly studied, spoken language of China, based on the dialect of the capital, Beijing) is actually one of the simplest of all Chinese dialects.

In *Putonghua* there are four tones (or five, if we count the 'zero' tone: see below). These tones are indicated in *Hanyu Pinyin* by the tone marks ū, ú, ǔ, and ù, written over the syllable like the accent in French (see above). Thus, *mā* is *m* + *a* (as described above) pronounced in the first tone, *má* is *m* + *a* pronounced in the second tone, and so on. The way in which the speaker uses the vocal chords to change the pitch can be written on a musical staff, as below. Note that it is only the contour of the pitch which determines the tone; thus a man's normal first tone will be a bit lower than a woman's. Pitch will normally be somewhere near the centre of the speaking voice and will vary according to the individual and his or her mood.[9]

The description of tones given here is the simplest and is the one most often presented in texts. It is intended to enable the student to pronounce words in isolation. In normal speech the tone may disappear from a syllable, and the syllable will be pronounced in a "neutral" or "zero" tone. In such cases in this book, the tone-marks have been omitted. In the case of two third tones in succession in a single expression, native speakers automatically change the first of them to a second tone: *hěn hǎo* becomes *hén hǎo*. We have indicated such changes in this book if the expression is a very common one. Some very common words change their tones regularly, depending on the tone of the following word, and in these cases we have indicated the tone appropriate to each expression. Problems of words in discourse are, however, more properly a subject for a textbook of modern spoken Chinese, which you are urged to consult for more specific information.

---

[9] The musical diagram is from Chao Yuen Ren, *A Grammar of Spoken Chinese* (Berkeley: University of California Press, 1968), p. 26.

1,062 BASIC CHARACTERS

and

Elements of the Writing System

ノ	ノ			PIĚ. left-falling stroke. LEFT rad. (4)(H4)
1 1 stroke				

人	ノ	人		RÉN, man. MAN rad. (9)(H23)
2 2 strokes				*Rén* is a picture — a rough stick drawing of a man. It occurs independently as a character and means "man" or "person". Learn to distinguish the "man" rad. from the "enter" rad. 入 (152, below).

丨	丨			SHÙ, downstroke. DOWN rad. (2)(H3)
3 1 stroke				Anciently, the "down" rad. was pronounced "*gǔn*", but nowadays everybody reads it as "*shù*", meaning "the vertical stroke." Learn to distinguish from the "hook" rad. (13, below).

亻	ノ	亻		RÉN, man. MAN rad. (9)(H21)
4 2 strokes				While traditional dictionaries classify this form as a special case of the "man" rad. (2, above), modern dictionaries make it a separate rad. It does not occur by itself as a character; it only occurs in combination with other rads. or with sound-components, as a part of characters. Sometimes called "side-man."

				YĬ, twist; the second "heavenly stem."
∟ (5, 1 stroke)				TWIST rad. (5)(H7; in H, the form 乙 — see p. 281a, below – and also the form ㇄ are classified as rad. 7)
				Yĭ occurs in early texts and means "fish guts." The character may originally have been a picture. Note that the character itself is bent and twisted.

				YĚ, also
也 (6, 3 strokes)				Note that 也 has "down" and "twist" in it. The other stroke is not a rad. in traditional dictionaries. In the form ㇆, however, it is used in modern dictionaries as a rad. (e.g., as H5). The history of 也 is very complicated; it involves the confusion of at least three different characters.

				TĀ, he, him
他 (7, 5 strokes)				他 is a sound-meaning compound. The "man" rad. (here, "sideman") suggests the meaning, the right half, *yě* (6, above) at one time suggested the sound, but now it is not such a good phonetic. Compare with 12 and 16, below.

				YĪ (YĬ, YÌ), one. ONE rad. (1)(H2)
一 (8, 1 stroke)				一 "one", 二 "two" (9, below), and 三 "three" (10, below) are probably the three simplest symbol-characters in the language. As a rad., this form is called 橫 *héng* "the horizontal stroke" (see p. 296a, below). 一 is pronounced as *yī* before a word in the fourth tone, and as *yì* before words in the first, second, or third tones.

				ÈR, two. TWO rad. (7)(H11)
二 (9, 2 strokes)				

三	一	二	三	**SĀN, three.**
10 3 strokes				

女	く	乆	女	**NǓ, woman. WOMAN rad. (38)(H73)** 女 is a picture — a rough stick drawing of a woman. It occurs independently as a character and means "woman." 女人 *nǚrén*, woman
11 3 strokes				

她	く	乆	女	**TĀ, she, her** This character is a sound-meaning compound. The "woman" rad. suggests the meaning, and *yě*, as in 他 *tā*, "he," (7, above) once suggested the sound. Note the logic in the writing system; the "man" rad. occurs in the character for "he;" the "woman" rad. occurs in the character for "she."
	如	妙	她	
12 6 strokes				

亅	亅			**JUÉ, hook. HOOK rad. (6)** The "hook" rad. has a little hook on the bottom of it. It differs from the "down" rad. (3, above): the "down" rad has no little hook. Note that *jué* is not a rad. in modern dictionaries, e.g. H. The hook occurred naturally, an elegant movement of the wrist, with the traditional brush; not so with the modern ball-point pen.
13 1 stroke				

扌	一	丨	扌	**SHǑU, hand. HAND rad. (64)(H55)** This form of the "hand" rad. does not occur by itself; it only occurs as a part of characters. We can call it the "side-hand" (some dictionaries call it 提手旁 *tí shǒu páng*, "side-hand with a rising stroke" (=the third stroke; 提 is 916, below). Distinguish from "thumb" 寸 (186, below) and "then" 才 (596).
14 3 strokes (4 strokes)				

牛	⟍	⟋	牛	**NIÚ, ox, cow; a family name. COW rad. (93)(H110)**
	牛			*Niú* is a picture. In older forms, it is easy to see a cow with horns drawn from the front. This form of the "cow" rad. occurs only as a part of characters; another form, 牛 (260, below) occurs as an independent character.
15 4 strokes				

牠	⟋	牛	牛	**TĀ, it**
	牛⟋	牛勿	牠	The student should compare *tā* with 他 "he" (7, above) and with 她 "she" (12, above). This *tā* "it" has the "cow" rad. for meaning; as in 他 and 她, the sound of 牠 "it" was once suggested by 也 (6, above). Note that *tā*, "it," is now usually written 它, and *tā* with the "cow" rad. is rarely seen.
16 7 strokes				

了	⟍	了		**LE; a particle that goes after verbs or after sentences; *le* basically means "changed status" or "completed action;" LIǍO, to finish, to conclude.**
17 2 strokes				

子	⟍	了	子	**ZǏ, child; first of the twelve "earthly branches." CHILD rad. (39)(H74)**
				子 is a picture. In older forms, it quite clearly resembles a child. 子 occurs often as an independent character and as a suffix to many nouns.
18 3 strokes				子女 *zǐnǚ*, sons and daughters; children

好	⟨	⟨	女	**HǍO, be good, be well; HÀO, to consider good; to like, to love**
	女⟋	女了	好	好 is a meaning-meaning compound. "Woman" beside "child" suggests "goodness, well-being, something desirable."
19 6 strokes				好人 *hǎorén*, good person; healthy person; a "good guy" who tries to get along with everybody, often sacrificing principle to do so.

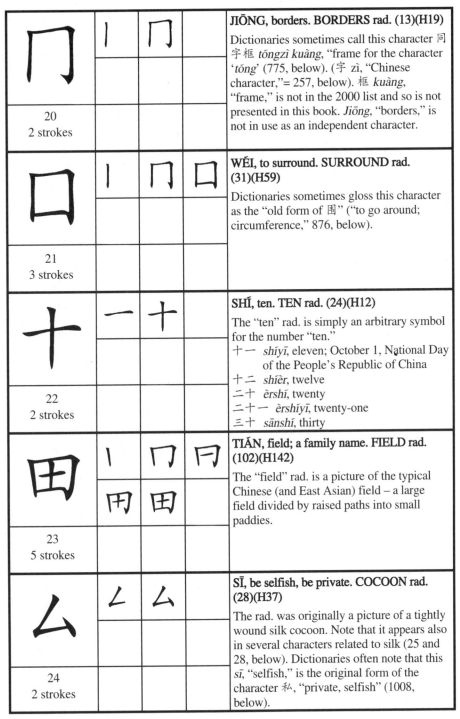

JIŌNG, borders. BORDERS rad. (13)(H19)

Dictionaries sometimes call this character 同字框 *tóngzì kuàng*, "frame for the character '*tóng*' (775, below). (字 *zì*, "Chinese character,"= 257, below). 框 *kuàng*, "frame," is not in the 2000 list and so is not presented in this book. *Jiōng*, "borders," is not in use as an independent character.

20
2 strokes

WÉI, to surround. SURROUND rad. (31)(H59)

Dictionaries sometimes gloss this character as the "old form of 围" ("to go around; circumference," 876, below).

21
3 strokes

SHÍ, ten. TEN rad. (24)(H12)

The "ten" rad. is simply an arbitrary symbol for the number "ten."
十一 *shíyī*, eleven; October 1, National Day of the People's Republic of China
十二 *shíèr*, twelve
二十 *èrshí*, twenty
二十一 *èrshíyī*, twenty-one
三十 *sānshí*, thirty

22
2 strokes

TIÁN, field; a family name. FIELD rad. (102)(H142)

The "field" rad. is a picture of the typical Chinese (and East Asian) field – a large field divided by raised paths into small paddies.

23
5 strokes

SĪ, be selfish, be private. COCOON rad. (28)(H37)

The rad. was originally a picture of a tightly wound silk cocoon. Note that it appears also in several characters related to silk (25 and 28, below). Dictionaries often note that this *sī*, "selfish," is the original form of the character 私, "private, selfish" (1008, below).

24
2 strokes

幺	ㄥ	幺	幺	**YĀO, coil; immature, tender, little. COIL rad. (52)(H76)**
25 **3 strokes**				The "coil" rad. originally was a picture of a coil of silk thread. Learn to distinguish "coil" from the "cocoon" rad. 厶 (24, above), from the "silk" rad. 糸 (28, below), and from the "dark" rad. 玄 (p. 248a).

八	ノ	八		**BĀ, eight. EIGHT rad. (12)**
26 **2 strokes**				The history of this character is problematical. Memorize it as an arbitrary symbol. Note that there are other forms of the "eight" rad. Only the form 八, seen as 98, below, appears as an independent character. See also 88.

小	亅	小	小	**XIĂO, be small, be little. SMALL rad. (42)(H79)**
27 **3 strokes**				Originally, this rad. was three small dots to suggest "small." Two of the dots remain, but the center dot has been replaced by a "hook" rad. 小人　*xiǎorén*, (archaic) a person of little social standing; a person of small moral worth 小子　*xiǎozi*, (colloquial) boy; bloke

糸	ㄥ	幺	幺	**SĪ, silk. SILK rad. (120) (the short form 纟 is H rad. 77)**
	纟	糸	糸	The "silk" rad. was a drawing of silk thread. Note that the modern form includes the "coil" rad. See also 174, below.
28 **6 strokes**				

累	丶	冂	冊	**LÈI, be tired; LĚI, pile up; be repeated**
	田	罒	罒	In ancient China, the men's main work was in the fields; the women's main work was sericulture (silk farming). 累 may be a meaning-meaning compound to suggest everybody's work, whence "be tired."
29 **11 strokes**	累	累	累	好累　*hǎolèi*, be very tired

彳	ノ	⼂	彳		**CHÌ, step. STEP rad. (60)(H62)**
30 3 strokes					Note that the "step" rad. includes the "side-man" (4, above), to which a stroke has been added — supposedly to suggest movement, a step taken. The "step" rad. occurs often in characters for action or movement.

艮	⼁	⼅	⼅		**GÈN, be stubborn; be blunt; be tough, leathery (of food or people). STUBBORN rad. (138)(H184)**
	艮	艮	艮		In early texts, 艮 is clearly a picture of a man with a big, staring eye — an obstinate type, an insolent fellow. In modern times, the spoken word *gèn* is dialect — used in certain localities, but not part of modern standard Chinese.
31 6 strokes					

很	ノ	⼂	彳		**HĚN, very**
	彳	彳	彳		This character is a sound-loan for *hěn* "very." Originally, it stood for a word that meant "to act stubborn, to resist" — a word that probably was cognate with *gèn* (31, above). The "stubborn" rad. was reclarified with the "step" rad., and sometime later the character was borrowed for *hěn*, "very."
32 9 strokes	很	很	很		

口	⼁	冂	口		**KŎU, mouth; a measure for human beings. MOUTH rad. (30)(H58)**
33 3 strokes					The "mouth" radical also occurs as an independent character and means "mouth." It is a picture. 人口 *rénkǒu*, population 三口人 *sān kǒu rén*, three people 口子 *kǒuzi*, hole, opening, cut, rip

灬	⼂	⼌	⼌		**HUŎ, fire. FIRE rad. (86)(H80)**
	灬				This is supposed to be a picture of the fire burning on the ground. This form of the "fire" rad. occurs only as a part of characters. It is called "fire-dots" or "four-dots fire." Compare the independent form 火 (414, below).
34 4 strokes					

馬 35 10 strokes	一	二	三	**MĂ, horse; a family name. HORSE rad. (187) (the short form is H rad. 75)** This character is a picture. The resemblance to a horse was clearer in older forms of the character. 小馬　*xiǎomǎ*, pony 马
	王	馬	馬	
	馬	馬	馬	

嗎 36 13 strokes	丨	口	口	**MA; a particle:** at the end of a sentence, it makes the sentence into a question; it may also appear in a sentence after the subject or topic to emphasize it. 嗎 is a sound-meaning compound — 馬 (35, above) for sound; the "mouth" rad. warning, as it often does, that the character is important for its sound, as a grammatical particle. 吗
	口一	口三	口丰	
	嗎	嗎	嗎	

亠 37 2 strokes	丶	亠		**TÓU, lid. LID rad. (8)(H9)** Originally, *tóu* had a more general meaning: "above; a thing that goes on top of something else, covering." It may be easier to remember as "lid" because it looks like a lid. Distinguish the "roof" rad. 宀 (127, below) and the "crown" rad. 冖 (47). Sometimes called 文字頭, *wénzìtóu*, "top of the character *wén* (360; for *tóu*, see 454).

言 38 7 strokes	丶	二	亠	**YÁN, word, words; family name. WORDS rad. (149)(H185; the short form, used as a part of characters, is H rad. 10)** Notice the mouth in "words." The other lines may be words pouring from the mouth, or "motion lines" to suggest the mouth moving. *Yán* often occurs independently and means "words, speech." The short form, 讠, appears only as a part of characters.
	言	言	言	
	言			

隹 39 8 strokes	丿	亻	亻	**ZHUĪ, dove. DOVE rad. (172)(H208)** Dictionaries often define *zhuī* as "short-tailed bird." In some ancient texts it specifically means "dove." The older forms of the character were clearly pictures of a bird.
	仁	仨	隹	
	隹	隹		

誰	丶	言	言	**SHÉI, who? whom? Also SHUÍ** This character is probably a sound-meaning compound. *Zhuī* (39, above) is supposed to suggest the sound.
	言	言	訁	
40 15 strokes	誰	誰	誰	谁
手	一	二	三	**SHŎU, hand. HAND rad. (64)(H111)** The "hand" rad. looks like this when it is an independent character meaning "hand." This form can also sometimes occur as a part of characters. Cp. the form 扌 (14, above) which always occurs in combination. Distinguish *shŏu* "hand" from *máo* "fur" 毛 (293, below). 小手 *xiǎoshŏu*, (dialect) pickpocket
41 4 strokes	手			
弋	一	弋	弋	**YÌ, dart. DART rad. (56)(H56)** The "dart" rad. is a picture. (H defines *yì* as "a retrievable arrow with string attached" and calls it "bookish.") Compare the "lance" rad. (43, below) and learn to distinguish "lance" from "dart."
42 3 strokes				
戈	一	弋	戈	**GĒ, lance. LANCE rad. (62)(H101)** The "lance" rad. is a picture. Note that "lance" has one more stroke than "dart," at the bottom. In museums you can see that the old weapon called *gē* had a blade like this at the lower end. The weapon is also sometimes called a "dagger-axe."
43 4 strokes	戈			
我	丶	二	于	**WŎ, I, me** The student should learn to distinguish *wŏ* from *zhǎo* "look for" 找 (508, below). *Wŏ* is "hand" + "lance;" *zhǎo* is "side-hand" + "lance."
	手	我	我	
44 7 strokes	我			

39

門	丨	冂	冂	**MÉN, gate. GATE rad. (169) (the short form is H rad. 46)**
				This character is a picture. It occurs often as an independent character and means "gate, door, entrance." Note that it resembles the swinging saloon doors in old Westerns.
	冃	冃'	門	
45 8 strokes	門	門		門口 *ménkŏu*, doorway, area by an entrance 门

們	丿	亻	们	**MÉN; suffix for pronouns and for certain nouns;** *mén* pluralizes the noun or pronoun
				A sound-meaning compound, *men* is used only with nouns or pronouns referring to people, so that the "man" rad. gives the meaning; *mén* (45, above) gives the sound.
	伀	伊	伊'	
46 10 strokes	們	們	們	们

冖	丿	冖		**MÌ, crown. CROWN rad. (14)(H18)**
				Mì had a general meaning of "to cover, a cover" — crown by metonymy (and as a useful mnemonic). Not used independently now, it appears at the top of characters. Distinguish "crown" from the "lid" rad. 亠 (37, above) and from the "roof" rad. 宀 (127). Called "平寶蓋" *píng bǎo gài* — "leveled-off top of 'bao' (平, see 543; 寶, p. 271b; 蓋, p. 295a).
47 2 strokes				

尔	丿	冖	冖	**ĔR, you**
				This character came to mean "you" by sound-loan. The history of the character is too complicated to go into here. Nowadays, it is a bookish character, not often seen.
	尒	尔		
48 5 strokes				

你	亻	伫	伫	**NĬ, you**
				Nĭ and *ĕr* (48, above) almost certainly are cognate words; *nĭ* is *ĕr* reclarified with the "man" rad.
	佇	你	你	你們 *nĭmen*, you (plural) 你好 *nĭ hǎo*, hello! hi! how are you!
49 7 strokes				

40

大	一	ナ	大	**DÀ, big. BIG rad. (37)(H52)**
50 3 strokes				大 is a man with arms extended: "big." 大小 *dàxiǎo*, size (abstract nouns are often formed of antonyms combined, as if to say "the big and little of it, the size:" cp. 高矮 *gāoǎi* (tall/short: height), 75, below; 多少 *duōshǎo* (many/few: how many?), 287; 輕重 *qīngzhòng* (light/heavy: weight), 1051; 寬窄 *kuānzhǎi* (broad/narrow: width), p. 254a, etc.)

夫	一	二	扌	**FŪ, husband, "big man"**
51 4 strokes	夫			大夫 *dàifū*, medical doctor (note that 大 "big" is pronounced *dài* in this expression) 夫人 *fūren*, Mrs.; Madam 馬夫人 *Mǎ fūren*, Mrs. Ma; Madam Ma

天	一	二	于	**TIĀN, heaven; day**
52 4 strokes	天			Heaven was anciently recognized as a diety in China. This character is supposed to be a picture of "an anthropomorphic diety." 天天 *tiāntiān*, every day 天子 *tiānzǐ*, the "Son of Heaven," the emperor

夭	丿	二	于	**YĀO, tender, gentle (with 天, *yāo* comprises H. rad. 90)**
53 4 strokes	夭			Learn to distinguish 夭 from 天 (52, above). The clue is: is there a "one" rad. or a "left" rad. across the top?

竹	丿	𠂉	𠂉	**ZHÚ, bamboo. BAMBOO rad. (118)(H178)**
54 6 strokes	𥫗	𥫗	竹	This character is a good picture of the slender, drooping leaves of the bamboo. 竹子 *zhúzi*, bamboo 竹馬 *zhúmǎ*, a stick used by children as a toy horse

竹	ノ	⺊	⺊	**ZHÚ, bamboo. BAMBOO rad. (118)(H178)**
				This form of the "bamboo" rad. only occurs as a part of characters. Compare the independent form that you just learned (54, above).
	竹	竹	竹	
55 6 strokes				

笑	ノ	⺊	⺊	**XIÀO, to laugh, smile; to ridicule**
				One scholar says, "When bamboo takes the wind, it leans back gently like a man who laughs." That is probably more useful as a mnemonic for the character than it is as a real explanation.
	竹	竹	竺	
56 10 strokes	竺	笋	笑	好笑 *hǎoxiào*, be easy to laugh at, be funny, be ridiculous

儿	ノ	儿		**RÉN, legs; ÉR, child, son; R. suffix to many nouns. LEGS rad. (10)(H29)**
				As *ér* and *r*, 儿 is used in place of 兒 (230, below). Distinguish the "legs" rad. from 兀 (58, below) and from the "table" rad. 几 (645, below).
57 2 strokes				

兀	一	丆	兀	**WÙ, stool, pedestal; man with amputated foot or feet**
				In modern times, this character stands for a bookish word meaning "towering" and also "bald" (of birds or mountains, not of people).
58 3 strokes				

尢	一	尢	尢	**WĀNG, be lame; YÓU, still; a family name. LAME rad. (43)(H53)**
				This is a picture of two legs, one shorter than the other to suggest lameness. The horizontal stroke serves to emphasize the unequal length of the two legs. Distinguish from "lack" 无 (60, below) and from "big" 大 (50, above). The pronunciation *yóu* comes from its use for 尤 (298, below).
59 3 strokes				

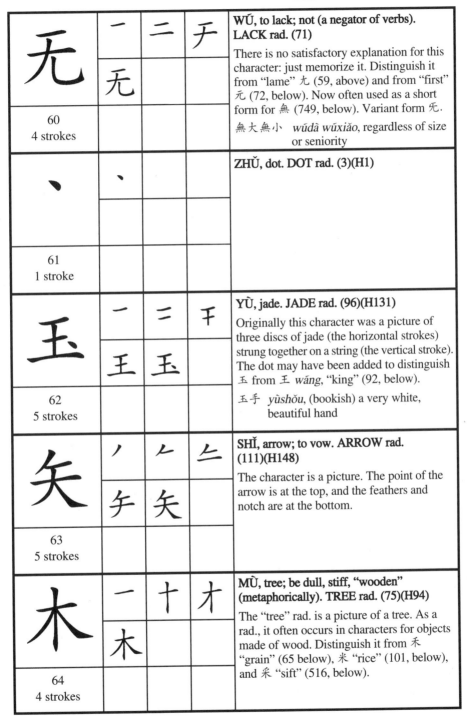

WÚ, to lack; not (a negator of verbs). LACK rad. (71)

There is no satisfactory explanation for this character: just memorize it. Distinguish it from "lame" 尢 (59, above) and from "first" 元 (72, below). Now often used as a short form for 無 (749, below). Variant form 无.

無大無小 *wúdà wúxiǎo*, regardless of size or seniority

60
4 strokes

ZHǓ, dot. DOT rad. (3)(H1)

61
1 stroke

YÙ, jade. JADE rad. (96)(H131)

Originally this character was a picture of three discs of jade (the horizontal strokes) strung together on a string (the vertical stroke). The dot may have been added to distinguish 玉 from 王 *wáng*, "king" (92, below).

玉手 *yùshǒu*, (bookish) a very white, beautiful hand

62
5 strokes

SHǏ, arrow; to vow. ARROW rad. (111)(H148)

The character is a picture. The point of the arrow is at the top, and the feathers and notch are at the bottom.

63
5 strokes

MÙ, tree; be dull, stiff, "wooden" (metaphorically). TREE rad. (75)(H94)

The "tree" rad. is a picture of a tree. As a rad., it often occurs in characters for objects made of wood. Distinguish it from 禾 "grain" (65 below), 米 "rice" (101, below), and 釆 "sift" (516, below).

64
4 strokes

43

禾	一	二	千	**HÉ, grain, especially rice. GRAIN rad. (115) (H149)**
	禾	禾		Note the similarity between 禾 "grain" and 木 "tree" (64, above). "Grain" has the left stroke across the top to represent the head of ripened grain. Distinguish "grain" from "sift" 采 (516, below).
65 5 strokes				

矮	ノ	㇄	㇄	**ĂI, be short (not tall)**
	矢	矢	矢	矮 is composed of "arrow" 矢 ＋ "grain" 禾 ＋ "woman" 女 — all things which, within their classes, are generally shorter: arrows than spears, grain than trees, women than men.
66 13 strokes	矮	矮	矮	矮子 *ăizi*, short person, dwarf 矮小 *ăixiăo*, be diminutive, under-sized

忄	ノ	㇀	忄	**XĪN, heart. HEART rad. (61)(H41)**
				This form of the "heart" rad. does not occur as an independent character; it occurs only as a part of characters. When printed, it often takes the form 忄 . Some dictionaries call it 竪心旁 "*shù xīn páng*: vertical heart, on the side" (竪, see p. 295b, below; 旁, 785.) Cp. the other form of "heart" 心 (70, below).
67 3 strokes (4 strokes)				

亡	丶	亠	亡	**WÁNG, to hide, to flee; be gone; to die; to subjugate (H rad. 43)**
				What is now "lid" (37, above) was once 入 "enter" (157, below) — a man entering a corner, to hide in it, basic meaning: "to hide." The other meanings are derived.
68 3 strokes				

忙	丶	丨	忄	**MÁNG, be busy**
	忄	忙	忙	忙 is supposed to be a sound-meaning compound. *Wáng* (68, above) supposedly suggests the sound, and "heart" suggests the meaning. 忙人 *mángrén*, a busy fellow
69 6 strokes				

心 70 4 strokes	丶 心	心	心	**XĪN, heart. HEART rad. (61)(H81)** In the old forms of 心, it is easy to see the picture of a heart. In this form, the "heart" rad. occurs as an independent character and as an element at the bottom of characters. Compare 67, above. 小心 *xiǎo xīn*, Be careful! 無心 *wúxīn*, not feel like, not be in the mood for; unintentionally
您 71 11 strokes	丿 伩 你	亻 竹 您	亻 你 您	**NÍN, you** 您 is deferential, used to address elders and superiors. Note that the top half of this character is 你 "you" (49, above).
元 72 4 strokes	一 元	二	元	**YUÁN, first** The "legs" rad. at the bottom of this character represents a man; the "two" rad. at the top is supposed to represent his head. From "head" comes the idea of "primary;" thus, 'first.' 元 is also commonly used to write 圓, "dollar" (733, below). 一元 *yìyuán*, one (Chinese) dollar
不 73 4 strokes	一 不	丁	不	**BÙ, a negative prefix for verbs and adverbs (H rad. 95)** *Bù* is pronounced *bú* before a word in the fourth tone. 不好 *bùhǎo*, It's not good; No good! 不很 *bùhěn*, not very… 很不 *hěn bù*, very un-… 不忙 *bùmáng*, There's no hurry; take your time
太 74 4 strokes	一 太	大	大	**TÀI, extremely** 太忙 *tàimáng*, be too busy 太太 *tàitai*, married lady, wife, Mrs. 田太太 *Tián tàitai*, Mrs. Tian 太子 *tàizi*, prince, crown prince

45

高	、	亠	宀	**GĀO, tall; to tower; a family name. TALL rad. (189)(H218)**
	亠	古	亠	高矮 *gāoǎi*, height (cf. 大小, under 50, above)
				高大 *gāodà*, be big and tall, be tall
75 10 strokes	高	高	高	高小 *gāoxiǎo*, higher primary school (short for 高級小學 *gāojí xiǎoxué*; 級, see p. 264a, below; 學 = 253)

阝	㇕	㇉	阝	**FÙ, mound. MOUND rad. (170)(H33)**
				Fù was a picture of stairs leading down from the mound. In form, "mound" and the "city" rad. (136, below) are the same, but "city" always appears at the far right in characters. Not an independent form. Dictionaries call "mound" 左耳朵 *zuǒ ěrduǒ*, "left ear." (左 = 572, below; 耳, 201; 朵, see p. 282b).
76 3 strokes (8 strokes)				

可	一	丁	丁	**KĚ, may, can; to suit; certainly**
	可	可		The origin of this character is unclear.
				可笑 *kěxiào*, be laughable
				可口 *kěkǒu*, to "suit your mouth," to taste good
				不可 *bùkě*, should not
77 5 strokes				可心 *kěxīn*, be satisfying, pleasing
				可可 *kěkě*, cocoa

阿	㇕	㇉	阝	**Ā, prefix for people's names**
	阝	阿	阿	This character originally meant "slope." The "mound" rad. suggested the meaning, and *kě* (77, above) suggested the sound. As a prefix, it is used by sound-loan.
	阿	阿		阿門 *āmén*, Amen (in prayer)
78 8 strokes				阿高 *Ā-Gāo*, (Old) Gao, (our friend or acquaintance, Mr.) Gao

啊	㇀	口	口	**Ā; a sentence-final particle — for questions, exclamations, commands, warnings, reminders, emphatic pauses, enumerations, direct address, and impatient statements.**
	口㇀	口㇉	叩	Sound-loan, reclarified with "mouth."
				好累啊 *hǎo lèi ā*, (I'm) really tired!
79 11 strokes	啊	啊	啊	小心啊 *xiǎo xīn ā*, Be careful!

丑	ㄱ	ㅋ	ㅋ	**JĬ, pig's head. PIG's HEAD rad. (58)(H70)** This character originally was a picture. This form of it does not occur independently (cp. 997, below). Certain older forms of the "hand" rad. look so much like this that even Chinese had trouble telling them apart. Modern dictionaries only give ヨ, ⺕, and ⺕ as forms of the "pig's head" rad.
80 3 strokes				
聿	ㄱ	ㅋ	ㅋ	**YÙ, brush. BRUSH rad. (129)** *Yù* is a picture of a hand holding a brush. The top part, 肀, is a rad. in many modern dictionaries (*i.e.*, H124). Such dictionaries often call the top part, as a rad., "top of the character 聿."
	ㅋ	聿	聿	
81 6 strokes				
曰	ㅣ	ㄇ	曰	**YUĒ, to say. SAY rad. (73)(H104)** *Yuē* has a stroke inside the mouth, perhaps to suggest the tongue moving. Learn to tell "say" 曰 from "sun" 日 (160, below). In "say" (but never in "sun") the inner stroke is usually incomplete (stops short of the right vertical stroke). Also "say" is shorter and fatter than "sun".
	曰			
82 4 strokes				
書	ㄱ	ㅋ	ㅋ	**SHŪ, book; letter; document; write** "Brush" + "say" = "book." (Not accurate historically, this explanation can help you remember the character.) 手書 *shǒu shū*, to write in your own hand; a personal letter 天書 *tiān shū*, a book from outer space — abstruse or illegible writing 书
	聿	書	書	
83 10 strokes	書	書	書	
卩	ㄱ	卩		**JIÉ, seal (as in "seal ring"). SEAL rad. (26)(H32)** Learn to tell "seal" from "mound" 阝 (76, above) and from "city" 阝 (136, below).
84 2 strokes				

47

又 85 2 strokes	ㄱ	又		**YÒU, again. RIGHT HAND rad. (29)(H35)** The character is a drawing of a right hand (cp. "left hand," 179, below). It means "again" by sound-loan. 又不 *yòu bù*, not at all… 又高又大 *yòu gāo yòu dà*, It's (He's/ She's) both tall and big. 又矮又小 *yòu ǎi yòu xiǎo*, It's (He's/ She's) both short and small.
土 86 3 strokes	一	十	土	**TǓ, earth. EARTH rad. (32)(H49)** Note that the "earth" rad. is a picture of a cross stuck into the earth ("The axis mundi!" say some scholars). It often occurs independently and means "earth, soil." Distinguish it from 士 *shì*, "knight" (134, below) — even though in H, they are both the same rad. 土人 *tǔrén*, a native, an aborigine 土木 *tǔmù*, building and construction
干 87 3 strokes	一	二	干	**GĀN, shield. SHIELD rad. (24)** The "shield" rad. is a picture. In modern texts, it is a common short form for 乾 (617, below) and for 幹 (p. 247a, below), as in the examples. 干笑 (乾笑) *gān xiào*, a hollow laugh (lit. "a dry laugh") 干嗎 (幹嗎) *gàn ma*, (colloquial) What the h---! What's this all about? OR, What shall we do?
⺍ 88 2 strokes	㇒	⺍		**BĀ, eight. EIGHT rad. (12)(H24)** This is the second form of the "eight" rad. that the student has learned. In printed characters the form of this rad. given as 26, above, is often used instead of this form. Compare 286, below.
幸 89 8 strokes	一 圭 幸	十 圭 幸	土 圭	**XÌNG, lucky** The student should learn to tell *xìng* from the "bitter" rad. 辛 (549, below); "lucky" has "earth" on top; the "bitter" rad. has "lid" on top. 幸好 *xìnghǎo*, fortunately, luckily 不幸 *bùxìng*, bad luck, adversity; be unlucky; unfortunately

報	土	耂	赱	**BÀO, to announce, report; newspaper; to requite**
	坴	幸	軐	The old form of this character meant "to requite" because it was a picture of a kneeling man with manacles and a hand to mete out the punishment. It stands for "announce" by sound-loan. It will have to be memorized as "lucky" + "seal" + "right hand."
90 12 strokes	軐	幇	報	小報 *xiǎobào*, tabloid　　　報

筆	丿	广	竺	**BǏ, brush, writing instrument**
	竹	笁	竺	*Bǐ* is a meaning-meaning compound: "bamboo" + "brush" = the traditional Chinese writing instrument, a brush made of bamboo.
91 12 strokes	筆	筀	筆	筆心 *bǐxīn*, pencil-lead; ball-point pen refill　　笔

王	一	二	王	**WÁNG, king; family name (H88)**
	王			*Wáng* is classified in traditional dictionaries under the "jade" rad. 玉 (62, above) although *wáng* has one less stroke. In such dictionaries, characters in which the rad. seems to be *wáng* will be found under "jade" but in modern dictionaries will be found, more logically, under 王 *wáng*, king.
92 4 strokes				

玩	一	二	干	**WÁN, to play, to amuse oneself**
	王	玕	玕	A sound-meaning compound. *Yuán* (72, above) suggests the sound. The "jade" rad. is supposed to help with the meaning, perhaps because toys were often made of jade; "toys" suggests "to play."
93 8 strokes	玕	玩		

金	丿	人	仐	**JĪN, gold, metals; a family name. GOLD rad. (167)(H209; short form = H rad. 147)**
	仐	全	全	The "gold" rad. occurs as an independent character and means "gold" or "metals." Often seen in characters for various metals or metallic objects.
94 8 strokes	余	金		金玉 *jīn yù*, (bookish) gold and jade; "treasures" (short form in combinations only: 钅)

49

山	丨	山	山	**SHĀN, mountain. MOUNTAIN rad. (46)(H60)** *Shān* is a picture. In the old form it is clearly three peaks sticking up. The "mountain" rad. often occurs independently as a character and means "mountain" and "hill." 山口 *shānkǒu*, mountain pass
95 3 strokes				

岡	丨	冂	冂	**GĀNG, ridge** Notice the "mountain" rad. in the center of *gāng*; it suggests the meaning. The rest of *gāng* is from an old character which gave the sound. 山岡 *shān gāng*, low hill, hillock
	冈	冈	冈	
96 8 strokes	岡	岡		冈

鋼	丿	𠂉	𠂉	**GĀNG, steel; GÀNG, to sharpen, whet** This character is a sound-meaning compound: the "gold" rad. for meaning, *gāng* (96, above) for sound. 鋼筆 *gāngbǐ*, pen
	𠂉	牟	余	
97 16 strokes	金	釘	鋼	钢

八	丿	八		**BĀ, eight. EIGHT rad. (12)(H24)** The student should compare this form of the "eight" rad. to the other forms he has learned (26 and 88, above). This is the form which is usually seen as an independent character. 王八 *wángbā*, tortoise; (vulgar, abusive) cuckold
98 2 strokes				

凸	几	几	凸	**YǍN, marsh** This character is not in common use now.
	凸			
99 5 strokes				

鉛	ノ	ᶥ	午	**QIĀN, lead (the metal)**
	金	金	釒	鉛筆 *qiānbǐ*, pencil
100 13 strokes	釚	鉛	鉛	铅

米	丶	ᶥ	丷	**MǏ, rice; a family name. RICE rad. (119)(H159)**
	半	米	米	The "rice" rad. was originally a picture of rice growing in a paddy. The horizontal stroke represented the water that stands in paddies. Distinguish "rice" from "sift" 釆 (516, below) from "grain" 禾 (65, above), and from "tree" 木 (64, above).
101 6 strokes				玉米 *yùmǐ*, maize, Indian corn

刀	ㄱ	刀		**DĀO, knife. KNIFE rad. (18)(H27; in H, the form ㄉ, seen in combinations, is classified as rad. 27)**
				刀 is a picture. Distinguish it from the "strength" rad. 力 (206, below).
				刀子 *dāozi*, knife
				刀口 *dāokǒu*, knife edge; a crucial point, point of best use; incision
102 2 strokes				刀筆 *dāobǐ*, writing of (legal) complaints and appeals; pettifoggery

分	ノ	八	分	**FĒN, to divide; a fraction, a very small part; FÈN, component; a share, one's lot**
	分			The "eight" rad. at the top is actually a picture of something being cut in two by the knife.
				分子 *fēnzi*, numerator; molecule
				分手 *fēnshǒu*, to part with somebody
103 4 strokes				分心 *fēnxīn*, to distract somebody's attention

粉	丶	ᶥ	半	**FĚN, dust, powder**
	半	米	米	Face powder used to be made of rice. *Fěn* is a sound-meaning compound: "rice" for meaning, *fēn* (103, above) to suggest the sound.
				米粉 *mǐfěn*, rice flour; rice-flour noodles
104 10 strokes	粉	粉	粉	粉筆 *fěnbǐ*, chalk (for writing with)

51

立	﹀	二	亠
	亣	立	
105 **5 strokes**			

LÌ, to stand. STAND rad. (117)(H126)

Lì is a picture: a man standing with feet planted firmly on the ground.

立言 *lìyán*, (old expression) write up your ideas; get a reputation through your writing

---

里	丨	冂	日
	日	旦	甲
106 **7 strokes**	里		

LǏ, village. VILLAGE rad. (166)(H195)

A meaning-meaning compound: "field" + "earth" = "village." A commentator says, "Where there's land by fields, you build a village." This character is also used by sound-loan for *li*, that is, a unit of distance (=1/3 English mile). *Lǐ*, "village," is a common short form for *lǐ*, "lining, inside" (449, below).

童	丶	二	亠
	立	音	音
107 **12 strokes**	音	童	童

TÓNG, child; children; bald; a family name

童女 *tóngnǚ*, virgin, maiden
童心 *tóngxīn*, childish disposition
童山 *tóngshān*, bare hills, bald mountains

鐘	ノ	𠂉	𠂉
	牟	金	釒
108 **20 strokes**	釒	鐕	鐘

ZHŌNG, clock; a family name

The "gold" rad. here signifies "some object made of metal," and the character *tóng* (107, above) suggests the sound.

十分鐘 *shí fēn zhōng*, ten minutes

钟

衣	丶	二	亠
	亣	衣	衣
109 **6 strokes**			

YĪ, gown. GOWN rad. (145)(H161)

This character is a picture. The gown's sleeves and skirt can be seen clearly in older forms. As a part of other characters, this rad. often means "clothing."

大衣 *dàyī*, overcoat

表	一	二	主
	主	声	耒
110 8 strokes	耒	表	

BIǍO, to show; surface, external; list, form

The "gown" rad. is not apparent in *biǎo*, but *biǎo* is classified under "gown" in old dictionaries (H puts it under 主, H89, which is not a traditional rad.) *Biǎo* once meant "overcoat" and came to mean "to show" by sound-loan — unless "overcoat" and "to show" were cognate words in old Chinese.

錶	ノ	𠂉	𠂤
	牟	余	余
111 16 strokes	金	鈝	錶

BIǍO, wristwatch, watch

The word for which this character stands may be cognate with *biǎo*, "to show." If so, this character is reclarified with the "gold" rad. This character may, however, be a simple sound-meaning compound.

手錶 *shǒubiǎo*, wristwatch

表

中	丨	冂	口
	中		
112 4 strokes			

ZHŌNG, middle; Chinese; ZHÒNG, hit the middle, fit perfectly; be hit or affected by (H rad. 105)

The downstroke through the center of the rectangle suggests "middle."

中心 *zhōngxīn*, center, core
中立 *zhōnglì*, "standing in the middle," i.e., neutrality

或	一	一	戸
	口	豆	或
113 8 strokes	或	或	

HUÒ, perhaps; or

This character is a sound-loan. Originally, it meant "nation" (see 114, below). As "nation," it was a combination of meanings: "lance" (for the army) + "mouth" (for a language) + "earth." "Earth" has been corrupted into "one" in the modern form.

國	丨	冂	冂
	同	冒	國
114 11 strokes	國	國	國

GUÓ, nation

Guó is 113, above, reclarified with the "surround" rad. to suggest the national boundaries.

中國 *Zhōngguó*, China
中立國 *zhōnglì guó*, a neutral nation

国

53

羊	丶	丷	丷	**YÁNG, sheep, goat; a family name. SHEEP rad. (123)(H157)**
				Yáng is a picture. The "eight" rad. at the top gives the horns. (H notes that 𦍌 and 龶 are alternate forms of this rad.)
丷	兰	羊		
115 6 strokes				山羊 *shānyáng*, goat 小羊 *xiǎoyáng*, lamb

美	丶	丷	丷	**MĚI, be beautiful**
				Supposed to be a meaning-meaning compound; one dictionary says, "If the sheep is big, it will be beautiful." Plumpness in women has often been considered beautiful.
丷	兰	羊		
116 9 strokes	羊	美	美	美國 *Měiguó*, America, the U.S.A. 美金 *měi jīn*, American money, the U.S.$ 美好 *měihǎo*, be fine, happy, glorious

夕	丿	夕	夕	**XĪ, dusk. DUSK rad. (36)(H64)**
				The character is a drawing of the moon, to suggest "dusk." Learn to tell "dusk" from the "chip" rad. 歹 (727, below).
117 3 strokes				

卜	丨	卜		**BǓ, to divine. DIVINE rad. (25)(H16)**
				In the Shang Dynasty (1751–1122 B.C.), the kings divined by scratching messages on tortoise sheels. A professional diviner applied heat to the shell until it cracked, then read the cracks to divine. The "divine" rad. is supposed to represent the divination cracks in the shell.
118 2 strokes				

外	丿	夕	夕	**WÀI, outside; relatives of one's mother, sisters, or daughters**
				Bernard Karlgren says, "… 'Moon' [dusk] and 'divine'… Moon may be phonetic… and the oracle crack appeared on the outside… of the shell when the inside was singed."
夕	外			
119 5 strokes				外国 *wàiguó*, foreign 外表 *wàibiǎo*, outward appearance, surface

目 120 5 strokes	丨 月	冂 目	月	**MÙ, eye. EYE rad. (109)(H141)** This character is a picture. The student should learn to distinguish the "eye" rad. from the "small nose" rad. 自 (515, below). 書目 *shūmù*, booklist, catalogue of book titles 目中無人 *mùzhōng wúrén*, be supercilious, haughty; consider no one to be worth your time
看 121 9 strokes	一 手 看	二 丢 看	三 看 看	**KĀN, to look at; KÀN, to look after, to take care of** A meaning-meaning compound: "hand" over "eye" to suggest "to look at." Note that the "hand" rad. (41, above) is slightly altered in this form. Distinguish "look at" from 着 (476, below). 看中 *kànzhòng*, to take a liking to, to pick out, to choose 看門 *kānmén*, to act as doorkeeper
西 122 6 strokes	一 襾	厂 襾	冂 西	**XIÀ, cover. COVER rad. (146)(H166)** This rad. is a picture — of a stopper or "cork" for a bottle, according to Karlgren (*Analytic Dictionary* 135). In H., it is combined with 西 *xī*, "west" (130, below) as rad. 166. As a modern rad., it will be seen in the form 西 at the top of characters.
貝 123 7 strokes	丨 月	冂 貝	月 貝	**BÈI, a cowrie; a family name. COWRIE rad. (156)(H106)** A cowrie is a small, yellowish-white shell "with a fine gloss, used by various peoples as money" (*Century Dictionary*). Cowries were money in China. We find the "cowrie" rad. in characters for value, money, business transactions, etc. 贝
貴 124 12 strokes	丶 中 貴	冖 虫 貴	口 串 貴	**GUÌ, expensive, be precious** *Guì* is a sound-meaning compound. The top part, no longer used as an independent character, gave the sound, and "cowrie" gave the meaning. 可貴 *kěguì*, be valuable; deserve commendation 貴人 *guìrén*, government VIP 贵

55

更	一	「	亓	**GÈNG, still more; GĒNG, to change; a "watch" (two-hour period of the night)**
	亓	百	事	The modern character is too much changed to make the explanation helpful.
125 **7 strokes**	更			更好 *gèng hǎo*, be better; even more

便	丿	亻	亻	**BIÀN, convenient; PIÁN, the first syllable of *piányi*, be inexpensive**
	仁	佢	佰	小便 *xiǎobiàn*, to piss, a piss 大便 *dàbiàn*, to shit, defecation 便衣 *biànyī*, street clothes, "civvies;" plainclothes man
126 **9 strokes**	便	便		

宀	丶	宀	宀	**MIÁN, roof. ROOF rad. (40)(H45)**
				The character is a picture. The top stroke may represent a chimney. The student will want to distinguish "roof" from "lid" 亠 (37, above) and from "crown" 冖 (47, above). Dictionaries sometimes call *mián* 寶蓋兒 *bǎo gàier*, "top of [the character] '*bao*'."
127 **3 strokes**				(For 寶, see p. 271b, below; for 蓋, see p. 295a; 兒 = 230, below).

且	｜	冂	月	**QIĔ, further**
	月	且		The character is a drawing of the ancestral tablet. Originally it stood for the word for ancestor or grandfather. Now it is used by sound-loan.
128 **5 strokes**				

宜	丶	八	宀	**YÍ, be appropriate**
	宀	宁	宜	The character is a picture of "the sacred pole of the altar of the soil, behung with… meat." It meant "sacrifice to the earth-god." It is used for "be appropriate" by sound-loan.
129 **8 strokes**	宜	宜		便宜 *piányi*, be inexpensive

西	一	冂	冂
	丙	西	西
130 6 strokes			

XĪ, west (H166, in the forms of 西 and 西)

The character is a picture of a bird in a nest and originally meant "to nest." It is used for *xī* "west" by sound-loan. Characters in which *xī* seems to be the radical will be found in traditional dictionaries under the "cover" rad. 西 (122, above). Distinguish the "wine" rad. 酉 (363, below).

要	一	一	冂
	西	西	西
131 9 strokes	要	要	要

YÀO, to want; to ask for; "wanted:" important, essential

要人 *yàorén*, important person (usually a government official)

要不 *yàobù*, otherwise, or else, or

要好 *yàohǎo*, be on good terms, be good friends; be eager to improve yourself

四	丶	冂	冖
	冖	冖	
132 5 strokes			

MÙ, eye. EYE rad. (109)

This form of the "eye" rad. occurs only as a part of characters (cp. 120, above). In form, it is identical to a form of the "net" rad. (637, below). As a classifying element for traditional dictionaries, this form is almost always "net" — and in H, always so.

買	冂	冖	冖
	四	罒	罒
133 12 strokes	胃	買	買

MǍI, to buy

Mǎi is a meaning-meaning compound. The eye is watching over the cowries (remember that cowries were used for money).

买

士	一	十	士
134 3 strokes			

SHÌ, knight. KNIGHT rad. (33). (In H, 士 and 土 (86, above) both = rad. 49.)

A *shì* organized ten 十 things into one 一 for his lord. Cp. "earth" 土 (86).

人士 *rénshì*, personage, notable person

士女 *shìnǚ*, young men and women, "guys and dolls"

女士 *nǚshì*, polite address for women, especially professionals; Ms.

貝女士 *Bèi Nǚshì*, Ms. Bei

賣	一	十	士	**MÀI, to sell**
	亠	声	声	買賣 *mǎimài*, business 賣國 *màiguó*, to sell out your country, to be a traitor
135 **15 strokes**	声	青	賣	卖

YÌ, city. CITY rad. (193)(H34)

阝	ㄱ	阝	阝	
				Learn to tell the "city" rad. from the "mound" rad. (76, above). When the form occurs far right in a character, it is always — in traditional dictionaries — "city" Dictionaries call "city" 右耳朵 *yòu ěrduǒ*, "right ear" (右 = 573, below; 耳 = 201; 朵, see p. 282b). This form does not occur independently.
136 **3 strokes** **(7 strokes)**				

BǏ, ladle. LADLE rad. (21)(H39)

| 匕 | ㄴ | 匕 | | This character is a picture. |
| **137**
2 strokes | | | | |

LǍO, be old. OLD rad. (125)(In H, the rad. is the form 耂 — 92)

老	一	十	土	*Lǎo*, say the dictionaries, is a picture of an old man with long hair and a cane. The modern form is very stylized (you can analyze it into "earth-left-ladle").
	尹	老	老	老人 *lǎorén*, an old person: "the old folks" — your grandparents (or very old parents)
138 **6 strokes**				老二 *lǎoèr*, second son or daughter

ZHĚ; a suffix to verbs: verb + *zhě* means "a person who…". Cp. English suffix "–er."

者	一	十	土	It may be hard to see in *zhě* the "old" rad., but we know it is there because *zhě* is classified under 老 "old" in traditional dictionaries.
	尹	耂	者	
139 **8 strokes**	者	者		老者 *lǎozhě*, an old fellow, an old man 筆者 *bǐzhě*, (bookish) the 'penner': I, the present writer

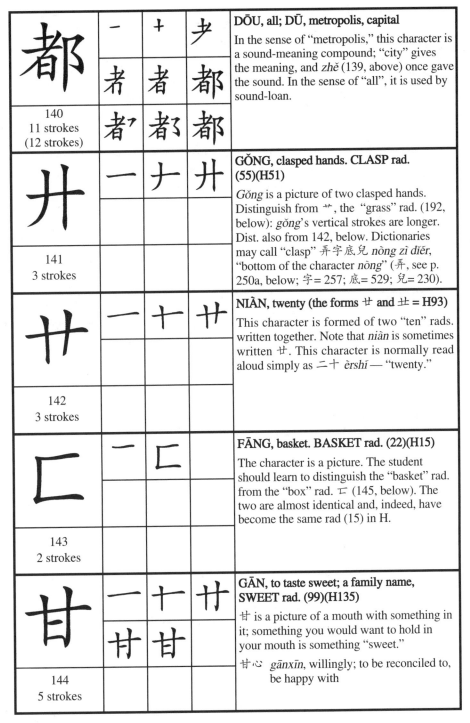

				DŌU, all; DŪ, metropolis, capital
都	一	十	少	In the sense of "metropolis," this character is a sound-meaning compound; "city" gives the meaning, and *zhě* (139, above) once gave the sound. In the sense of "all", it is used by sound-loan.
140 11 strokes (12 strokes)	者 者 都			
	者 者 都			

				GŎNG, clasped hands. CLASP rad. (55)(H51)
廾	一	𠂇	廾	*Gǒng* is a picture of two clasped hands. Distinguish from 艹, the "grass" rad. (192, below): *gǒng*'s vertical strokes are longer. Dist. also from 142, below. Dictionaries may call "clasp" 弄字底兒 *nòng zì dǐer*, "bottom of the character *nòng*" (弄, see p. 250a, below; 字= 257; 底= 529; 兒= 230).
141 3 strokes				

				NIÀN, twenty (the forms 廿 and 卅 = H93)
廿	一	十	廿	This character is formed of two "ten" rads. written together. Note that *niàn* is sometimes written 卅. This character is normally read aloud simply as 二十 *èrshí* — "twenty."
142 3 strokes				

				FĀNG, basket. BASKET rad. (22)(H15)
匚	一	匚		The character is a picture. The student should learn to distinguish the "basket" rad. from the "box" rad. 匸 (145, below). The two are almost identical and, indeed, have become the same rad (15) in H.
143 2 strokes				

				GĀN, to taste sweet; a family name, SWEET rad. (99)(H135)
甘	一	十	廿	甘 is a picture of a mouth with something in it; something you would want to hold in your mouth is something "sweet."
144 5 strokes	廿 甘			甘心 *gānxīn*, willingly; to be reconciled to, be happy with

				XǏ, box. BOX rad. (23)(H15)
匚	一	匚		The character is a picture. Note that, unless we assume the box is tipped on its side, the right-hand side of the box is not drawn in. Cp. 143, above.
145 **2 strokes**				

				PǏ, mate, one-half of a pair
匹	一	匚	匹	一匹馬 *yì pǐ mǎ*, a horse 匹夫 *pǐfū*, ordinary man; "dummy," stupid fellow
	匹			
146 **4 strokes**				

				SÌ, four
四	丨	冂	叼	This is an arbitrary symbol; memorize it. 四書 *sìshū*, "The Four Books," the "core classics" of Confucianism.
	四	四		
147 **5 strokes**				

				WǓ, five
五	一	丆	五	五金 *wǔjīn*, the five metals (gold, silver, copper, iron, and tin); metals generally
	五			
148 **4 strokes**				

				LIÙ, six
六	丶	亠	六	六書 *liùshū*, the six categories of Chinese characters (see pp. 12–14, above).
	六			
149 **4 strokes**				

七	一	七	**QĪ, seven** The student will want to distinguish 七 from the "ladle" rad. 匕 (137, above). Printed form: 七 七夕 *qīxī*, the seventh night of the seventh lunar month — the one night of the year, according to myth, that the legendary lovers "the Cowboy" and "the Weaver Girl" get to spend together
150 2 strokes			
九	丿	九	**JIŬ, nine** 九天 *jiŭtiān*, "Ninth Heaven," the highest of heavens (the Western world has "seventh heaven")
151 2 strokes			
入	丿	入	**RÙ, to enter. ENTER rad. (11) (In H, with 人 (2, above), = rad. 23) Distinguish "enter" from 人 (=2).** 入口 *rùkŏu*, entrance 入門 *rùmén*, to start well; primer 入手 *rùshŏu*, put your hand in; get started, make a beginning 入木三分 *rù mù sān fēn*, be written in a forceful hand; be profound
152 2 strokes			
甚	一 十 廿 廿 甘 其 甚 甚 甚		**SHÉN; the first syllable of *shénme* (*shémme*), what? SHÈN, very** Originally this character stood for a word meaning "peace and happiness." It was a meaning-meaning compound: "sweet" + "mate." Now the character is used by sound-loan.
153 9 strokes			
厂	一 厂		**HĂN, slope, cliff. SLOPE rad. (27)(H13)** *Hăn* is a picture of a slope. The student will want to note that this character is usually seen, in modern texts, as the short form for 廠 *chăng*, "factory" (p. 264b, below). In H, besides H13 there is a look-alike form 厂, identified as rad. 22, but H22 is the rad. only in 反 (308, below) and 盾 (p. 277b) and in the short forms for 後 (452) and 質 (p. 256b).
154 2 strokes			

广	`	亠	广	**YǍN, lean-to. LEAN-TO rad. (53)(H44)**
155 3 strokes				The character is a picture. Learn to distinguish "lean-to" from the "slope" rad. 厂 (154, above) and from the "sick" rad. 疒 (531, below). *Yǎn*, "lean-to," will most often be seen in modern texts as the short form for *guǎng* 廣 (972, below) and will then, of course, be pronounced *guǎng*.

林	一	十	才	**LÍN, forest; a family name**
	木	朮	村	*Lín* is a meaning-meaning compound: "tree" beside "tree" = "forest, woods." Cp. 森 *sēn* (p. 266a, below), which also means "forest." 林立 *línlì*, to stand in great numbers, like forest trees
156 8 strokes	村	林		林木 *línmù*, woods; a forest tree 山林 *shānlín*, mountain forest; wooded hills or mountains

麻	`	亠	广	**MÁ, hemp; be rough, coarse, pock-marked; a family name. HEMP rad. (221)**
	广	斤	斤	The old form was a picture of plants beside a curved line (now "lean-to"), perhaps the inside of a river bend (hemp grows well in damp grounds). 麻木 *mámù*, numb, apathetic
157 11 strokes	床	麻	麻	麻子 *mázi*, pockmarks; a person with a pocky face 大麻 *dàmá*, hemp; marijuana

么	丿	么	么	**YĀO, puny; one (in dice games)**
158 3 strokes				Variant 幺. Compare 25, above. *Yāo* is often seen in modern texts as the short form for 159, below — and then it is pronounced *me*.

麼	`	亠	广	**ME; the second syllable of *shénme* (*shémme*), what?**
	斤	斤	麻	甚麼 *shénme* (*shémme*), what? (*Shémme* is much more commonly written now as 什麼 or 什么 [for 什, see p. 281b, below].)
159 14 strokes	麻	麼	麼	么

日	丨	冂	日	**RÌ, sun. SUN rad. (72)(H103)** *Rì* is a picture. Learn to tell "sun" from the "say" rad. 曰 (82, above): 1) "sun" will be taller and thinner, or 2) the inner line in "say" will be incomplete, or 3) the two will be indistinguishable, and in a traditional dictionary, you might have to look up a character under both rads. before you could find it.
160 4 strokes	日			
杲	丶	冖	曰	**GǍO, to shine (bookish)** This character is a meaning-meaning compound: "sun" above "tree" suggests "to shine."
	旦	旦	早	
161 8 strokes	杲	杲		
桌	丨	卜	卜	**ZHUŌ, table** The "tree" rad. at the bottom of this character gives you a hint that it refers to some object made of wood. 桌子 *zhuōzi*, table 書桌 *shūzhuō*, writing desk
	占	占	卣	
162 10 strokes	卓	卓	桌	
奇	一	ナ	大	**QÍ, be weird** *Qí* is said to be a meaning-meaning compound, but it is not clear why "big" + "be able" should suggest "be weird." 好奇 *hàoqí*, be curious, be interested in odd things or just in many things 好奇心 *hàoqíxīn*, curiosity
	広	夻	夻	
163 8 strokes	奇	奇		
椅	一	十	才	**YǏ, chair** *Yǐ* is supposed to be a sound-meaning compound. The "tree" rad. helps with the meaning, and *qí* (163, above) is supposed to help with the sound. 椅子 *yǐzi*, chair
	木	杧	杧	
164 12 strokes	椅	椅	椅	

東	一	厂	戸
	両	百	東
165 **8 strokes**	東	東	

DŌNG, east

Lexicographers now explain *dōng* as a meaning-meaning compound; "the sun tangled in the branches of a tree" is supposed to suggest "sunrise" and, therefore, "east." Actually the character originally meant "bundle" and was a picture. "East" is by sound-loan.

东

戔	一	七	戋
	戋	戋	戋
166 **8 strokes**	戔	戔	

JIĀN, thin

Jiān originally meant "be fierce, be cruel." It was a meaning-meaning compound: two lances to suggest "fierce." It is "thin" by sound-loan.

戋

錢	ノ	𠂆	𠂉
	牟	牟	金
167 **16 strokes**	金	錢	錢

QIÁN, money; a family name

The "gold" rad. gives the meaning, and *jiān* (166, above) suggests the sound in this sound-meaning compound.

九分錢 *jiǔ fēn qián*, nine cents
金錢 *jīnqián*, money

钱

古	一	十	寸
	古	古	
168 **5 strokes**			

GŬ, ancient; a family name

According to the usual explanation, *gǔ* is a meaning-meaning compound. "Ten" + "mouth" suggests something which has been passed through ten generations of mouths (people); therefore, ancient.

古老 *gǔlǎo*, be ancient, be age-old
古玩 *gǔwán*, antique, curio

固	丨	冂	冃
	冊	冊	固
169 **8 strokes**	固	固	

GÙ, be hard, be strong

Gǔ (168, above) helps give the sound. There is no satisfactory explanation for the "surround" rad.

個	╱	亻	亻	**GÈ; a "counter" or "measure", used to enumerate nouns in the construction "number + gè + noun;" individual (adjective)**
	佀	佀	佀	三個 *sān gè*, three … 個人 *gèrén*, each person, everyone; oneself, personal
170 10 strokes	佀	個	個	个

| 辶 | 丶 | 氵 | 辶 | **CHUÒ, to halt. HALT rad. (162)(H47)**
 The character was a picture of a foot halted at a crossroads. This form of the "halt" rad. does not occur as an independent character but only as a part of characters. The independent form appears as 983, below. Its traditional printed form is 辶 (sometimes counted as four strokes). |
| 171
 3 strokes
 (7 strokes) | | | | |

這	丶	亠	宀	**ZHÈI, ZHÈ, this** *Zhèi* normally appears in the construction "*zhèi* + 'measure'" or "*zhèi* + 'measure' + noun" (cp. 170, above).
	言	言	言	這個 *zhèi gè*, this, this one 這麼 *zhème*, so, thus, in this case; in this way, to this extent or degree
172 10 strokes	言	言	這	这

那	刁	习	弓	**NÈI, NÀ, NÈ, that** *Nèi* normally appears in the construction "*nèi* + 'measure'" or "*nèi* + 'measure' + noun" (cp. 170 and 172, above).
	月	那	那	那個 *nèi gè*, that, that one 那麼 *nème*, that being so, in that case; in that way, to that extent or degree
173 7 strokes	那			

糸	乚	纟	幺	**SĪ, silk. SILK rad. (120)(H77 in the short form 纟)** This is another way to write 糸 (28, above). The student should learn to recognize both forms of the "silk" rad.
	幺	糸	糸	
174 6 strokes				

仝	丿	人	스

JÍ, to get together, to come together

The character is explained as "three things gathered around a single space." Not in current use as an independent character.

175
3 strokes

合	丿	人	스
	今	合	合

HÉ, to join, to bring together.

The root meaning of *hé* is "to join or close," as one would two panels of a double door. Early dictionaries call this character a meaning-meaning compound and say, "to close, like the mouth."

176
6 strokes

合口 *hékǒu*, to taste good; (of a wound) to heal up
合金 *héjīn*, combined metals, i.e., an alloy

給	ㄥ	纟	纟
	纟	纟	纟
	紁	紷	給

GĚI, to give; to allow; for (someone)…; JǏ, to supply

給我書 *gěi wǒ shū*, gives me books
給我看 *gěi wǒ kàn*, let me look
給我買 *gěi wǒ mǎi*, buy for me

177
12 strokes

給

月	丿	刀	月
	月		

YUÈ, moon. MOON rad. (74)(H118)

The "moon" rad. is a picture. In a traditional dictionary, you cannot be sure whether this form is the "moon" rad. or the "meat" rad. (326); you may have to try under both rads. before you find a character. H puts all such characters under the "meat" rad. (=H118), perhaps because "meat" is by far the commoner of the two, as a rad.

178
4 strokes

𠂇	一	𠂇	

ZUǑ, left hand (H14)

This is a picture of a left hand. Compare the right hand (85, above). Not in current use as an independent character. The student will also want to note that the form is a rad. in H but not in traditional dictionaries.

179
2 strokes

有	一	ナ	才
	冇	有	有
180 6 strokes			

YǑU, to have; there is, there are

The earliest forms show a hand taking hold of a piece of meat. Later lexicographers lost sight of it, so *yǒu* came to be classified under "moon" 月 (in H, under 广 "left hand," 179 above).

有钱 *yǒuqián*, be rich
固有 *gùyǒu*, be inherent, be innate

氵	丶	冫	氵
181 3 strokes (4 strokes)			

SHUǏ, water. WATER rad. (85)(H40)

To distinguish this form of the "water" rad. from the other form 水 (362, below), this form is called 三點水 *sān diǎn shuǐ*, "three-dots water" (for 點, see 282, below). The three-dots form often appears in characters for liquids and fluids.

汗	丶	冫	氵
	汀	汗	汗
182 6 strokes			

HÀN, sweat

Hàn is a sound-meaning compound. The "three-dots water" rad. suggests the meaning; *gān* (87, above) suggests the sound.

殳	丿	几	殳
	殳		
183 4 strokes			

SHŪ, club, to club. CLUB rad. (79)(H119)

Shū is a picture: a right hand holds the club. Distinguish "club" from these characters: "branch" 支 (271, below), "knock" 攵 (384), "pattern" 文 (360), "follow" 夂 (319), and "slow" 夂 (337).

Shū, "club," is not now in common use.

沒	丶	冫	氵
	沪	沪	沒
184 7 strokes	沒		

MÒ, to inundate. MÉI; negates *yǒu* (180, above) and, in certain grammatical situations, negates other verbs. 没 negates *yǒu* and other verbs by sound-loan. Sometimes written 没.

沒有 *méiyǒu*, there isn't, there aren't; doesn't have; has not (done something)
沒買 *méi mǎi*, did not buy, has not bought (yet)

身	´	⼈	勹	**SHĒN, torso. TORSO rad. (158)(H200)**
	甹	自	身	*Shēn* is a picture of a person in which the torso is the most prominent part. It also means "self."
185 7 strokes	身			可身 *kěshēn*, to fit well (clothes) 合身 *héshēn*, to fit well (clothes) 身分 *shēnfèn*, position, rank

寸	一	寸	寸	**CÙN, thumb; inch. THUMB rad. (41)(H54)**
				The "thumb" rad. is a picture of a hand, with the dot added to indicate the thumb. Learn to distinguish "thumb," "side-hand" 扌 (14, above), and "then" 才 (596, below).
186 3 strokes				

射	´	⼈	勹	**SHÈ, to shoot**
	甹	自	身	The character has been corrupted through time. Originally, the "torso" was a picture of an arrow on a bow, and the "thumb" was a hand drawing on a bow, whence "to shoot."
187 10 strokes	射	射		射門 *shèmén*, to shoot (at the goal, in sports) 射手 *shèshǒu*, marksman, sharpshooter

謝	﹅	⼆	言	**XIÈ, thanks; to thank; excuse oneself; a family name**
	言	訁	訃	*Xiè* is a sound-meaning compound; the "words" rad. gives the meaning, and *shè* (187, above) suggests the sound.
188 17 strokes	訝	謝		謝謝 *xièxiè*, Thank you. 不謝 *bùxiè*, You're welcome.　　謝

吉	一	十	士	**JÍ, lucky; a family name**
	士	吉	吉	An early dictionary says the character is a meaning-meaning compound: "scholar" (or "knight") + "mouth" = "lucky."
189 6 strokes				吉日 *jírì*, a "lucky day" on the traditional calendar; a good day for taking action 吉他 *jítā*, guitar

喜	一	十	士	**XǏ, to enjoy, to give enjoyment to**
	吉	壴	壴	The top part of this, what is now "knight-mouth-eight-one," used to be a picture of a drum. *Xǐ* was a meaning-meaning compound: "drum" + "mouth" = "to sing and play drums, to enjoy yourself."
190 **12 strokes**	壴	喜	喜	喜人 *xǐrén*, be satisfying 喜好 *xǐhào*, to like, to love, be fond of

欠	丿	⺈	夕	**QIÀN, yawn; to owe; to lack. YAWN rad. (76)(H120)**
	欠			Note that the lower part of this character is the "man" rad. If it helps you to remember the character, think of the upper part as his hand covering his mouth as he yawns.
191 **4 strokes**				欠錢 *qiànqián*, to owe money, to be in debt

⺾	一	㇇	一一	**CǍO, grass. GRASS rad. (140)**
	⺾			This is a picture of two little shoots of grass breaking through the soil. It occurs only as part of characters. Distinguish this form of the "grass" rad. from "clasp" 廾 (141, above). Printed ⺿. Some dictionaries call this form 草字頭兒 *cǎo zì tóur*, "top of the character 'grass'." 草 = 992, below; 字 =257; 頭 =454; 兒 =230.
192 **4 strokes** **(6 strokes)**				

雚	㇇	⺊⺊	廿	**GUÀN, heron**
	茁	艹	苐	This character is not at present used as an independent character.
193 **18 strokes**	雚	雚	雚	(口 33)

歡	艹	茁	芇	**HUĀN, be pleased**
	雚	雚	雚	*Guàn* (193, above) suggests the sound. The "yawn" rad. suggests the meaning, perhaps as a mouth open to smile or to laugh rather than to yawn.
194 **22 strokes**	雚	歡	歡	喜歡 *xǐhuān*, to like 歡笑 *huānxiào*, to laugh delightedly 歡心 *huānxīn*, favor (noun), love (noun)　　欢

69

止	丨	卜	止	**ZHǏ, to stop. TOE rad. (77)(H102)**
	止			The "toe" rad. is a picture of a foot. From "foot" came derived meanings, actions of the foot; "to march; to halt." Only the meaning "to halt" has stayed with the character to modern times.
195 4 strokes				不止三個 *bù zhǐ sān gè*, not stopping at three, not only three

足	丶	口	口	**ZÚ, foot; be sufficient. FOOT rad. (157)(H196)**
	尸	尸	尸	A picture. The bottom part of 足 is, in fact, the "toe" rad. (195, above). In 197, below, the "foot" ràd. appears as part of the character; note that in the form used in compounds, the "toe" can clearly be seen.
196 7 strokes	足			十足 *shízú*, sheer, total, absolute, utter

跟	口	尸	足	**GĒN, heel; to follow, to go with; with**
	足	趵	趵	*Gēn* is a sound-meaning compound; the "foot" rad. gives the meaning; *gēn* (31, above) gives the sound.
197 13 strokes	趵	跟	跟	跟上 *gēnshang*, to keep up with, keep pace with

青	一	二	丰	**QĪNG, be green or blue. GREEN rad. (174)(H202)**
	主	丰	青	Note that the bottom half of "green" resembles "moon." *Qīng* by itself, however, is recognized as a rad. The character also occurs independently and means "green" and sometimes other "colors of nature," like azure, or even greenish black or gray. Often printed 青.
198 8 strokes	青	青		

請	丶	二	二	**QǏNG, to invite; please…**
	言	言	言	This character is a sound-meaning compound; "words" gives the meaning, and *qīng* (198, above) gives the sound.
199 15 strokes	計	請	請	誰請 *shéi qǐng*, Who's paying? 请

問	丨	ㄇ	ㄇ
	ㄖ	ㄇㄧ	門
200 11 strokes	門	門	問

WÈN, to ask (for information)
"Mouth" gives the meaning, and *mén* once gave the sound in this sound-meaning compound.
請問 *qǐngwèn*, Would you please tell me…

(口　33)　　问

耳	一	厂	丌
	丅	耵	耳
201 6 strokes			

ĔR, ear. EAR rad. (128)(H163)
The "ear" rad. is a picture.
耳目 *ĕrmù*, hearsay, "scuttlebutt," information; a spy, informer, "fink"
木耳 *mùĕr*, edible tree fungus

聞	丨	ㄇ	ㄇ
	ㄖ	ㄇㄧ	門
202 14 strokes	門	門	聞

WÉN, to hear
Notice that *mén* (45, above) functions here, as in 200, above, to suggest the sound *wen*. In *wén* "to hear," the meaning is given by the "ear" rad.
聞人 *wénrén*, famous person
耳聞 *ĕrwén*, to hear about, especially superficially, or from others (in contrast to seeing with one's own eyes)　闻

閒	丨	ㄖ	ㄇㄧ
	門	門	閒
203 12 strokes	閒	閒	閒

XIÁN, leisure
閒, the moon shining through a crack in a gate, originally meant "crack, break." "Leisure" may be an extension of meaning, as in English a rest is "a break." Now usually = 閑, which looks like a meaning-meaning compound: "put a tree across your door so you won't be disturbed."　闲

間	丨	ㄖ	ㄇㄧ
	門	門	間
204 12 strokes	閒	間	間

JIÀN, space; be separated from; to separate, "drive a wedge between," sow discord.
JIĀN, space, area; between; a 'measure-word' for rooms.
This once was a mere variant of 203.
中間 *zhōngjiān*, between, among; the middle, center
田間 *tiánjiān*, farm, field
人間 *rénjiān*, the human world, the world of human affairs　间

刂 205 2 strokes	⼁	刂	

DĀO, knife. KNIFE rad. (18)(H17)

This form of the "knife" rad. occurs only as a part of characters. Cp. the independent form 刀 (102, above), and note that this dependent form and the form 刀 are different radicals in H. Some dictionaries call this form 立刀旁兒 lì dāo pángr, "standing side-knife." (旁 = 785, below; 兒 = 230).

力 206 2 strokes	ㄱ	力

LÌ, strength. STRENGTH rad. (19)(H28)

The student should distinguish "strength" from the "knife" rad. 刀 (102, above)

四匹馬力 sì pǐ mǎlì, four horsepower
賣力 màilì, "put your back" into a job; do something "with all your might"

另 207 5 strokes	⼂	⼌	口
	号	另	

LÌNG, separately

另外 lìngwài, in addition

別 208 7 strokes	⼂	⼌	口
	尸	另	别
	別		

BIÉ, to separate, to part; Don't…!

分別 fēnbié, leave each other; sort out, differentiate; difference
別人 biérén, other people
別買 biémǎi, Don't buy it!
個別 gèbié, specific; very few; be exceptional

朋 209 8 strokes	⼃	刀	月
	月	肌	朋
	朋	朋	

PÉNG, friend

The character originally stood for a fabulous bird and was a picture of the wing of that bird. It means "friend" by sound-loan. The character is classified in traditional dictionaries under the "moon" rad. 月 (178, above). In H, it is classified under rad. 118 ("moon/meat").

友	一	ナ	友	**YǑU, friend**
	友			A meaning-meaning compound: "left hand" + "right hand" = "friend." The character perhaps is supposed to suggest the Chinese gesture of parting from friends: clasping your own hands in front of you and bowing over them.
210 4 strokes				朋友 *péngyǒu*, friend

父	'	八	父	**FÙ, father. FATHER rad. (88)(H108)**
	父			父老 *fùlǎo*, elders (as in a district)
211 4 strokes				

毋	乚	口	毋	**WÚ, Don't! DON'T rad. (80)**
	毋			The character is supposed to be a picture of a woman in irons. The relation of that to its present meaning is unclear. Learn to distinguish the "don't" rad. from 母 *mǔ*, "mother" (216, below).
212 4 strokes				

亲	丶	二	六	**ZHĒN, hazel tree**
	六	立	立	This character is not in modern use except as a short form for 親 *qīn* (215, below), in which usage it is, of course, pronounced "*qīn.*"
213 9 strokes	辛	亲	亲	

見	丨	冂	冂	**JIÀN, to see; to perceive. SEE rad. (147)(H107)**
	冃	目	貝	The modern form of "see" = "eye" over "legs." It comes from a drawing of a man in which the eye was drawn large to suggest "to see; to perceive." It is now often
214 7 strokes	見			explained (inaccurately) as "the eye running out to gather information for the looker." 见

73

親	`	⺀	六	**QĪN, kin; hold dear; in person; QÌNG, relatives by marriage**
	立	辛	亲	*Zhen* (213, above) for sound, eye for meaning (so say the lexicographers). 父親 *fùqīn*, father 六親 *liù qīn*, the six (most important) relatives: father, mother, elder brothers, younger brothers, wife, children 親人 *qīnrén*, kinfolk
215 16 strokes	親	親	親	亲

MǓ, mother

母	ㄥ	母	母	*Mǔ* is a picture of a woman with two dots to emphasize the breasts. Learn to distinguish "mother" from the "don't" rad. 毋 (212, above).
	母	母		母親 *mǔqīn*, mother 父母 *fùmǔ*, parents, your father and mother
216 5 strokes				

GĒ, older brother

哥	一	丁	丁	哥哥 *gēge*, older brother 大哥 *dàgē*, oldest brother; also used to address politely a man about your own age 表哥 *biǎogē*, older male cousin such that the two of you are children or grandchildren of a brother and a sister, or of two sisters
	可	可	哥	
217 10 strokes	哥	哥		

GŌNG, bow. BOW rad. (57)(H71)

弓	ㄱ	ㄱ	弓	The "bow" rad. is a picture of a bow. 弓子 *gōngzi*, bow (e.g., a violin bow)
218 3 strokes				

DIÀO, to pity

弔	ㄱ	ㄱ	弓	This character is supposed to be a picture of an arrow stayed on the bow, hence "to pity." In modern use, this character has been replaced by 吊, which Bernhard Karlgren calls "a vulgar corruption" (*Analytic Dictionary* 989).
	弔			
219 4 strokes				

弟

220
7 strokes

DÌ, younger brother

弟弟 *dìdi*, younger brother; younger male cousin
二弟 *èrdì*, second younger cousin

姐

221
8 strokes

JIĚ, older sister

姐姐 *jiějie*, older sister
大姐 *dàjiě*, oldest sister; also used to address politely a woman about your own age
小姐 *xiǎojiě*, Miss

未

222
5 strokes

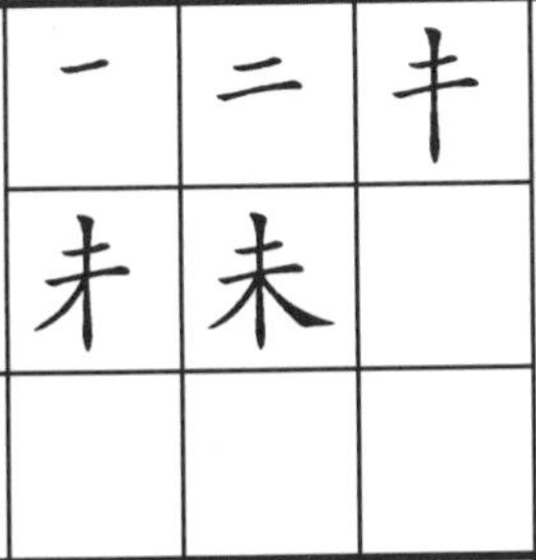

WÈI, not yet; the eighth "earthly branch"

Distinguish 未 "not yet" from 耒 (1029, below) and from 末 (p.301b).

未可 *wèikě*, cannot, be unable to

妹

223
8 strokes

MÈI, kid sister

妹妹 *mèimei*, younger sister
姐妹 *jiěmèi*, sisters
妹夫 *mèifū*, brother-in-law (precisely, younger sister's husband)
表妹 *biǎomèi*, younger female cousin such that the two of you are children or grandchildren of a brother and a sister, or of two sisters

氏

224
4 strokes

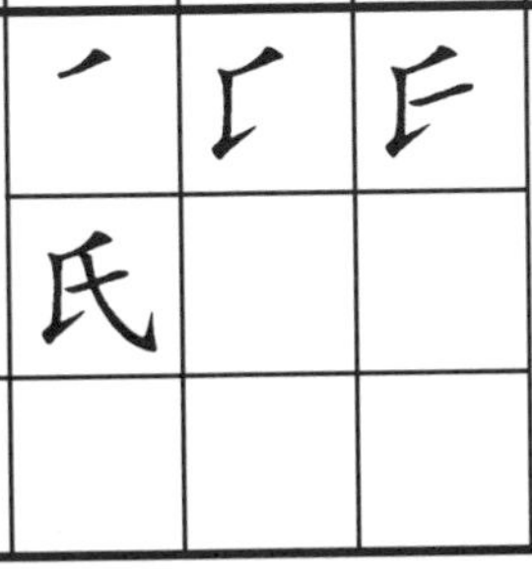

SHÌ, clan. CLAN rad. (83)(H122)

The student may find it difficult to remember how to write rads. which, like the "clan" rad., do not make a clear picture of anything. But the number of such non-representational rads. is small, and the student will find that a little extra work solves the problem.

田王氏 *Tián Wáng shì*, Mrs. Tian, whose maiden name is Wang

紙

225
10 strokes

ZHǏ, paper

A sound-meaning compound. The "silk" rad. gives the meaning; *shì* (224, above) suggests the sound.

手紙 *shǒuzhǐ*, toilet paper
報紙 *bàozhǐ*, newspaper, newsprint

纸

長

226
8 strokes

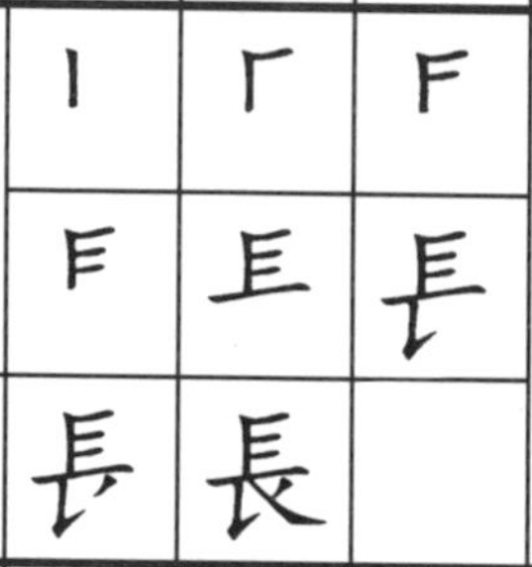

CHǍNG, be long; ZHǍNG, to grow; senior. LONG rad. (168). (In modern dictionaries, not a rad.; the short form is classified under *piě* [1, above])

The character is a drawing of a man with a long beard.

長大 *zhǎngdà*, to grow up
長子 *zhǎngzi*, eldest son

长

張

227
11 strokes

ZHĀNG, to open out, to open up; a measure for objects coming in sheets; a family name

三張紙 *sān zhāng zhǐ*, three sheets of paper
張弓 *zhāng gōng*, draw a bow

(弓 218)

张

畫

228
12 strokes

HUÀ, a painting

一張畫 *yì zhāng huà*, a painting
畫報 *huàbào*, an illustrated magazine
國畫 *guóhuà*, "national painting," i.e., traditional Chinese painting

(田 23)

画

臼

229
6 strokes

JIÙ, mortar. MORTAR rad. (134)(H179)

Jiù is the drawing of a mortar (a vessel in which to grind things up).

兒	′	亻	白	**ÉR, son, child; R. a noun-suffix (rarely, a verb-suffix)** This character is said to be a picture of a child with open fontanel. 兒子 *érzi*, son 女兒 *nǚér*, daughter 兒童 *értóng*, child
230 8 strokes	白	白	白	
	臼	兒		儿

白	′	亻	白	**BÁI, be white; a family name. WHITE rad. (106)(H150)** The student should distinguish "white" from the "sun" rad. 日 (160, above) and from the "nose" rad. 自 (515, below). 白天 *báitiān*, in the daytime 白給 *báigěi*, to give free of charge 白人 *báirén*, white guy, white girl 表白 *biǎobái*, to vindicate
231 5 strokes	白	白		

勹	′	勹		**BĀO, to wrap. WRAP rad. (20)(H26)** The character is a picture of a wrapper. As part of a character, the "wrap" rad. usually appears wrapped around other rads. or parts of the character. Some modern dictionaries call the "wrap" rad. "包字頭兒," *bāozì tóur* — top of the character 'bao' (包 = 509, below; 字 = 257; 頭 = 454).
232 2 strokes				

勺	′	勹	勺	**SHÁO, spoon; frying pan** 勺子 *sháozi*, spoon 木勺 *mùsháo*, wooden ladle
233 3 strokes				

的	′	亻	白	**DE; a suffix to nouns and pronouns; a grammatical particle; DÌ, bull's-eye** 我的 *wǒde*, my, mine 有的 *yǒude*, some 目的 *mùdì*, aim, purpose
234 8 strokes	白	白	白	
	的	的		

本	一	十	才	**BĚN, root; volume (book); capital (money); principal (money); a measure for books**
	木	本		*Běn* is a picture of a tree with a horizontal stroke at the bottom to signify that the meaning is "root." 日本 *Rìběn*, Japan
235 5 strokes				一本書 *yì běn shū*, a book 本人 *běnrén*, I, myself; in person 本錢 *běnqián*, capital (money)

對	丶	丷	业	**DUÌ, to face; facing; to match; be correct**
	业	业	业	對了 *duìle*, That's right! 對手 *duìshǒu*, adversary, opponent 對鐘 *duì zhōng*, to set a clock
236 14 strokes	业	业	對	对

兄	丶	冂	口	**XIŌNG, older brother**
	尸	兄		兄弟 *xiōngdì*, brothers 表兄 *biǎoxiōng*, older male cousin on the mother's side
237 5 strokes				

兌	丶	丷	丷	**DUÌ, to hand over**
	兯	台	户	兌給 *duìgěi*, to pay to
238 7 strokes	兌			

稅	丿	二	千	**SHUÌ, tax**
	禾	禾	秒	The peasantry in China traditionally paid their taxes in grain, so "to hand over" + "grain" was a good meaning-meaning compound for "tax."
239 12 strokes	秒	秒	稅	報稅 *bàoshuì*, to make a customs declaration, to declare goods on which duty is owed

説	`	ン	言
	言	言	訡
240 14 strokes	訲	詺	説

SHUŌ, to speak; SHUÌ, try to persuade

This is a sound-meaning compound: the "word" rad. for meaning, *duì* (238, above) for sound. (When the character was invented, *duì* gave the sound more accurately than it does now.)

説笑 *shuōxiào*, to talk and laugh together, to yuk it up

説一不二 *shuō yī bú èr*, to mean what you say   説

千	ノ	二	千
241 3 strokes			

QIĀN, one thousand; a family name (rare)

The "ten" rad. gives a clue that the character stands for a number.

千里 *qiān lǐ*, many miles; long journey
千里馬 *qiānlǐ mǎ*, a superb horse, a horse that can run many miles
千古 *qiāngǔ*, eternal, of the ages

重	ノ	二	二
	育	盲	重
242 9 strokes	重	重	

ZHÒNG, be heavy; CHÓNG, over again, to repeat by mistake, to duplicate

重要 *zhòngyào*, be important
買重了 *mǎichóng le*, has/have bought an extra one (one too many)
貴重 *guìzhòng*, be valuable
重了 *chóng le*, be done twice, get repeated

董	一	十	十一
	艹	芏	苦
243 13 strokes	菁	萤	董

DǑNG, to correct, to supervise; a family name

古董 *gǔdǒng*, an antique; an old fart

懂	`	十	忄
	忄	忄	忄
244 16 strokes	惜	懂	懂

DǑNG, to understand

This character may stand for the same word as 243, above: "be correct (in the mind) about, to understand." Note that in form it is identical to 243, with the addition of the "heart" rad. (often glossed as "heart/mind").

看不懂 *kànbudǒng*, be unable to read

79

| 疋 | 一 | 下 | 下 | **PǏ, bolt (of cloth). BOLT rad. (103)(H156)** |
| 245
5 strokes | 疋 | 疋 | | |

是	丶	口	日	**SHÌ, am, is, are; be right (H rad. 213)** 不是 *bûshì*, "No!"; a fault 是的 *shìde*, "Yes!", "That's right!" 可是 *kěshì*, but 要是 *yàoshi*, if
	日	旦	早	
246 9 strokes	早	昰	是	

| 先 | 丿 | 一 | 屮 | **XIĀN, to precede; late (deceased)**
先父 *xiānfù*, my late father
先夫 *xiānfū*, my late husband
先天 *xiāntiān*, innate, inborn |
| 247
6 strokes | 生 | 步 | 先 | |

| 生 | 丿 | 一 | 仁 | **SHĒNG, to bear (give birth to). BIRTH rad. (100)**
先生 *xiānsheng*, "Mr."; teacher
生女兒 *shēng nǚér*, to bear a daughter
女生 *nǚshēng*, a coed
生日 *shēngrì*, birthday
生手 *shēngshǒu*, green hand, green horn |
| 248
5 strokes | 牛 | 生 | | |

李	一	十	才	**LǏ, plum tree; a family name** 李子 *lǐzi*, plum 李先生 *Lǐ Xiānsheng*, Mr. Li
	木	杢	李	
249 7 strokes	李			

亥	丶	亠	亡	**HÀI, the twelfth "earthly branch"**
	歺	亥	亥	亥, originally a picture of a boar, is still similar in form to the "pig" rad. 豕 (389, below). The boar is the symbolical animal of the twelfth category in the "earthly branches" cycle. *Hài* gives the sound in a number of common characters (usually as *hai*, sometimes as *gai*).
250 **6 strokes**				

孩	⁊	了	孑	**HÁI, child**
	孑	孑	孖	The "child" rad. gives the meaning; *hài* (250, above) gives the sound. 孩子 *háizi*, child 孩童 *háitóng*, children 小孩兒 *xiǎoháir*, child (colloquial)
251 **9 strokes**	孩	孩	孩	

爻	ノ	メ	爻	**YÁO, crisscross. CRISSCROSS rad. (89)**
	爻			
252 **4 strokes**				

學	⸍	⸜	⸝	**XUÉ, to study, to learn** The "child" rad. is, of course, the student. "Mortar" was once two hands guiding the student to write characters (the "crisscross" rad.) properly. Anciently, 學 and *jiāo* "teach
	臼	臼	臼	(386 below) were the same character. 學生 *xuéshēng*, student 大學 *dàxué*, university (子 18)
253 **16 strokes**	學	學	學	学

男	丶	冂	日	**NÁN, male** According to the classic dictionary *Shuō wén jiě zì*, 男 is a meaning-meaning
	田	田	男	compound: "it's the *males* who use their strength 力 in the fields 田." 男人 *nánrén*, man 男生 *nánshēng*, male student 長男 *zhǎngnán*, eldest son 男女 *nánnǚ*, men and women
254 **7 strokes**	男			

81

姓	㇑	女	女	**XÌNG, surname; to be surnamed**
	女	女	女	您貴姓 *nín guì xìng*, What is your name? (polite)
255 **8 strokes**	姓	姓		我姓李 *wǒ xìng Lǐ*, My (sur)name is Li. 姓氏 *xìngshì*, surname

名	㇒	ク	夕	**MÍNG, name**
	夕	名	名	Ancient Chinese dictionaries say that *míng* is a meaning-meaning compound: "dusk" (117, above) + "mouth." In the "dark" you can't see someone, so you "mouth" (call) his name.
256 **6 strokes**				姓名 *xìngmíng*, full name 有名 *yǒumíng*, be famous

字	丶	丷	宀	**ZÌ, written character**
	宀	宁	字	The original meaning is "bring up, cherish," and the character is meaning-meaning: "a child under your roof." The character means "written character" by sound-loan.
257 **6 strokes**				名字 *míngzi*, name 字母 *zìmǔ*, alphabet; letter 別字 *biézì*, mispronounced or wrongly written character

丩	㇄	丩		**JIŪ, to connect**
				This character is not in modern use except as a part of other characters.
258 **2 strokes**				

叫	㇑	冂	口	**JIÀO, to call; to be called; to order a person to do something**
	叩	叫		"Mouth" gives the meaning; *jiū* (258, above) gives the sound.
259 **5 strokes**				叫甚麼 *jiào shémme*, What's it called (named)? 馬叫 *mǎ jiào*, the horse neighs

牛	丿	二	二	**NIÚ, cow, COW rad. (93)**
	牛			This character is a picture (cp. 15, above). This form occurs as a part of characters and also as an independent character. Learn to distinguish "cow" from *wǔ* "noon" 午 (594, below).
260 4 strokes				

告	丿	二	牛	**GÀO, to inform**
	牛	牛	告	The original meaning of this character was "muzzle for cows." The character was a meaning-meaning compound: "cow" + "mouth" suggested the device. By sound-loan it means "inform."
261 7 strokes	告			報告 *bàogào*, to report; a report, a lecture

斤	丿	厂	厂	**JĪN, axe. AXE rad. (69)(H115)**
	斤			The "axe" rad, is a picture. The character now stands also for a measure of weight, a *jīn* or "catty," which equals about 1.5 pounds.
262 4 strokes				

斥	丿	厂	厂	**CHÌ, to scold**
	斤	斥		
263 5 strokes				

訴	丶	二	言	**SÙ, SÒNG, to inform**
				告訴 *gàosù*, to inform
				訴説 *sùshuō*, to tell, to relate
	言	言	言	上訴 *shàngsù*, (legal term) to appeal to a higher court
264 12 strokes	訂	訢	訴	诉

83

知 265 8 strokes	ノ	㇄	㇁
	乍	矢	矢
	知	知	

ZHĪ, to know

The early lexicographers pretty much agree that this is a meaning-meaning compound — "arrow" (63, above) + "mouth" — "because when you know, your mouth is sharp and far-reaching, like an arrow."

知心 *zhīxīn*, to understand each other
先知 *xiānzhī*, a person having foresight; a prophet, soothsayer

首 266 9 strokes	`	㇀	丷
	䒑	产	产
	首	首	首

SHŎU, chief; the head. CHIEF rad. (185)

The student should distinguish the "chief" rad. from the "head" rad 頁 (333, below) and from the "face" rad. 面 (610, below). "Chief" was originally a picture of a head with horns or some big headdress.

首都 *shŏudū*, capital city

道 267 12 strokes	`	丷	丷
	䒑	产	首
	首	道	道

DÀO, road; to say; the Way

知道 *zhīdào*, to know
道謝 *dàoxiè*, to thank
道喜 *dàoxǐ*, to congratulate
道士 *dàoshì*, Taoist (Daoist) priest
道學 *dàoxué*, Neo-Confucianism

| 此 268 6 strokes | ㇑ | ㇜ | ㇊ |
| | 止 | 此 | 此 |

CǏ, this

The form of the character can be analyzed as "toe" + "ladle," but the meaning cannot be explained on that basis. The student will just have to memorize it.

此外 *cǐwài*, furthermore, in addition

| 些 269 8 strokes | ㇜ | 止 | 此 |
| | 此 | 些 | 些 |

XIĒ, few

好些 *hǎoxiē*, quite a few
這一些書 *zhèi yìxiē shū*, this lot of books
大些 *dà xiē*, a bit larger

位	ノ	イ	イ	**WÈI, position, standpoint; seat; a polite measure for persons** 三位小姐 *sān wèi xiǎojiě*, three young ladies 位子 *wèizi*, seat 學位 *xuéwèi*, academic degree
---	仁	仁	付	
270 7 strokes	位			

支	一	十	支	**ZHĪ, branch; to prop up; to pay or draw (money). BRANCH rad. (65)** The student will need to distinguish the "branch" rad. from "club" 殳 (183, above), "knock" 攴 (384, below), "pattern" 文 (360), "follow" 夂 (319), "slow" 夊 (337), and the 攵 form of "knock" (p. 276a).
---	支			
271 4 strokes				

枝	一	十	才	**ZHĪ, branch; a measure for pens, pencils, chalk, etc.** In this character, 271, above, has been reclarified with the "tree" rad. 枝子 *zhīzi*, (tree) branch 一枝筆 *yì zhī bǐ*, a pen
---	木	村	枋	
272 8 strokes	枝	枝		

己	⁊	コ	己	**JǏ, self; the sixth "heavenly stem." SELF rad. (49)(H72)** As a cyclical character ("heavenly stem"), this was probably a symbol. The meaning "self" is probably by sound-loan. Learn to tell "self" from "already" 已 (274, below), from *sì* 巳 (275), and from "seal" 㔾 (760). 知己 *zhījǐ*, "bosom" or "intimate" (as in "bosom friend")
---				
273 3 strokes				

已	⁊	コ	已	**YǏ, already; to end, to cease** See the note under 273, above, for characters with which 已 is likely to be confused.
---				
274 3 strokes				

巴	ㄱ	コ	巴	**SÌ**, the sixth "earthly branch" (巳, as well as 己 (273, above) = H rad. 72.)
275 **3 strokes**				*Sì* is originally supposed to have been a drawing of a fetus, with a large head and curled up lower part. The student should learn to distinguish *sì* from 273 and 274, above.

巴	ㄱ	コ	コ	**BĀ**, open hand; palm; to stick to; to hope for
	巴			In ancient texts, this character meant python — as the dictionaries call it, "the elephant snake" — and it was a picture. It came to mean "open hand" by sound-loan.
276 **4 strokes**				

吧	丨	口	口	**BA**; a sentence-final particle; indicates supposition ("…, I guess") or suggestion
	口ㄱ	口コ	口コ	吧 is a sound-meaning compound. 好吧 *hǎo ba*, Okay! Bravo! Fine! 你知道吧 *nǐ zhīdào ba*, You know, I suppose.
277 **7 strokes**	吧			

央	丶	冂	凸	**YĀNG**, center
	央	央		中央 *zhōngyāng*, center, central
278 **5 strokes**				

英	一	十	艹	**YĪNG**, be bold; flower (bookish); a family name
	艹	艹	苎	The original meaning was "flower, to flower;" "grass" gave the meaning, and *yāng* (278, above) suggested the sound. "Bold" is by sound-loan.
279 **9 strokes**	苴	英	英	英國 *Yīngguó*, England 英里 *yīng lǐ*, English mile

86

黑	丶	冂	冂	**HĒI, black. BLACK rad. (203)(H223)**
	冂	回	回	*Hēi* is said to be the picture of a man painted up with war paint and decorated with tattooing.
280 12 strokes	甲	里	黑	黑心 *hēixīn*, a "black heart," an evil mind 黑白不分 *hēi bái bù fēn*, cannot distinguish between right and wrong.

占	丨	卜	卜	**ZHĀN, to divine; ZHÀN, seize; constitute**
	占	占		占 is a meaning-meaning compound: the "divine" rad. (118, above) + "mouth" = "to explain (orally) the divination cracks." Other meanings by sound-loan.
281 5 strokes				占有 *zhànyǒu*, to possess; to occupy 占便宜 *zhàn piányi*, get an unfair advantage; advantageous

點	丶	冂	冂	**DIĂN, dot**
	回	甲	里	五點鐘 *wǔ diǎn zhōng*, 5:00 三點六 *sān diǎn liù*, 3.6 點心 *diǎnxīn*, snack, pastry, "dim sum" 要點 *yàodiǎn*, main points, essential point or points
282 17 strokes	黑	點	點	点

雨	一	一	冂	**YǓ, rain, RAIN rad. (173)(H204)**
	雨	雨	雨	The "rain" rad. is a picture of raindrops falling from clouds.
283 8 strokes	雨	雨		雨點 *yǔdiǎn*, raindrop 雨衣 *yǔyī*, raincoat

令	丿	人	亼	**LÌNG, to command; command; your (respectful); LǏNG, ream**
	今	令		Usually printed 令.
284 5 strokes				令兄 *lìng xiōng*, (respectful) your older brother 一令紙 *yì lǐng zhǐ*, a ream of paper

87

零	一	厂	雨	**LÍNG, zero; tiny bit**
	雨	雨	雨	The original meaning of this character was "drop," and it was a compound of "rain" for meaning and *líng* (284, above) for sound. The meaning "zero" may be an extension: "drop" > "tiny bit" > "virtually nothing" > "nothing"; or it may be a case of sound-loan. Usually printed 零.
285 **13 strokes**	雯	零	零	

半	丶	丷	丷	**BÀN, half**
	半	半		The vertical stroke bisects the "eight" rad. and the two "one" rads, to suggest "half." 一大半 *yī dà bàn*, majority 三點半 *sān diǎn bàn*, 3:30 半天 *bàntiān*, long time
286 **5 strokes**				

多	丿	夕	夕	**DUŌ, be numerous**
	多	多	多	多半 *duōbàn*, the greater part; for the most part, probably 好多了 *hǎo duō le*, Much better! 多謝 *duōxiè*, Many thanks!
287 **6 strokes**				

少	丿	小	小	**SHǍO, be few; SHÀO, be young**
	少			多少 *duōshǎo*, How much? How many? 少了三個 *shǎo le sān gè*, to be three short 少不了 *shǎo bu liǎo*, cannot do without, must have; to be unavoidable 少女 *shàonǚ*, young girl
288 **4 strokes**				

句	丿	勹	勹	**JÙ, sentence; verse line; measure for sentences and verse lines**
	句	句		句子 *jùzi*, sentence
289 **5 strokes**				

够	ノ	勹	勹
	句	句	句
290 11 strokes	夠	够	够

GÒU, enough

Duō "be numerous" (287, above) suggests the meaning; *jù* (289) once suggested the sound.

够朋友 *gòu péngyǒu*, to be a friend indeed

鬼	ノ	′	白
	白	甶	甶
291 10 strokes	鬼	鬼	鬼

GUǏ, ghost. GHOST rad. (194)(H216)

This character is said to be a picture of a ghost. That is a statement difficult to deny.

心里有鬼 *xīnlǐ yǒu guǐ*, to have a guilty conscience. 里 here is the short form for 449, below

鬼點子 *guǐdiǎnzi*, (dialect) dirty trick, evil plan

塊	一	十	土
	圡	圫	坤
292 13 strokes	坤	塊	塊

KUÀI, clod, lump; a measure for dollars

The "earth" rad. gives the meaning; *guǐ* (291, above) suggests the sound.

七塊錢 *qī kuài qián*, seven dollars
一塊田 *yī kuài tián*, a piece of land, a field

块

毛	ノ	二	三
	毛		
293 4 strokes			

MÁO, fur; a measure for dimes; a family name. FUR rad. (82)(H112)

Máo is a picture of an animal's pelt. Distinguish from 手 "hand" (41, above).

毛筆 *máobǐ*, writing brush
毛衣 *máoyī*, (wool) sweater
汗毛 *hànmáo*, fine body-hair (on people)

相	一	十	才
	木	木	机
294 9 strokes	相	相	相

XIĀNG, mutually, each other; XIÀNG, face, appearance; to examine

The original meaning was "to examine." The character is supposed to show someone studying a tree or piece of wood with his eye; a carpenter checking material.

相對 *xiāngduì*, relative (not absolute)
首相 *shǒuxiàng*, prime minister

想	一	十	才
	木	相	相
295 13 strokes	相	想	想

XIĂNG, to think

This character may stand for a word cognate with 294, above. The "heart" rad. means "mind" (as it often does), and 想 can be explained as "to examine in the mind, to think." The character is then a reclarified compound.

想要 *xiăngyào*, to feel like, to want to

得	ノ	ク	彳
	彳	彳	彳
296 11 strokes	彳	得	得

DĔI, must; DÉ, to get; DE; a grammatical particle

得了 *dé le*, That does it! Enough!
貴得多 *guì de duō*, be much more expensive
看得見 *kàndejiàn*, be able to see
巴不得 *bābude*, (colloquial) be eager to do something, really want to do something

共	一	十	廿
	丗	共	共
297 6 strokes			

GÒNG, all together, collectively, joint

Older forms have "clasp" (141, above) twice.

一共 *yìgòng*, all together
中共 *Zhōng Gòng*, Chinese Communists (from 中國共產黨 *Zhōngguó Gòngchăndăng*, Chinese Communist Party [產 = 626, below; 黨 = 625])

尤	一	ナ	尢
	尤		
298 4 strokes			

YÓU, still more; a family name

姓尤的 *xìng Yóu de*, someone surnamed "Yóu"
尤毛氏 *Yóu Máo shì*, Mrs. *Yóu*, whose maiden name was *Máo*

京	、	亠	宀
	亠	亠	宁
299 8 strokes	亨	京	

JĪNG, capital

The character is a picture of a tall building (cp. 75, above), and this was its original meaning. It soon came to mean "tall buildings: capital."

京都 *Jīngdū*, Kyoto
東京 *Dōngjīng*, Tokyo

就	丶	二	古
	亠	京	京
300 12 strokes	亣	就	就

JIÙ, then; only; to go to; to go with

就是 *jiùshì*, be precisely …; namely …;
That's right!
就有三個 *jiù yǒu sān gè*, to have only three

直	一	十	亠
	市	市	甴
301 8 strokes	直		

ZHÍ, straight; to keep on; be a certain length

A meaning-meaning compound: ten + eyes
目 inspect the line — and find it to be
straight. (Usually printed 直.)

一直 *yìzhí*, so far, straight on
直言 *zhíyán*, to speak bluntly

真	一	十	亠
	市	市	甴
302 10 strokes	直	真	真

ZHĒN, be real, be true; truly

Of *zhēn*, the bottom part was originally 兀
(58, above). 真 was analyzed: ten eyes
check out something put in plain view, on a
pedestal, so it must be real, genuine. Often
printed 真.

真相 *zhēnxiàng*, true picture
真是的 *zhēn shì de*, That's really too bad!
真好 *zhēn hǎo*, Great!

現	一	二	干
	王	玎	珇
303 11 strokes	珇	珼	現	现

XIÀN, present, now

現錢 *xiànqián*, ready money
兌現 *duì xiàn*, to cash a check, to fulfill a
promise

在	一	犬	犬
	在	在	在
304 6 strokes			

ZÀI, be at, in, on

現在 *xiànzài*, now
在我看 *zài wǒ kàn*, as I see it
不在了 *bú zài le*, to no longer exist; to be
dead

良	丶	㇋	㇋	**LIĂNG, good**
				The student should distinguish *liăng* from the "stubborn" rad. 艮 (31, above). *Liăng* has the extra dot at the top.
	㇌	自	艮	良心 *liángxīn*, conscience
305				良好 *liánghǎo*, be good, be well
7 strokes	良			良友 *liángyǒu*, good companion

食	丿	人	人	**SHÍ, food, to eat. FOOD rad. (184)(H217)**
				The "food" rad. is a picture of a jar commonly used to hold food.
	今	今	今	零食 *língshí*, snack
				日食 *rìshí*, solar eclipse
306	食	食	食	月食 *yuèshí*, lunar eclipse
9 strokes				食言 *shíyán*, to break a promise, to go back on your word

兩	一	厂	冂	**LIĂNG, two; a tael (ancient unit of weight equaling 50 grams)**
				兩塊錢 *liǎng kuài qián*, two dollars
	帀	兩	兩	一兩金子 *yì liǎng jīnzi*, a tael of gold
307				兩口子 *liǎng kǒuzi*, husband and wife
8 strokes	兩			两

反	一	厂	厂	**FĂN, to turn back; to rebel**
				相反 *xiāngfǎn*, the opposite of
	反			反對 *fǎnduì*, to oppose
308				反射 *fǎnshè*, reflex; reflection
4 strokes				反目 *fǎnmù*, to quarrel, to have a falling out (especially of husband and wife)

食	丿	𠂉	𠂊	**SHÍ, food, to eat. FOOD rad. (148)(The short form is H rad. 68.)**
				Compare this with the form of "food" rad. above (306). The form here (309) is the form the "food" rad. usually takes when it is part of a character; 306 is the independent form.
	𠂤	𠂤	𠂤	
309				
8 strokes	食	食		飠
(9 strokes)				

92

飯	ノ	⺀	今
	𩙿	𩙿	𩙿
310 12 strokes	𩙿	飰	飯

FÀN, cooked rice, food

Fàn is a sound-meaning compound. The "food" rad. gives the meaning; *fǎn* (308, above) suggests the sound.

米飯 *mǐfàn*, cooked rice
要飯 *yàofàn*, to beg for food or money

饭

唐	、	一	广
	广	户	庐
311 10 strokes	庐	唐	唐

TÁNG; the name of the Tang (T'ang) dynasty; family name

The *Shuō wén jiě zì* dictionary says that this character originally meant "to talk big," that is, to boast rudely. The mouth rad., of course, helped with this meaning; the top part — anciently *gēng* 庚 (p. 271a, below) — may have suggested the sound. Tang (dynasty), then, by sound-loan.

糖	、	⺌	丷
	半	米	籿
⟍ 312 16 strokes	籿	糒	糖

TÁNG, sugar, candy

The "rice" rad. helps with the meaning; it often appears in characters for words that mean a powdery substance, grain, or granular foodstuffs. *Táng* (311, above) is, of course, phonetic.

白糖 *báitáng*, white sugar, refined sugar
糖水 *tángshuǐ*, syrup

舌	一	二	千
	千	舌	舌
313 6 strokes			

SHÉ, tongue. TONGUE rad. (135)(H177)

Shé is a picture of a tongue sticking out of a mouth.

學舌 *xuéshé*, to learn "by tongue," i.e., so that you can parrot the teacher's words without really understanding them; (colloquial) gossipy

話	、	二	亠
	言	言	言
314 13 strokes	言	訐	話

HUÀ, speech, language

Huà combines meanings: "words" + "tongue" = "speech, language."

説話 *shuōhuà*, to speak, talk
中國話 *Zhōngguó huà*, the Chinese language
白話 *báihuà*, the ordinary spoken language, contrasted to "classical Chinese" 文言: see 360

话

舍	ノ	人	스
	스	仐	仝
315 **8 strokes**	舍	舍	

SHÈ, home; SHĚ, to give up, to give charity

Note the form of "man" at the top. *Shè* now = "man" + "tongue," which doesn't help much with the meaning "home." The character was originally a meaning-meaning compound, but its form has been corrupted. Memorize it.

舍弟 *shèdì*, my younger brother

事	一	一	一
	戸	写	写
316 **8 strokes**	事		

SHÌ, affair, event

This character shows a hand holding a writing instrument. Originally, it meant "to hold office, to serve" and was supposed to suggest the scribes who were early rulers' most important servants.

董事 *dǒngshì*, member of a board of directors

情	`	忄	忄
	忄	忄=	忄丰
317 **11 strokes**	忄丰	情	情

QÍNG, emotion; circumstances

事情 *shìqing*, affair, business
情人 *qíngrén*, sweetheart
説情 *shuōqíng*, to beg for mercy or understanding on behalf of someone; to intercede

歌	丁	丁	可
	可	哥	哥
318 **14 strokes**	歌	歌	歌

GĒ, song

The "yawn" rad. (to suggest the opening mouth) combines with *gē* (217, above) in this sound-meaning compound.

國歌 *guógē*, national anthem
歌手 *gēshǒu*, singer
情歌 *qínggē*, love song

夂	ノ	ク	夂
319 **3 strokes**			

ZHǏ, to follow. FOLLOW rad. (34)(H65)

The student should compare this with the "slow" rad. (337, below). The two rads. are identical in form. When the form occurs in characters above other elements, it is "follow" (as in 320, below); when the form occurs below other elements, it is "slow" (as in 340 below). Both forms are H rad. no. 65.

94

| 各 320 6 strokes | ノ | ク | 夂 |
| | 冬 | 各 | 各 |

GÈ, each; various

各個 *gègè*, every one; one by one
各國 *gèguó*, various nations
各位 *gèwèi*, everybody (used in addressing an audience, to get people's attention); each person

客 321 9 strokes	丶	宀	宀
	宀	宁	安
	客	客	客

KÈ, guest

客人 *kèrén*, guest
請客 *qǐngkè*, to give a party
説客 *shuōkè*, an (informal) emissary, an eloquent fellow sent to win others to your point of view

| 乞 322 3 strokes | ノ | ⺀ | 乞 |

QǏ, to beg

This character once was identical to the "breath" rad. (324, below) and meant "breath, vapours, exhalations." It was probably by sound-loan that it came to mean "to beg."

乞食 *qǐshí*, beg for food

| 吃 323 6 strokes | 丨 | 口 | 口 |
| | 口 | 吵 | 吃 |

CHĪ, to eat

吃飯 *chīfàn*, to eat
吃的東西 *chīde dōngxī*, food, things to eat
吃力 *chīlì*, to require strength and exertion; arduous

| 气 324 4 strokes | ノ | ⺁ | 乞 |
| | 气 | | |

QÌ, breath, vapours, exhalations, BREATH rad. (84)(H109)

The character is a picture of breath passing off in waves.

氣	ノ	ｒ	ｆ	**QÌ, breath, animus, energy, soul**
	气	气	気	客氣 *kèqì*, polite; to stand on ceremony 生氣 *shēngqì*, to get angry 元氣 *yuánqì*, vitality, personal energy, vigor
325 10 strokes	氧	氣	氣	气

月	ノ	刀	月	**RÒU, meat. MEAT rad. (130)(H118)**
	月			Note that when the "meat" rad. occurs as a part of characters, it is identical in form to the "moon" rad. (178, above). The "meat" rad. as an independent character, however, has a different form (928, below). As part of a character, this *form* is H. rad. 118 whether it originally meant "meat" or "moon."
326 4 strokes (6 strokes)				

能	ㄥ	ㄙ	ㄅ	**NÉNG, to be able to**
	月	自	訇	*Néng* is listed in traditional dictionaries under the "meat" rad. (326, above); that is the only way we know that this form is "meat." 能力 *nénglì*, ability 能夠 *nénggòu*, to be able to
327 10 strokes	能	能	能	

曾	ˋ	˘	˘˘	**CÉNG, already; ZĒNG, relationship between great-grandparents and great-grandchildren through the male line; a family name**
	竹	竹	尚	
328 12 strokes	尚	迪	曾	(日 160)

尸	ㄱ	コ	尸	**SHĪ, corpse. CORPSE rad. (44)(H67)**
				The character was originally a picture of a man lying down. The student should learn to distinguish the "corpse" rad. from the "door" rad. 戸 (391, below).
329 3 strokes				

會 330 13 strokes	ノ	人	人	**HUÌ, to know how to, to be able to; to meet; a while; KUÀI, to calculate**
	令	侖	侖	會客 *huìkè*, to receive a guest 學會 *xuéhuì*, to learn, to master; an academic society 一會子 *yī huìzi*, a moment
	侖	會	會	会

| 以
331
4 strokes
(5 strokes) | ＇ | V | ﾚ | **YǏ, using; taking; because of** |
| | ﾚﾉ | 以 | | 可以 *kěyǐ*, may, be permitted to
以東 *yǐdōng*, to the east of
以外 *yǐwài*, beyond, outside of, in addition to |

原 332 10 strokes	一	厂	厂	**YUÁN, origin; a plain** The character originally was "slope" + "white" + "water" and meant "spring" (i.e., a water-source). "Water" was corrupted into "small."
	尺	厈	盾	原子 *yuánzi*, atom 原先 *yuánxiān*, at first; previously
	原	原	原	

頁 333 9 strokes	一	一	丆	**YÈ, head. HEAD rad. (181)(H170)** The character was a picture of a man's head. The student should learn to distinguish "head" from the "chief" rad. 首 (266, above) and from the "face" rad. 面 (610, below).
	丆	百	百	
	頁	頁		页

願 334 19 strokes	一	厂	厂	**YUÀN, willing** The short form (below) is probably a better sound-meaning compound than the traditional form, willingness often being a matter of the heart, not of the head.
	盾	原	原	心願 *xīnyuàn*, heart's desire 情願 *qíngyuàn*, voluntarily
	原	願	願	愿

97

音	丶	二	亠
	亠	立	立
335 9 strokes	音	音	音

YĪN, tone. TONE rad. (180)(H211)

The old form of the "tone" rad. was a mouth blowing on a flute — a pretty good way to suggest "tone." The modern form has been corrupted into "stand" over "say."

口音 *kǒuyīn*, voice; accent
他的口音很重 *tāde kǒuyīn hěn zhòng*,
   He has a very thick accent.

意	丶	亠	立
	音	音	音
336 13 strokes	意	意	意

YÌ, idea, opinion, motive

This character is often explained as "the tone in the heart" = "idea, motive, etc."

願意 *yuànyì*, be willing
意見 *yìjiàn*, opinion
意外 *yìwài*, be unforeseeable (lit., "beyond thought"); accident

夂	丿	勹	夂
337 3 strokes			

SUĪ, slow. SLOW rad. (35)(H65)

The student will remember that "slow" is identical in form to the "follow" rad. (319, above) and may want to review the entry under 319 for clarification of their relation. In modern dictionaries like H, these two forms are put together as one rad. (=H65).

爫	丷	丷	丷
	爫		
338 4 strokes			

ZHǍO, claws. CLAWS rad. (87)(H116)

This is the form of the "claws" rad. that is used as a part of characters. (For the independent form, see p. 273a.) It is a picture.

受	丷	丷	丷
	爫	爫	爫
339 8 strokes	受	受	

SHÒU, to receive

The "crown" rad. is said to be an object being received from the "claws" (fingernails, hand) by the right hand.

受累 *shòulèi*, to be hassled, to be put to a lot of trouble
受累 *shòulěi*, to get involved for somebody else
受看 *shòukàn*, to be easy on the eyes
受氣 *shòuqì*, get pushed around

	一	灬	灬	**ÀI, to love**
愛				Over "heart" for meaning, old forms have a character that is phonetic — or that means "to swallow": to take into your heart, is to love. Modern "love" is much corrupted, but "heart" remains.
	灬	悉	悉	愛情 *àiqíng*, love (man and woman's)
340	愛	愛	愛	愛人 *àirén*, lover, wife, husband 愛國 *àiguó*, patriotic 喜愛 *xǐài*, to be fond of, to love　　爱
13 strokes				

	ノ	イ	仁	**RÉN, humaneness, kindness**
仁	仁			It is supposed that this word *rén* and the word *rén* 人 "man; be human" are cognates. The "two" rad., then, is a reclarification. The "two" is often explained philosophically: "two" = "another, other," and kindness is the most important virtue toward others.
341 **4 strokes**				

	ノ	ト	乍	**ZHÀ, suddenly**
乍	乍	乍		乍看 *zhà kàn*, at first sight 乍有乍沒 *zhà yǒu zhà méi*, now it's here, 　　now it's not (idiomatically: "now you 　　see it, now you don't")
342 **5 strokes**				

	ノ	イ	亻	**ZUÒ, to do, to make**
作	仁	作	作	Sometimes foreign students have trouble distinguishing this character in meaning from the homonymous 做 "make, produce, act, act as, be…" (p. 267a, below).
343	作			作對 *zuòduì*, to oppose 作者 *zuòzhě*, writer, author 合作 *hézuò*, to cooperate
7 strokes				

	丶	冂	日	**CHĀNG, sunlight; splendor; a family name**
昌	日	日	昌	This is a meaning-meaning compound: "sun" + "sun."
344	昌	昌		昌言 *chāngyán*, (bookish) frank and open 　　speech or remarks
8 strokes				

99

唱 345 11 strokes	丶	冂	口
	叮	叩	叩
	唱	唱	唱

CHÀNG, to sing; a family name

The "mouth" gives the meaning; *chàng* (344, above) suggests the sound.

唱歌 *chànggē*, to sing
合唱 *héchàng*, a chorus (group of singers)
賣唱 *màichàng*, to sing for a living

| 上 346 3 strokes | 丨 | 卜 | 上 |

SHÀNG, up, upon, above; to come or go up

上個月 *shàngge yuè*, last month
上千人 *shàng qiān rén*, to be nearly a thousand people
上學 *shàng xué*, to go to school
上馬 *shàngmǎ*, to get on a horse; to start a project

寫 347 15 strokes	丶	宀	宀
	宀	宀	宀
	宮	寫	寫

XIĚ, to write

寫字 *xiězì*, to write
寫作 *xiězuò*, to write (e.g., a novel, a poem)
寫生 *xiěshēng*, (artist's expression) to draw from life

(勹 232, 灬 34)   写

思 348 9 strokes	丶	冂	曰
	田	田	田
	思	思	思

SĪ, to think, thought

This character was originally "head" + "heart"; "head" was corrupted to "field."

思想 *sīxiǎng*, thought
意思 *yìsī*, idea

皀 349 7 strokes	丿	亻	白
	白	白	白
	皀		

XIĀNG, be fragrant; the sweet smell of grain

The character originally was a pan over a spoon and was perhaps supposed to suggest the smell of cooking grain. "Pan" has been corrupted into "white." *Xiāng* is not used in modern Chinese, but it is seen as a sound component in modern characters.

鄉	㇛	㇔	纟
	纟	纟	纳
350 13 strokes	纳	绑	鄉

XIĀNG, country (opposite of city)

Often printed 鄉.

思鄉 *sīxiāng*, be homesick, to suffer nostalgia
鄉音 *xiāngyīn*, local accent, accent of your native place
鄉土 *xiāngtǔ*, native soil; local

乡

下	一	丁	下
351 3 strokes			

XIÀ, below

下個月 *xiàge yuè*, next month
鄉下 *xiāngxià*, in the country; rural
以下 *yǐxià*, from now on; just after
上山下鄉 *shàngshān xiàxiāng*, go and work in the countryside and in the mountainous back-country (educated young people did it as part of a socialist education)

巾	丨	冂	巾
352 3 strokes			

JĪN, cloth. CLOTH rad. (50)(H57)

The character is a picture of a small piece of cloth — a kerchief, napkin, or towel — hanging down.

毛巾 *máojīn*, towel
手巾 *shǒujīn*, small towel, face towel
紙巾 *zhǐjīn*, paper towel

冒	丨	冂	冃
	日	尸	冃
353 9 strokes	冐	冒	冒

MÀO, to cover the eyes; to rush blindly forward, act rashly; to try to "pull the wool over people's eyes," to fool or defraud them; to emit

The top part of this character is the cover, over the eye(s).

冒名 *màomíng*, to use someone else's name
冒雨 *mào yǔ*, to brave the rain
冒氣 *mào qì*, to emit steam

帽	丨	冂	巾
	巾	巾⼀	帽
354 12 strokes	帽	帽	帽

MÀO, hat

The "cloth" rad. gives the meaning; *mào* (353, above) gives the sound.

帽子 *màozi*, hat, cap
筆帽兒 *bǐ màor*, cap of a pen
帽舌 *màoshé*, peak of a cap; visor

新	`	㇒	立	**XĪN, new**
				新聞 *xīnwén*, news
	辛	亲	亲	重新 *chóngxīn*, again, anew; fresh
355 **13 strokes**	新	新	新	(亲 213)

舊	一	㇖	⺍	**JIÙ, old (things, not people)**
				The original meaning of this character was "owl." The "grass" rad. represented the bird's "horns," the dove rad. helped further fix the meaning, and *jiù* (229, above) gave the sound. The meaning "old" is by sound-loan.
	艿	莋	崔	
356 **18 strokes**	雈	雈	舊	(臼 229) 旧

異	丶	冂	田	**YÌ, strange; separate; regard as strange**
				奇異 *qíyì*, weird, bizarre, strange
	田	甲	畀	異己 *yìjǐ*, person belonging to a different party
				異鄉 *yìxiāng*, alien land
	畀	異	異	日新月異 *rì xīn yuè yì*, to change or develop every day
357 **11 strokes**				(田 23) 异

戋	一	十	土	**CÁI, to wound**
				The "lance" rad. gives the meaning; the other part of this character once gave the sound.
	兺	戋	戋	Not in use as an independent character in modern writing.
358 **6 strokes**				

戴	十	土	吉	**DÀI, to wear (hats, glasses, gloves, etc.); honor; a family name**
				戴帽子 *dài màozi*, to wear a hat
	壴	壹	橐	愛戴 *àidài*, love and honor
359 **17 strokes**	戴	戴	戴	

文 360 4 strokes	丶 文	二	宁	**WÉN**, pattern; language, literature, culture; civil (opposed to military); a family name. PATTERN rad. (67)(H84) This was a picture: a man with patterns worked onto his shirt. Distinguish "hand over" 交 (401, below). 中文 *zhōngwén*, the Chinese language 文學 *wénxué*, literature 文言 *wényán*, classical Chinese (cp. 白話 "spoken language" in 314)
茶 361 10 strokes	一 艹 苳	十 艾 茶	艹 苳 茶	**CHÁ**, tea 吃茶 *chīchá*, to drink tea 茶點 *chádiǎn*, refreshments 茶會 *cháhuì*, tea party, reception
水 362 4 strokes	亅 水	刁	水	**SHUǏ**, water; a family name. WATER rad. (85)(H125) The character is a picture of a stream of running water. This is the independent form of the rad.; you have already learned the other form, "three-dots water" (181, above). 水土 *shuǐtǔ*, climatic conditions 汗水 *hànshuǐ*, perspiration (especially a large amount)
酉 363 7 strokes	一 丙 酉	丆 西	冂 西	**YǑU**, wine; the tenth "earthly branch." WINE rad. (164)(H193) The "wine" rad. is a picture of a wine-jug; the horizontal stroke inside represents the liquid in it. The student should distinguish the "wine" rad. from "west" 西 (130, above).
酒 364 10 strokes	丶 氵 洒	冫 沔 酒	氵 洒 酒	**JIǓ**, wine, alcoholic beverage *Jiǔ* combines meanings: "water" + "wine" = "wine, alcoholic beverage." 酒鬼 *jiǔguǐ*, an alcoholic, wino, lush 酒會 *jiǔhuì*, cocktail party 酒意 *jiǔyì*, mild high from drink; tipsy feeling

取	一	厂	丌
	耵	耳	耳
365 8 strokes	耴	取	

QǓ, to grab, to take hold of

The form, of course, is "right hand" + "ear;" the hand is supposed to be grabbing the ear, hence the meaning "to grab."

取得 *qŭdé*, to get, to obtain
取笑 *qŭxiào*, to make fun of, to tease

最	丶	冂	日
	旦	昂	昂
366 12 strokes	昂	昂	最

ZUÌ, most

最好 *zuìhǎo*, the greatest; the best thing to do, is …

尚	丨	丬	小
	丬	뉴	尚
367 8 strokes	尚	尚	

SHÀNG, still; respect; a family name

尚且 *shàngqiě*, still, even, yet
高尚 *gāoshàng*, lofty, noble

常	丶	丬	小
	丬	尚	尚
368 11 strokes	常	常	常

CHÁNG, often; as a rule; a family name

常常 *chángcháng*, often
常見 *chángjiàn*, common, ordinary
常會 *chánghuì*, regular meeting

革	一	十	廿
	廿	苫	苫
369 9 strokes	莒	莗	革

GÉ, hide (as in "cowhide"); a family name. HIDE rad. (177)(H212)

The character is a picture of a hide split and spread out to dry.

104

堇

370
11 strokes

JIĀN, difficult, in difficulty

In the old forms, some scholars see the picture of a man with his hands tied behind his back, hence "to be in difficulty." Not in modern use as an independent character.

艱

371
17 strokes

JIĀN, difficult

This is the same word as 370, above; the character is reclarified with the "stubborn" rad. The student should distinguish *jiān* from *nán* (372, below). In 艱 *jiān*, the right-hand element is "stubborn;" in 難 *nán*, the right-hand element is "dove."

艰

難

372
19 strokes

NÁN, difficult; NÀN, a tough time; disaster, adversity

難吃 *nánchī*, to taste bad
難道 *nándào*, It couldn't be that…? You don't mean…?
艱難 *jiānnán*, difficult, in difficulty
難得 *nándé*, rare; difficult to get; rarely

难

谷

373
7 strokes

GǓ, valley. VALLEY rad. (150)(H199)

The character is a picture.

山谷 *shāngǔ*, ravine

容

374
10 strokes

RÓNG, to allow; face; a family name

容人 *róngrén*, tolerant, to put up with people
笑容 *xiàoróng*, a smile, smiling face

勿	丿	勹	勾
	勿		
375 4 strokes			

WÙ, must not; Don't!

This is said to be a picture of an old warning flag — "Stop!" — from which the meaning "must not" derives.

易	丨	冂	日
	日	月	昻
376 8 strokes	昜	易	

YÌ, to change; easy; family name

Yì originally meant "chameleon" and was a picture of the chameleon. The meaning "to change" is an easy extension of "chameleon." The meaning "easy" is probably by sound-loan.

容易 *róngyì*, be easy

囪	丿	厂	冂
	冂	囪	囪
377 7 strokes	囪		

CŌNG, smoke-hole, chimney, flue

The character is a picture.

悤	丿	亻	冂
	囪	囪	囪
378 11 strokes	悤	悤	悤

CŌNG, excited; hurried.

Cōng (377, above) gives the sound; the "heart" rad. gives the meaning.

A popular variant is 匆.

聰	一	厂	丌
	耳	耳	耵
379 17 strokes	聅	聰	聰

CŌNG, intelligent

Cōng originally meant "to be quick of hearing, to be quick of apprehension," from which it easily came to mean "to be quick to understand, to be intelligent." The character is a sound-meaning compound. *Cōng* (378, above) gives the sound; the "ear" rad. gives the meaning.

聰

明	丨	冂	月	**MÍNG, bright**

"Sun" + "moon" = "light, bright"

聰明 *cōngmíng*, intelligent
明白 *míngbái*, to understand
明天 *míngtiān*, tomorrow
黑白分明 *hēi bái fēnmíng*, in sharp contrast (literally, with black and white clearly marked)

380
8 strokes
日 旳 明 明 明

TĪNG, to listen

聽
一 丅 耳
耳 耳 耵
聐 聼 聽

Sometimes explained, perhaps fancifully, as: to get your heart 心 set straight 直 (301 above, with the eye on its side) through the ear 耳, i.e., because you really listened to your guru. The part under the ear gave the sound. Cp. 965.

聽說 *tīngshuō*, to hear it said that
聽見 *tīngjiàn*, to hear
(罒 132, 心 70)

听

381
22 strokes

JĪN, present, contemporary

今
丿 人 스
今

今天 *jīntiān*, today
古今 *gǔjīn*, past and present
今日 *jīnrì*, today, the present time, "these days"
今生 *jīnshēng*, this life

382
4 strokes

NIÀN, to study

念
人 스 今
今 念 念
念

This character is supposed to be a meaning-meaning compound: "present" + the "heart" rad. (for "mind") = "to have present in the mind, to study."

念書 *niànshū*, to study, to do some serious reading
想念 *xiǎngniàn*, to miss, to remember longingly

383
8 strokes

PŬ, knock. KNOCK rad. (66)(H113)

攵
乀 ケ 攵

"Knock" is a picture of a hand knocking with a stick. This form is the form usually seen as a part of characters. (For the independent form, see p. 276a.) Distinguish "knock" from "club" 殳 (183, above), "branch" 支 (271), and "pattern" 文 (360).

384
4 strokes

107

孝	一	十	土	**XIĀO, filial piety; family name**
	耂	耂	孝	The character combines meanings: the "old" rad. (138, above) + the "child" rad. = "filial piety." Note that the "old" rad. is abbreviated.
385 7 strokes	孝			孝心 *xiàoxīn*, filial piety, love and respect for parents 孝子 *xiàozǐ*, filial son

教	土	耂	耂	**JIĀO, to teach; JIÀO, to tell; religion; family name**
	孝	孝	孝	教 looks like a meaning-meaning compound: old + child + a hand holding a stick (for discipline). In fact, "old" used to be "crisscross" and was the character the child was being taught; 教 is now often written, more correctly, as 教. Cp. 253, above.
386 11 strokes	教	教	教	教書 *jiāoshū*, to teach

曷	丶	冂	日	**HÉ, what? why?**
	曰	𡰪	号	The form at the top is the "say" rad., not the "sun" rad. This character is now bookish.
387 9 strokes	号	曷	曷	

喝	丨	冂	口	**HĒ, to drink; HÈ, to shout**
	叩	叩	叩	*Hé* (387, above) gives the sound; the "mouth" rad. gives the meaning. 喝茶 *hē chá*, to drink tea
388 12 strokes	喝	喝	喝	大吃大喝 *dà chī dà hē*, to pig out, to eat and drink extravagantly

豕	一	丆	丅	**SHǏ, pig. PIG rad. (152)(H194)**
	豖	豕	豕	The character is a picture of a pig.
389 7 strokes	豕			

家	丶	八	宀	**JIĀ, home, house, family; specialist; a family name (rare)** *Jiā* combines meanings: "pig" under "roof" = "home." Some commentators say the pig is really outside the house. 家鄉 *jiāxiāng*, hometown, ancestral home 家母 *jiāmǔ*, my mother 家長 *jiāzhǎng*, head of a family
	宀	宀	宀	
390 10 strokes	家	家	家	
户	丶	⺈	弖	**HÙ, door; family name. DOOR rad. (63) (H85)** This character is a picture. The student should distinguish it from "corpse" 尸 (329, above). Usually printed 戶. 户口 *hùkǒu*, population; household 三户人家 *sān hù rénjiā*, three households
	户			
391 4 strokes				
方	丶	亠	方	**FĀNG, square; direction; locality; family name. SQUARE rad. (70)(H85)** *Fāng* may originally have been a picture of a man leaning heavily to one side — the original character for 旁 *páng* "side" (785). By tradition = the "square" rad. 方便 *fāngbiàn*, be convenient 東方 *dōngfāng*, the East, the Orient 方言 *fāngyán*, dialect
	方			
392 4 strokes				
房	丶	⺈	弖	**FÁNG, house, building; family name** "Door" gives the meaning; *fāng* (392, above) gives the sound. 房東 *fángdōng*, landlord 房子 *fángzi*, house, building; room 房事 *fángshì*, sexual intercourse (between husband and wife)
	户	户	庐	
393 8 strokes	房	房		
婁	丶	口	毌	**LÓU, a constellation's name; family name** *Lóu* once had 毋 *wú* (212, above) over 中 *zhōng* (112) over 女 *nǚ* (11) and meant "seclusion," as in the women's quarters. It came to stand for words meaning "tether" and "to drag." Now it gives the sound in several characters. 婁子 *lóuzi*, (colloquial) blunder 娄
	毌	呂	婁	
394 11 strokes	婁	婁		

109

樓	一	十	木	**LÓU, a building of two or more stories; family name**
	朴	杪	档	樓房 *lóufáng*, building of two or more stories 下樓 *xiàlóu*, to go downstairs 樓下 *lóuxià*, downstairs
395 15 strokes	樓	樓	樓	楼

至	一	工	云	**ZHÌ, to reach, to arrive at. REACH rad. (133)(H171)** The character is a picture of a bird alighting, from which came the idea "to reach, to arrive at."
396 6 strokes	云	至	至	至今 *zhìjīn*, up to the present time 至少 *zhìshǎo*, at least

屋	一	一	尸	**WŪ, a room** The "corpse" rad. here is supposed to mean "to lie or sit," and the character is explained: "where you come (reach) to lie or sit down — your room."
	尸	戶	层	
397 9 strokes	居	屋	屋	屋子 *wūzi*, room 房屋 *fángwū*, houses, buildings

地	一	十	土	**DÌ, the earth, soil; place** 地方 *dìfāng*, place 土地 *tǔdì*, land 地位 *dìwèi*, job, status 謝天謝地 *xiètiān-xièdì*, Thank Heaven! 別有天地 *bié yǒu tiān-dì*, a place of great beauty
398 6 strokes	扣	坳	地	

成	一	厂	厂	**CHÉNG, to perfect; to become; family name** 成就 *chéngjiù*, accomplishment 成立 *chénglì*, to set up 兌成美金 *duìchéng Měijīn*, to change into American money 成人 *chéngrén*, an adult
399 7 strokes	万	成	成	
	成			

城	一	十	土	**CHÉNG, city wall; city**
	圹	圹	坊	The "earth" rad. gives the meaning, and *chéng* (399, above) gives the sound in this character.
400 **9 strokes** **(10 strokes)**	城	城	城	城鄉 *chéng xiāng*, town and country 長城 *Chángchéng*, the Great Wall

交	、	亠	亠	**JIĀO, to hand over, to exchange**
	六	亣	交	The original meaning of this character was "to cross;" it was a picture of a man with crossed legs. The student should distinguish it from "pattern" 文 (360, above).
401 **6 strokes**				交易 *jiāoyì*, to trade 交情 *jiāoqíng*, friendship

校	一	十	才	**JIÀO, to check; to collate; XIÀO, school**
	木	术	杧	校對 *jiàoduì*, to proofread 學校 *xuéxiào*, school 校長 *xiàozhǎng*, principal; college president
402 **10 strokes**	柠	栌	校	

用	丿	几	月	**YÒNG, to use. USE rad. (101)**
	月	用		Early scholars say, "The vertical stroke in the center is an arrow shot into the bull's eye, therefore 'apt (fit to the purpose, usable), to use.'"
403 **5 strokes**				別有用心 *bié yǒu yòngxīn*, to have hidden motives or an axe to grind 作用 *zuòyòng*, to have an effect on; function; effect; motive

甫	一	厂	万	**FǓ, to begin; just, only (bookish)**
	月	月	甫	
404 **7 strokes**	甫			

鋪 405 15 strokes	丿	𠂉	乍
	牟	金	金
	釘	鋪	鋪

PÙ, to store; PŪ, to spread

The character is a sound-meaning compound. The "gold" rad. gives the meaning, and *fū* (404, above) suggests the sound.

鋪子 *pùzi*, store, shop
鋪張 *pūzhāng*, extravagant

铺

| 㠯 406 5 strokes | 丨 | 厂 | 尸 |
| | 𦥑 | 㠯 | |

YǏ, using, taking; because of

This is another way to write 以 (331, above). The student should distinguish this character from "bureaucrat" 臣 (491, below) and from "chief, large, great" 巨 (496, below).

官 407 8 strokes	丶	丷	宀
	宀	宁	官
	官	官	

GUĀN, mandarin; organ (of the body)

Some scholars say this was once a picture of many people under a roof: "the people's roof," i.e., city hall; by metonymy, it became the personnel there, the mandarins. Cf. 408, below.

官話 *guānhuà*, "Mandarin" language
官方 *guānfāng*, governmental; official
五官 *wǔ guān*, the five organs (ears, eyes, lips, nose, tongue)

館 408 16 strokes	丿	人	𠂊
	今	𣪚	食
	食	飠	館

GUǍN, public building (e.g., embassy, museum); public accommodation (e.g., hotel, eatery, tea-house); family name

Guān (407) gives the sound — and maybe the meaning; for "eatery," the "food" rad. gives, or helps with, the meaning.

飯館 *fànguǎn*, restaurant
下館子 *xià guǎnzi*, eat in a restaurant
天文館 *tiānwénguǎn*, planetarium
(天文 = astronomy)

馆

| 尼 409 5 strokes | ⁊ | ⁊ | 尸 |
| | 尼 | 尼 | |

NÍ, nun

Looking now like "corpse" 尸 (329, above) + "ladle" 匕 (137, above), this character was once "man" beside "man" and meant "beside, near." The meaning "nun" appears to have come by sound-loan.

112

呢	` `	`口`	`口`	**NE; a grammatical practical; NǏ, wool-stuff** *Nǐ* (409, above) gives the sound; the mouth here warns that the character may be a particle. The meaning "wool-stuff" comes by sound-loan.
	`口'`	`口'`	`呓`	我呢 *wǒ ne*, What about me?
410 8 strokes	`呢`	`呢`		呢大衣 *ní dàyī*, wool overcoat

所	`'`	`彳`	`彳`	**SUǑ, place; which? what? family name** "Door" and "axe" here are supposed to combine to give the meaning "to build a living place," whence "place." The meanings "which? what" are by sound-loan.
	`户`	`戶`	`所`	所以 *suǒyǐ*, therefore
411 8 strokes	`所`	`所`		交易所 *jiāoyìsuǒ*, stock exchange

車	`一`	`厂`	`冖`	**CHĒ, car; family name. CAR rad. (159)(the short form is H rad. 100)** The character is a picture of a car or chariot.
	`冃`	`日`	`車`	車房 *chēfáng*, garage 車夫 *chēfū*, chauffeur 客車 *kèchē*, passenger train; bus
412 7 strokes	`車`			车

汽	`丶`	`冫`	`氵`	**QÌ, gas, steam** The character combines meanings: "water" + "breath" (vapor) = "steam."
	`汽`	`汽`	`汽`	汽車 *qìchē*, automobile 汽水 *qìshuǐ*, carbonated drink, soda water
413 7 strokes	`汽`			

火	`丶`	`丷`	`少`	**HUǑ, fire. FIRE rad. (86)(H83)** The character is a picture of flames rising. This is the independent form of "fire dots" (34, above)
	`火`			火車 *huǒchē*, (railroad) train 火山 *huǒshān*, volcano
414 4 strokes				鬼火 *guǐhuǒ*, will-o'-the-wisp (literally, "ghost-fire")

舟 415 6 strokes	´	ノ	力	**ZHŌU, boat (bookish). BOAT rad. (137)** **(H812)** The "boat" rad. is a picture of a boat. 舟車 *zhōuchē*, (bookish) boat and car; 　　　　journey 舟子 *zhōuzǐ*, (bookish) boatman
	舟	舟	舟	

船 416 11 strokes	´	ノ	力	**CHUÁN, boat** *Zhōu* (415, above) gives the meaning; 㕣 *yǎn* (99, above) once gave the sound. 下船 *xiàchuán*, to disembark 汽船 *qìchuán*, steamship 船長 *chuánzhǎng*, captain, master of a ship 船首 *chuánshǒu*, the bows of a boat, prow
	舟	舟	舟	
	舟	舟	船	

飛 417 9 strokes	乀	飞	飞	**FĒI, to fly. FLY rad. (183)** *Fēi* is a picture of a flying bird. 飛船 *fēichuán*, blimp 飛舟 *fēizhōu*, a very fast boat
	飞	飞	飛	
	飛	飛	飛	飞

丝 418 6 strokes	∠	幺	幺	**YŌU, small** Note that this character is the "coil" rad. 幺 (25, above) doubled. It is not in modern use as an independent character.
	红	丝	丝	

幾 419 12 strokes	幺	丝	丝	**Jǐ, a few, several; how many** Scholars say: 戍 (shù), man with lance, "frontier guard," plus *yōu* "small," means the guards noticed the smallest things, and "small" suggests "few." 幾個人 *jǐ ge rén*, a few people, several 　　　　people; how many people? 幾點了 *jǐ diǎn le*, What time is it?
	丝	丝	幾	
	幾	幾		幾年 *jǐ nián*, a few years, several 　　　　years; how many years?　几

機	一	十	木	**JĪ, machine, mechanism; crucial point, opportunity; be quick-witted**
	杉	松	機	飛機 *fēijī*, airplane 機子 *jīzi*, (colloquial), loom, small machine, trigger 機會 *jīhuì*, opportunity 唱機 *chàngjī*, a record-player, phonograph
420 16 strokes	機	機	機	机

行	ノ	ク	彳	**XÍNG, to go, to do, to perform; HÁNG, business firm, "hong." GO rad. (144)**
	彳	彳	行	The left half of "go" is "step" (30, above). Originally the right half was identical (the similarity is still clear), and the character was easily explained: "step" + "step" = "to go."
421 6 strokes				行房 *xíngfáng*, (bookish) have sexual relations (between spouses)

圭	一	十	土	**GUĪ, jade tablets or jade batons used in the old days as symbols of authority**
	圭	圭	圭	Note that in *guī* "earth" appears twice. These jade symbols were the tokens used in conferring fiefs (land).
422 6 strokes				圭錶 *guībiǎo*, old Chinese sundial (it measured the length of the year and of the 24 solar terms)

街	ノ	ク	彳	**JIĒ, a street**
	彳	彳	彳	*Jiē* is a sound-meaning compound. The "go" rad. gives the meaning; *guī* (422, above) at one time gave the sound.
	街	街	街	唐人街 *Tángrén jiē*, Chinatown 大街 *dàjiē*, boulevard
423 12 strokes				

定	丶	八	宀	**DÌNG, to settle (a matter); family name**
	宀	宁	宁	The character combines meanings: first "set right" 正 (493, below) things under your "roof" 宀 (127) to have a settled life. 正 now looks more like 疋 (245). 一定 *yídìng*, certainly
424 8 strokes	定	定		定錢 *dìngqián*, money on deposit 定報 *dìngbào*, to subscribe to a newspaper 定親 *dìngqīn*, marriage engagement (arranged by parents)

115

	ノ	⺅	亻
怎	乍	乍	乍
425 9 strokes	怎	怎	怎

ZĚN, how? why?

The character is supposed to be a meaning-meaning compound: "suddenly" (342, above) + "heart" (mind) = "bewilderment" = the questions "how? why?"

怎麼 zěnme, how? why?
不怎麼 bùzěnme, not very

	ノ	人	从
从	从		
426 4 strokes			

CÓNG, to follow; from

The character is a picture of one man following another. Compare 427, below.

	ノ	⺅	彳
從	彳	彷	徉
427 11 strokes	徉	從	從

CÓNG, to follow; from

This is the same word as 426, above. The character has been "reclarified" with various additions.

從三點鐘 cóng sān diǎn zhōng, since 3:00
從小 cóng xiǎo, from childhood

从

	l	冂	冂
回	冋	回	回
428 6 strokes			

HUÍ, to return; time, occurrence; Muslim; a family name

The character is supposed to symbolize going around something until you return to the starting point.

回家 huíjiā, to go home
下回 xiàhuí, next time
回見 huíjiàn, So long! See you later!

	一	工	云
到	云	至	至
429 8 strokes	到	到	

DÀO, to arrive at; verb-ending, indicating successful completion of the action of the verb; family name

The "reach" rad. gives the meaning; dāo (205, above) gives the sound.

到了 dào le, [some subject] has arrived
看到 kàndào, to see
想不到 xiǎngbudào, unexpected

坐	丿	人	人人
	丛	半	坐
430 7 strokes			

ZUÒ, to sit down; to travel by

Zuò is a picture of two men sitting on the earth.

坐下 *zuòxià*, to sit down
坐船 *zuòchuán*, to travel by boat
坐飛機 *zuòfēijī*, to travel by plane

來	一	厂	丆
	夾	來	來
431 8 strokes	來	來	

LÁI, to come; a family name

This character originally meant "wheat" and was a picture of growing wheat. The meaning "to come" is by sound-loan.

下來 *xiàlái*, to come down
從來 *cónglái*, customarily (in the past)
未來 *wèilái*, the future

来

去	一	十	土
	去	去	
432 5 strokes			

QÙ, to go; to cause to go; get rid of (H rad. 133)

Qù was a cup (now "cocoon" 厶, 24, above) with a lid (now "earth," 土, 86). Why it means "to go" is unclear.

下去 *xiàqù*, to go down
說來說去 *shuō lái shuō qù*, to say over and over
去火 *qùhuǒ*, (traditional medical term) to reduce internal heat

站	丶	二	亠
	立	立	立
433 10 strokes	站	站	站

ZHÀN, (taxi, bus) stand, to stand

The "stand" rad. gives the meaning; *zhàn* (281, above) gives the sound.

火車站 *huǒchēzhàn*, train station
汽車站 *qìchēzhàn*, bus station
站長 *zhànzhǎng*, stationmaster

走	一	十	土
	丰	丰	走
434 7 strokes	走		

ZǑU, to walk. WALK rad. (156)(H189)

The character originally was a meaning-meaning compound: "man" + "foot." The modern character is somewhat corrupted.

他走了 *tā zǒu le*, He's left.
走吧 *zǒu ba*, I suggest we leave. Let's go! Let's get outta here!

	土	丰	丰
起	走	走	起
435 10 strokes	起	起	

QǏ, to rise, to raise

Jī (273, above) suggests the sound in this character; the "walk" rad. is supposed to help with the meaning.

Often printed 起.

站起來 *zhàn qǐlái*, to stand up
起飛 *qǐfēi*, to take off (airplane)

	ˋ	冂	日
昨	日	日/	日/
436 9 strokes	昨	昨	昨

ZUÓ, yesterday

The "sun" rad. suggests the meaning; *zhà* (342, above) once gave the sound.

昨天 *zuótiān*, yesterday
昨兒 *zuór*, (colloquial) yesterday

	ˋ	冂	日
旦	日	旦	

437
5 strokes

DÀN, dawn

The character is a picture of the sun just above the horizon to suggest "dawn."

元旦 *Yuándàn*, New Year's Day
旦夕 *dànxī*, (bookish) in the morning or the evening — pretty soon
一旦 *yí dàn*, in one day, pronto, right away

	ˋ	冂	日
早	日	旦	早

438
6 strokes

ZǍO, be early; long ago; Good morning!

早點 *zǎodiǎn*, breakfast
早飯 *zǎofàn*, breakfast
早就 *zǎojiù*, long ago
早上 *zǎoshang*, early morning

	ˊ	ˊ	ˊ
兔	刍	刍	刍
439 7 strokes	兔	兔	

MIǍN, to escape

Miǎn is supposed to be a picture of a running hare, whence "to escape." Do not confuse it with *tù* 兔 "hare" (p. 284b).

免稅 *miǎnshuì*, to be exempt from taxes
免得 *miǎndé*, to save (from inconvenience); to avoid

118

晚	｜	⼐	日
	日ʹ	日ʹʹ	昡
440 12 strokes	晘	睁	晚

WǍN, be late; evening; family name

Miǎn (439, above) used to give the sound of this character; "sun" gives the meaning.

晚飯 *wǎnfàn*, supper
昨晚 *zuówǎn*, yesterday evening
早晚 *zǎowǎn*, morning and evening; sooner or later

故	一	十	士
	古	古	古ʹ
441 9 strokes	故	故	

GÙ, ancient; to die; cause; intentionally

故事 *gùshi*, story
故意 *gùyì*, on purpose
故去 *gùqù*, to pass away, to die
故土 *gùtǔ*, "the old country," one's native land

巛	〱	巜	巛
442 3 strokes			

CHUĀN, river. "RIVER" rad. (47)(H78)

This character is a picture of flowing water. The form given here is not seen independently but only as a part of other characters. (For the independent form, see p. 245b.) Cp. 560, below, for another form of "river" which may appear as a part of characters.

工	一	丁	工
443 3 strokes			

GŌNG, work. WORK rad. (48)(H48)

Gōng is a picture of a carpenter's square.

工作 *gōngzuò*, work, job
木工 *mùgōng*, carpenter
工夫 *gōngfū*, free time
分工 *fēngōng*, to divide the labor

坙	一	〱	巜
	巛	巠	坙
444 7 strokes	坙		

JĪNG, warp (of fabric)

This character is a picture of threads run across a loom. Not in modern use as an independent character.

經	ㄥ	幺	幺	**JĪNG, warp (of fabric); to pass through; literary classics; family name**
	幺	糸	糸	In the sense of "warp," this is 444, above, reclarified with "silk." The other meanings are derived from "warp."
445 13 strokes	經	經	經	已經 *yǐjīng*, already 曾經 *céngjīng*, have already done something/had some experience 经

网	l	冂	冈	**WǍNG, net. NET rad. (122)**
	冈	网	网	The character is a picture of a net. 一張网 *yì zhāng wǎng*, a net 网子 *wǎngzi*, net
446 6 strokes				

睘	、	冖	罒	**HUÁN, to return; still; as before**
	罒	睘	睘	Note that the "gown" rad. (109, above) appears in this character without its top dot. The explanation of *huán* is very complicated and unsatisfactory. It occurs as part of characters to give the sound. Not now used as an independent character.
447 13 strokes	睘	睘	睘	(口 33)

還	罒	罒	睘	**HUÁN, to return; HÁI, still, yet**
	睘	睘	睘	還鄉 *huánxiāng*, to return to your native place 還是 *háishi*, still, yet 還有 *háiyǒu*, furthermore, in addition
448 16 strokes	睘	還	還	还

裏	丶	亠	亠	**LǏ, lining, inside**
	亠	亯	車	The character combines the meanings of "gown" and the sound of *lǐ* (106, above). 裏子 *lǐzi*, lining 城裏 *chénglǐ*, in the city 這裏 *zhèlǐ*, here
449 13 strokes	車	裏	裏	里

| 刖 450 6 strokes | 丿 | 刀 | 月 |
| | 月 | 刖 | 刖 |

YUÈ, to cut off the foot (or feet) as punishment

This was one of the punishments prescribed by ancient Chinese law. It is, of course, no longer the practice. The character is a sound-meaning compound: "knife" is for meaning, *yuè* (178, above) for sound.

前 451 9 strokes	丶	丷	丷
	广	六	前
	首	前	前

QIÁN, front, in front of

從前 *cóngqián*, in the past
前兩天 *qián liǎng tiān*, the past two days
前門 *qiánmén*, (at) the front door

後 452 9 strokes	丿	彳	彳
	彳	彳	彳
	移	移	後

HÒU, back, in back of

前後 *qiánhòu*, in front and back; from beginning to end
後來 *hòulái*, and then, after that
後天 *hòutiān*, (on) the day after tomorrow

后

豆 453 7 strokes	一	一	一
	口	戸	豆
	豆		

DÒU, flask; bean, pea. FLASK rad. (151)(H191)

The character is a picture of a flask. The meaning "bean, pea" is by sound-loan.

豆子 *dòuzi*, bean, pea
土豆 *tǔdòu*, potato

頭 454 16 strokes	一	口	豆
	豇	頭	頭
	頭	頭	

TÓU, the head; a suffix used to form nouns and noun-phrases; a bulb (of garlic); a measure-word for certain animals

Dòu (453, above) suggests the sound; the "head" rad. gives the meaning

一頭牛 *yì tóu niú*, a cow
木頭 *mùtóu*, wood
後頭 *hòutóu*, in back

头

寺	一	十	土
	圭	寺	寺
455 6 strokes			

SÌ, (Buddhist) monastery

The character = "earth" over "thumb." There is no satisfactory explanation. *Sì* occurs as a part of many characters to give the sound, and in these characters it usually indicates the sound *shi*.

時	丨	刀	日
	日	日一	日十
456 10 strokes	旪	時	時

SHÍ, time

The "sun" rad. gives the meaning; *sì* (455, above) gives the sound.

時事 *shíshì*, current events
不時 *bùshí*, from time to time
時常 *shícháng*, often
四時 *sìshí*, spring, summer, fall, winter

时

候	丿	亻	亻
	伫	伫	伫
457 10 strokes	侯	候	候

HÒU, to wait; to pay the bill; climate; a period of time

時候 *shíhou*, time
問候 *wènhòu*, to ask after someone
火候 *huǒhòu*, time required to cook something

百	一	丆	丆
	百	百	百
458 6 strokes			

BǍI, one hundred

Bái (231, above) gives the sound; the "one" rad. suggests that the meaning is numerical.

老百姓 *lǎobǎixìng*, the common people

為	丶	丿	丆
	丷	尹	爭
459 12 strokes	爭	爲	為

WÈI, for; WÉI, to be, to act, to do

The character is supposed to be the picture of some animal, variously given as "monkey," "elephant," etc. The present meanings are all sound-loan. Common variant 为.

為什麼 *wèi shénme*, why?
為人 *wéirén*, to behave like a human being, to act properly; character

为

122

主	、	ニ	二	**ZHŬ, lord, host; principal; to indicate**
	宁	主		*Zhǔ* (61, above) gives the sound; the character "king" gives the meaning.
460 5 strokes				主人 *zhǔrén*, host, landlord 主張 *zhǔzhāng*, to advocate, to propose 主意 *zhǔyì*, idea, plan

住	ノ	イ	イ	**ZHÙ, to live; to stay; to stop**
	仁	仨	住	住户 *zhùhù*, group of people living under one roof; family 站住 *zhànzhù*, to stop, to halt
461 7 strokes	住			問住 *wènzhù*, to stump with a question 止不住 *zhǐbuzhù*, cannot stop

第	ノ	ゟ	ゟ	**DÌ; a prefix to numbers (forms ordinals)**
	竺	竺	竺	第一 *dìyī*, first, the first 第四天 *dìsì tiān*, the fourth day 第三者 *dìsānzhě*, the third one
462 11 strokes	笃	第	第	

年	ノ	ゟ	乍	**NIÁN, year**
	乍	乍	年	The rad. of 年 in traditional dictionaries is "shield" 干 (87, above); in H, the rad. is ノ (H20).
463 6 strokes				去年 *qùnián*, last year 今年 *jīnnián*, this year 明年 *míngnián*, next year 百年 *bǎinián*, a hundred years; a lifetime

凵	L	凵		**KĂN, bowl. BOWL rad. (17)(H38)**
				Kǎn is a picture of a bowl.
464 2 strokes				

123

屮	㇄	凵	屮
465 3 strokes			

CHÈ, sprout. SPROUT rad. (45)(H61)

The "sprout" rad. is a picture of a sprout.

出	㇄	凵	屮
	出	出	
466 5 strokes			

CHŪ, to come out, to go out; to produce

出 is supposed to be a picture of a sprout pushing out of a bowl.

出來 *chūlái*, to come out
出門 *chūmén*, to go out (of the house)
出國 *chūguó*, to go abroad
出汗 *chūhàn*, to sweat

等	ノ	⺊	⺋
	𥫗	竺	笁
467 12 strokes	笁	等	等

DĚNG, to wait; to equal; rank; … "and similar (things);" etc.; signals the end of a list

等候 *děnghòu*, to wait for
馬牛羊等 *mǎ niú yáng děng*, horses, cows, sheep, etc.
等到 *děngdào*, by the time that…
等外 *děngwài*, be sub-standard

把	一	丁	扌
	扌	扚	扣
468 7 strokes	把		

BǍ, to grasp; handful; to guard; a particle used to bring direct objects in front of the verb; a measure for things with handles (knives, spoons, teapots) or that you grasp (chairs, handfuls of rice, bunches of flowers); BÀ, handle

一把米 *yì bǎ mǐ*, a handful of rice
一把勺 *yì bǎ sháo*, a spoon
把門 *bǎmén*, to guard a door or gate
把兄弟 *bǎxiōngdì*, sworn brothers

夬	㇇	ユ	𠃋
	夬		
469 4 strokes			

JUĒ, archer's thimble; GUÀI, to divide

The character may be a picture of a man drawing his bow or fitting the thimble before he draws. It occurs as a part of characters to give sometimes the sound *jue*, sometimes the sound *guai* (or *kuai*).

124

				KUÀI, fast; soon; happy; sharp
快	丶	丨	忄	快車 *kuàichē*, express train
	忄	忄	快	快刀 *kuàidāo*, sharp knife
470	快			飛快 *fēikuài*, be very fast; be very sharp
7 strokes				快點 *kuàidiǎn*, "Faster, please."

				MÀN, long; to stretch out; graceful
曼	丶	冂	曰	
	曰	昌	昌	
471	昌	曼	曼	
11 strokes				

				MÀN, slow
慢	丶	丨	忄	慢車 *mànchē*, local train
	忄	忄	惧	快慢 *kuàimàn*, "the fast and the slow of it," i.e. speed
472	惧	慢	慢	慢走 *mànzǒu*, Watch your step! "Take care of yourself!" (said to a departing guest)
14 strokes				

				RǍN, tender, flexible; whiskers; a family name
冉	丨	冂	冂	The character originally was a picture of whiskers.
	冉	冉		冉冉 *rǎnrǎn*, (bookish) slowly, little by little
473				
5 strokes				

				ZÀI, again; another, more
再	一	冂	再	再見 *zàijiàn*, Goodbye!
	再			再給三個 *zài gěi sān gè*, to give three more
474				再說 *zài shuō*, and furthermore
6 strokes				

羊	丶	ソ	业	**YÁNG, sheep. SHEEP rad. (123)(H157)** The student already has learned one form of the "sheep" rad. (see 115, above). The form here is used as a part of characters and does not occur as an independent character.
	业	羊	羊	
475 6 strokes				
着	丶	ソ	业	**ZHÈ**, a verb-suffix: continuing to, to be in process of doing; **ZHÁO**, to be ignited; to touch; verb ending: to succeed in …; **ZHĀO**, to suffer from; That's right!
	业	羊	羊	Note: 着 is not 看 (see 121, above). 跟着 *gēnzhe*, to occur immediately after, to follow close on the heels of
476 11 strokes (12 strokes)	羊	养	着	着火 *zháohuǒ*, to catch fire
件	丿	亻	亻	**JIÀN**; a measure for events, official documents, articles of clothing, pieces of furniture
	仁	仁	件	零件 *língjiàn*, component; spare part, accessory 文件 *wénjiàn*, documents, papers
477 6 strokes				一件事 *yī jiàn shì*, an event, a matter, an affair
曲	丨	冂	冂	**QŪ**, to twist; to curve and curl, twisted; family name; **QŬ**, song
	内	曲	曲	曲 once was a picture of an earthworm and had the meanings "earthworm; to twist." The rad. is now the "say" rad. (82, above).
478 6 strokes				唱曲 *chàngqǔ*, to sing a song 作曲 *zuòqǔ*, to compose (music)
豊	丨	冂	冂	**LĬ**, ritual dish
	曲	曹	曹	*Lǐ* was a picture of a vessel (the "flask" rad.) holding flowers. The flowers have been corrupted to "twist." Not in modern use as an independent character.
479 13 strokes	豊	豊	豊	(口 33)

126

| 礻 480 4 strokes (5 strokes) | 、 丆 礻 礻 | **SHÌ, sign. SIGN rad. (113)(H87)** *Shì* means "sign" in various senses, including "signs from heaven" and omens as well as the sense of "to exhibit, to show, to proclaim." It is supposed to be a picture of a wooden sign — perhaps of an ancestral tablet. Distinguish from the 衤 form of "gown" (910, below). Often printed 示. |

| 禮 481 17 strokes | 礻 礻 礻 礻 神 禮 禮 禮 禮 禮 禮 禮 | **LǏ, ritual; manners** This character is 479, above, reclarified with the "sign" rad. Here, as often, the "sign" rad. occurs in a character related to religion or religious matters. 禮帽 *lǐmào*, top hat 禮金 *lǐjīn*, cash given in congratulation or as a sign of respect ·· 礼 |

| 拜 482 9 strokes | 一 二 三 手 手 拜 拜 | **BÀI, to worship** The rad. in this character is the "hand" rad. (41, above). Note that its form here is slightly distorted (cp. 121, above). *Bài* originally had two "hands" + "to lower." "Lower the hands" = "to worship." 禮拜 *lǐbài*, to worship; week |

| 拿 483 10 strokes | 丿 人 人 合 合 合 合 拿 | **NÁ, to pick up** The character combines meanings: "to join" + "hand" = "to pick up." 拿起來 *náqǐlái*, to pick up 拿走 *názǒu*, to take away 拿住 *názhù*, to hold onto firmly |

| 進 484 11 strokes | 丿 亻 亻 隹 隹 隹 隹 谁 進 | **JÌN, to enter** 進去 *jìnqù*, to enter 進口 *jìnkǒu*, to import 進行 *jìnxíng*, to make progress with; to pull strings ·· 进 |

127

送	`	⸌	⸜
	⸜	羊	关
485 9 strokes	关	送	送

SÒNG, to send off; to see off; to see home

送行 *sòngxíng*, to see off
送禮 *sònglǐ*, to send a present
不送 *búsòng*, (by guest) Don't bother seeing me off; (by host) Excuse me for not seeing you off.
買一送二 *mǎi yī sòng èr*, buy one, get one free

因	∣	⼌	冂
	冈	冈	因
486 6 strokes			

YĪN, cause, because

Karlgren says the basic meaning is "cause" in a legal sense and explains the character as "a man (the 'big' rad.) in prison."

因為 *yīnwèi*, because
因此 *yīncǐ*, because of this

信	ノ	亻	亻
	仁	佇	信
487 9 strokes	信	信	信

XÌN, sincerity; to believe; letter (as in "business letter," "personal letter")

The character shows "a man standing by his word," whence "sincere, to believe."

相信 *xiāngxìn*, to believe
信用 *xìnyòng*, trustworthiness
信件 *xìnjiàn*, mail, letters
音信 *yīnxìn*, mail; message

禸	∣	冂	冂
	禸	禸	
488 5 strokes			

RǑU, to track (as in "track a bear")
TRACK rad. (114)

The character, especially in its old forms, looks like the view of an animal walking away from the viewer: you can see its hind-legs, its tail, and the arch of its back.

禺	⸜	冂	曰
	曰	甲	禺
489 9 strokes	禺	禺	禺

YÚ, monkey

The character is a picture of a monkey. Not in modern use as an independent character.

萬	一	十	艹	**WÀN, ten thousand; family name**
				This character was a picture of a scorpion, and the original meaning was "scorpion." It is used to mean "ten thousand" by sound loan.
	艿	苩	芦	
490 13 strokes	萬	萬	萬	千萬 *qiānwàn*, ten million; by all means 萬里長城 *wàn lǐ Chángchéng*, the Great Wall 万

臣	一	厂	厂	**CHÉN, bureaucrat. BUREAUCRAT rad. (131)(H164)**
				Learn to distinguish the "bureaucrat" rad. from "using, taking" 臣 (406, above) and from "chief, large, great" 巨 (496, below).
	臣	臣	臣	
491 7 strokes (6 strokes)	臣			大臣 *dàchén*, important official, minister (in a monarchy)

緊	臣	臤	臤	**JǏN, tense, urgent, tight**
				太緊 *tài jǐn*, be too tight (as in shoes) 緊張 *jǐnzhāng*, be excited; be tense; be exciting 要緊 *yàojǐn*, be important
	臤	堅	堅	
492 14 strokes	緊	緊	緊	緊

正	一	丁	下	**ZHÈNG, true; truly; straight, upright; in the midst of (doing something)**
				正吃飯 *zhèng chīfàn*, in the midst of eating 正在 *zhèngzài*, in the midst of 正好 *zhènghǎo*, just right; it just happens that… 正直 *zhèngzhí*, honest
	正	正		
493 5 strokes				

必	丶	心	心	**BÌ, must**
				必得 *bìděi*, must 必要 *bìyào*, necessary, essential 必定 *bìdìng*, certainly 未必 *wèibì*, not necessarily
	必	必		
494 5 strokes				

夜	、	亠	广	**YÈ, night**
	疒	疠	疹	The character is classified under the "dusk" rad. 夕 (117, above) in some dictionaries, but in H. under the "lid" rad. (37, above). Logically, to classify it under 夕 works better; but formally, under "lid."
495 **8 strokes**	夜	夜		半夜 *bànyè*, midnight

巨	一	厂	匚	**JÙ, chief, large, great, gigantic**
	臣	巨		*Jù* was traditionally classified under the "work" rad. 工 (443, above), distorted. 巨 is supposed to have been a picture of "a large carpenter's square, with handle." In modern dictionaries, the rad. is "basket" or "box" (143 and 145, above), these now being taken as one rad.
496 **5 strokes**				艱巨 *jiānjù*, to be onerous

戊	一	厂	仄	**WÙ, the fifth "heavenly stem" (H rad. 138)**
	戊	戊		The character used to mean "lance, halberd" and was a picture. Learn to tell it from *xū* (498, below).
497 **5 strokes**				

戌	一	厂	仄	**XŪ, the eleventh "earthly branch."**
	戌	戌	戌	The original meaning of *xū* was "to destroy, to kill." The "one" rad. is a wound made by the lance or halberd (497, above). Note that *xū* 戌 is not *shù* 戍, discussed in 419, above. In *shù* 戍, the internal stroke is "dot;" in *xū* 戌, the internal stroke is the "one" rad. (a very short "one").
498 **6 strokes**				

歲	卜	止	止	**SUÌ, harvest; year; years old**
	止	此	岸	他幾歲了 *tā jǐ suì le*, How old is he? (assuming less than ten)
499 **13 strokes**	歲	歲	歲	歲月 *suì yuè*, years 〈止 195〉 岁

130

忘 500 7 strokes	丶 亠 忘 忘	亠 忘	亡 忘

WÀNG, to forget

The "heart" rad. gives the meaning; *wáng* (68, above) gives the sound. Compare 69, above, and note that *wáng* + "heart" at the side means "be busy" while *wáng* + "heart" below means "to forget."

忘八 *wángbā*, tortoise; cuckold (abusive) (note the change to *wáng*)

差 501 9 strokes (10 strokes)	丶 丷 半 羊 羞	丷 羊 差	丷

CHÀ, to differ, to fall short, to owe; CHĀ, differ; difference (arithmetical); mistake; CHĀI, to send; to commission; official

差不多 *chàbuduō*, almost the same
差別 *chābié*, difference
差事 *chāishì*, work, job, official assignment

开 502 4 strokes	一 开	二	于

JIĀN, to raise in both hands

Not in modern use in this pronunciation and meaning. Cf. 503, below (short form).

開 503 12 strokes	丨 門 閁	冂 門 開	冂 門 開

KĀI, to open

開門 *kāimén*, to open the door
開車 *kāichē*, to drive a car
水開了 *shuǐ kāi le*, The water's boiling.
開會 *kāihuì*, to hold a meeting, to attend a meeting
開夜車 *kāiyèchē*, to work late into the night (literally, "to drive the night train") 开

丱 504 5 strokes	∠ 丱	屮 丱	屮

GUÀN, the two tufts of hair on a child's head (a traditional way to dress hair)

The character is a picture of the two tufts of hair sticking up. It is not in modern use as an independent character.

131

緃 505 11 strokes				**GUĀN, (in weaving) to run the threads through a web** The "coil" rad. (repeated) represents the silk or other thread in this process, and *guàn* (504, above) gives the sound. Not in modern use as an independent character.

GUĀN, to shut; barrier; family name

關門 *guānmén*, to shut the door
關心 *guānxīn*, concerned about
關稅 *guānshuì*, customs duty

506
19 strokes

关

KÈ, quarter of an hour; to engrave or carve; stingy; sarcastic

The original meaning was "carve." "Knife" gave the meaning; *hài* (250, above) gave the sound.

三點一刻 *sān diǎn yí kè*, 3:15
木刻 *mùkè*, a woodcut, a wood engraving
立刻 *lìkè*, immediately, right away

507
8 strokes

ZHǍO, to look for; to visit; to give change

The student should distinguish *zhǎo* from *wǒ* 我 (44, above)

找不着 *zhǎobuzháo*, can't find
找到 *zhǎodào*, to find
找事 *zhǎoshì*, to go job-hunting; to pick a quarrel

508
7 strokes

BĀO, to wrap; a family name

包起來 *bāoqǐlái*, to wrap up
包工 *bāogōng*, to do contract work
包飯 *bāofàn*, to board at a place
書包 *shūbāo*, book-bag, school satchel

509
5 strokes

跑	`	冖	口	**PǍO, to run**
				The "foot" rad. gives the meaning; *bāo* (509, above) suggests the sound.
	𧾷	𧾷	𧾷	跑道 *pǎodào*, racetrack; runway (for airplanes) 跑馬 *pǎomǎ*, a horse race; to ride a horse
510 12 strokes	𧾷	趵	跑	飛跑 *fēipǎo*, to go very fast

骨	`	冖	冎	**GǓ, bone. BONE rad. (188)(H 219)**
				The top part is supposed to show the bone in the flesh. Note the "meat" rad. (flesh) at the bottom.
	冎	冎	𩰡	骨頭 *gǔtóu*, bone 頭骨 *tóugǔ*, "head-bone," i.e., skull
511 10 strokes	骨	骨	骨	

冎	l	冖	冂	**GUǍ, skeleton; bone with the meat stripped off**
				This character is the "bone" rad. minus its lower part, the "meat" rad.
	冎	冎	冎	
512 6 strokes				

咼	l	冖	冂	**KUĀI, puckered mouth**
				The "mouth" rad. gives the meaning in this character; *guǎ* (512, above) gives the sound. This character occurs in a number of characters to give the sounds *guo* or *huo*. Not in modern use as an independent character.
	冎	冎	冎	
513 9 strokes	咼	咼	咼	

過	冂	冂	冎	**GUÒ, to go over**
				過來 *guòlái*, to come over 過去 *guòqù*, to go over; to die; in the past 過年 *guònián*, to celebrate the New Year
	咼	咼	過	
514 12 strokes	過	過		过

133

自 515 6 strokes	′ 自	亻 自	竹 自	**ZÌ, nose; self; from. SMALL NOSE rad. (132)(H180)** The character is supposed to be a picture of a nose. It is called "small nose" to distinguish it from the "big nose" rad. 鼻 (p. 295a) that also means "nose." Distinguish 自 from "eye" 目 (120, above). 自來水 *zì lái shuǐ*, tap water, running water
釆 516 7 strokes	一 釆	丷	丷 釆	**BIÀN, to sift. SIFT rad. (165)(H197)** Note that "sift" = "left" + "rice." If it helps, the student can think of the "left" rad. as the sifter with the rice falling through below it. Distinguish from *cǎi* "cull" (517, below) and from "grain" 禾 and "tree" 木 (65 and 64, above).
采 517 8 strokes	′ 采 采	亻	爫 采	**CǍI, to cull; bright colors** Though this character seems to be composed of "claws" over "tree," it is found in dictionaries under the "sift" rad. (516, above). The "claws" are supposed to represent a hand picking fruit from a tree, whence "to cull." The meaning "bright colors" is by sound-loan.
菜 518 12 strokes	一 艹 苹	十 艹 莘	艹 艹 菜	**CÀI, vegetables; course or dish in a Chinese meal** 點菜 *diǎncài*, to order dishes (in a restaurant) 一道菜 *yí dào cài*, a course (of a meal) 菜地 *càidì*, plot of vegetables
丁 519 2 strokes	一	丁		**DĪNG, person; nail; be strong; single; the fourth "heavenly stem;" a family name** 尼古丁 *nígǔdīng*, nicotine 一丁點兒 *yì dīng diǎnr*, (dialect) a tiny bit, a trifle 丁零 *dīnglíng*, tinkle tinkle (onomatopoeic) 丁字 *dīngzì*, T-shaped

				DĂ, to beat; from; DĀ, a dozen
打	一	丁	扌	打開 *dăkāi*, to open
	扌	打		打入 *dărù*, to branch out (in business); to force a way into
520				打聽 *dătīng*, to inquire
5 strokes				打字機 *dăzìjī*, typewriter

				SUÀN, to add up; to add in; to consider as
算	ノ	⺊	⺮	打算 *dăsuàn*, to plan to
	竹	竻	筲	算了 *suàn le*, That's enough! Forget it!
				心算 *xīnsuàn*, to do arithmetic in your head
521	筲	算	算	筆算 *bĭsuàn*, to do arithmetic with pencil and paper
14 strokes				

				RÈN, knife edge, blade
刃	フ	刀	刃	The character is "knife" with an additional stroke to call attention to the blade.
522				刀刃 *dāorèn*, knife-blade; crucial point
3 strokes				

				RĔN, to bear, to endure
忍	フ	刀	刃	The "heart" rad. gives the meaning; *rèn* (522, above) gives the sound.
	刃	忍	忍	忍受 *rĕnshòu*, to endure, to "stand"
				忍心 *rĕnxīn*, hard-hearted enough (to do such-and-such a deed)
523	忍			忍不住 *rĕnbuzhù*, unable to bear
7 strokes				

				RÈN, to recognize; to admit
認	、	二	言	認得 *rènde*, to recognize
	言	訂	訒	認為 *rènwéi*, to think, to feel, to deem
				認真 *rènzhēn*, conscientious; take seriously
524	認	認	認	認字 *rènzì*, literate
14 strokes				认

135

戠 525 13 strokes	丶	亠	宀
	立	立	音
	戠	戠	戠

ZHĪ, to command; weapon; to stick to
Karlgren explains the character by analyzing the "tone" rad as "speak, give commands" and says, "the man with a lance who gives commands." This character gives the sound in a number of common modern characters; it is not in modern use as an independent character.
(日 82)

識 526 19 strokes	一	二	言
	言	誩	諳
	識	識	識

SHÍ, to know; knowledge; ZHÌ (bookish), to remember; a mark or sign
認識　*rènshi*, to recognize, to know
識字　*shízì*, literate
常識　*chángshí*, general knowledge

识

放 527 8 strokes	丶	二	宀
	方	方	方
	放	放	

FÀNG, to lay down; to put; to tend; to lend; to fire (a weapon)
放手　*fàngshǒu*, to let go of
放心　*fàngxīn*, at ease about
放學　*fàngxué*, to get out of class, to get out of school

| 氐 528 5 strokes | 一 | 匚 | 氐 |
| | 氐 | 氐 | |

DǏ, foundation; bottom; to go down
The little horizontal stroke at the bottom gives the meaning; the rest of the character, *shì* (224, above), once gave the sound. In modern usage, this character has been replaced by 529, below.

底 529 8 strokes	丶	二	广
	广	庀	庀
	底	底	

DǏ, foundation; bottom
The word is the same as 528, above; the character is reclarified with "lean-to."
底子　*dǐzi*, background, origin, foundation; original copy
底下　*dǐxià*, underneath, below
年底　*niándǐ*, year's end

路	丶	口	卩
	卩	𧾷	𧾷
530 13 strokes	𧾷	𧾷	路

LÙ, road; kind, sort; family name

The "foot" rad. gives the meaning; the rest of the character once gave the sound.

路過 *lùguò*, to go past
走路 *zǒulù*, to walk
思路 *sīlù*, train of thought

疒	丶	亠	广
	广	疒	
531 5 strokes			

NÌ, sick. SICK rad. (104)(H127)

The character represents a man stretched out on his bed, whence "be sick." Compare the "bed" rad. (849, below). *Nì* is not in modern use as an independent character.

内	丨	冂	内
	内		
532 4 strokes			

NÈI, inside

Nèi is a picture of a man entering a space marked off by the "borders" rad. (The traditional rad. is "enter," not "man.")

内地 *nèidì*, interior (of a country)
三天内 *sān tiān nèi*, within three days
内人 *nèirén*, my wife (old-fashioned, sexist)

丙	一	厂	冂
	丙	丙	
533 5 strokes			

BǏNG, fish tail; the third "heavenly stem"

Bǐng looks like a picture of a fish tail.

丙等 *bǐngděng*, the third in a series; third category

病	丶	亠	广
	广	疒	疒
534 10 strokes	疖	病	病

BÌNG, sickness, sick

The character combines the "sick" rad. for meaning with *bǐng* (533, above) for sound.

看病 *kànbìng*, to see a doctor; to examine a patient
生病 *shēngbìng*, to get sick, to come down with a disease

137

封	一	十	土	**FĒNG, to seal up; a measure for letters; a family name**
	圭	丰	圭	一封信 *yì fēng xìn*, a letter 信封 *xìnfēng*, envelope 封口 *fēngkǒu*, to seal (a letter) to heal up (of a wound); to say something that ends debate
535 **9 strokes**	圭	封	封	

帛	ノ	⼂	⼓	**BÁI, silk; riches; a family name**
	白	白	白	The character has "cloth" for meaning, *bái* (231, above) for sound. Not in modern use as an independent character.
536 **8 strokes**	帛	帛		

幫	一	十	土	**BĀNG, to help; clique, group**
	圭	圭	封	幫忙 *bāngmáng*, to help 幫手 *bāngshǒu*, helper 一幫人 *yì bāng rén*, a group, a band, a clique
537 **17 strokes**	封	幇	幫	帮

垂	ノ	二	千	**CHUÍ, to droop** *Chuí* was originally a picture of a tree with drooping leaves. The character is now classified under the "earth" rad. 土 in some dictionaries (but in H, under the "left" rad. [1, above]).
	千	壬	丢	
538 **8 strokes**	垂	垂		垂老 *chuílǎo*, (bookish) to be getting old 垂青 *chuíqīng*, (bookish) to appreciate (a person), to look with favor on a person

睡	丨	刀	目	**SHUÌ, to sleep; to lie down** In this character, *chuí* (538, above) is probably there to give the sound. *Shuì* can also be explained as a meaning-meaning compound: "eye" + "to droop" = "to sleep."
	目	盯	盯	
539 **13 strokes**	盯	睡	睡	睡衣 *shuìyī*, pajamas 睡意 *shuìyì*, sleepiness, desire to sleep

帶	一	十	卅	**DÀI**, belt; to wear around the waist; to bring along
540 11 strokes	卅	卅	卅	帶孩子 *dài háizi*, to bring children along 帶頭 *dàitóu*, to take the lead, to set an example 帶路 *dàilù*, to act as a guide
	卅	帶	帶	帶

DÀI, belt; to wear around the waist; to bring along

帶孩子 *dài háizi*, to bring children along

帶頭 *dàitóu*, to take the lead, to set an example

帶路 *dàilù*, to act as a guide

犬

541
4 strokes

一　ナ　大

犬

QUǍN, dog. DOG rad. (94)(H96)

The student will note that the "dog" rad. = "big" + "dot." Care should be taken to distinguish "dog" from "big" 大 (50, above) and from 太 "extremely" (74, above).

哭

542
10 strokes

丶　口　口

叩　吅　罒

哭　哭

KŪ, to cry, to howl

Kū combines meanings: "dog" + "mouth" = "to howl, to cry." This was originally the top part of 喪 "to mourn" (p. 291a, below); the bottom part was a person, hidden away (in the grave).

哭笑不得 *kū-xiào bu dé*, to not know whether to laugh or cry; find a thing both painful and amusing

---

平

543
5 strokes

一　丷　二

平　平

PÍNG, to weigh; even, calm, level, flat

Píng is a picture of a scale in balance.

平常 *píngcháng*, ordinary

平等 *píngděng*, equal

平原 *píngyuán*, a plain (flatland)

應

544
17 strokes

丶　亠　广

庁　府　庐

雁　應　應

YĪNG, to promise; ought; a family name;
YÌNG, to respond; to turn out to be true

應用 *yīngyòng*, to put into practice

應得的 *yīng déde*, ought to be gotten; deserved

(亻 4)　应

當	⟍	⟍	⟍	**DĀNG**, to serve as; in the presence of; the very same; **DǍNG**, to think (mistakenly) that; **DÀNG**, to think (mistakenly) that; to pawn
	业	半	严	
545 13 strokes	严	當	當	應當 *yīngdāng*, ought to (do) 當時 *dāngshí*, (at) that time 丁當 *dīngdāng*, ding-dong　　　　当

法	⟍	⟍	⟍	**FǍ**, method, way, law; doctrine
	⟍	汁	注	法官 *fǎguān*, a judge 説法 *shuōfa*, way of saying something; version, argument; *shuōfǎ*, to expound Buddha's doctrine
546 8 strokes	法	法		法國 *Fǎguó*, France

怕	⟍	丨	忄	**PÀ**, to fear
	忄	忄	怕	"Heart" + "white" = "to fear." *Bái* "white" (231, above) is probably there to give the sound.
547 8 strokes	怕	怕		怕太太 *pà tàitai*, henpecked 可怕 *kěpà*, frightening, scary 怕事 *pàshì*, timorous, afraid of getting into trouble

完	⟍	八	宀	**WÁN**, to finish; family name
	宀	宁	完	完成 *wánchéng*, to complete 用完 *yòng wán*, to use up, to be used up 玩兒完 *wánr wán*, (colloquial), kaput, finished, "done for"
548 7 strokes	完			

辛	⟍	二	亠	**XĪN**, bitter, toilsome; the eighth "heavenly stem;" family name. BITTER rad. (160)(H186)
	亠	立	产	There is no helpful explanation of this rad. The student should be careful to distinguish it from *xìng* "be lucky" 幸 (89, above).
549 7 strokes	辛			艱辛 *jiānxīn*, hardship

辩	、	二	亠
	亠	立	立
550 14 strokes	辛	辛二	辩

BIÀN, to wrangle

Biàn is supposed to combine meanings. The "bitter" rad. repeated = "bitter against bitter:" "to recriminate, to wrangle, to dispute." In modern times, reclarified (logically enough) with "words" (rad. 149): 辩.

辦	、	二	亠
	亠	立	辛
551 16 strokes	剙	勃	辦

BÀN, to manage; to punish

Biàn (550, above) suggests the sound; the "strength" rad. (suggesting exertion) helps with the meaning.

辦公　*bàn gōng*, to work (in an office), to take care of official business
辦法　*bànfǎ*, method, way
辦事　*bànshì*, to do a job, to work, manage things

办

覺	𠄎	乞	⺋
	臼	臼	𦥑
552 20 strokes	𦥔	學	覺

JUÉ, to feel; JIÀO, to sleep

覺得　*juéde*, to feel
睡覺　*shuìjiào*, to sleep
聽覺　*tīngjué*, sense of hearing

(見 214)

觉

昔	一	十	廿
	卅	井	芷
553 8 strokes	昔	昔	

XĪ, ancient

The original meaning of this character was "meat dried in the sun; to age," and the top part of the old character was a picture of meat. The sun can still be found in the modern character. The meaning "ancient" derives from the earlier meaning "to age."

錯	丿	𠆢	乍
	𠂉	余	余
554 16 strokes	金	鉳	錯

CUÒ, to make a mistake

不錯　*búcuò*, pretty good
錯過　*cuòguò*, to miss a chance
錯覺　*cuòjué*, illusion, wrong impression
錯字　*cuòzì*, incorrectly written character; misprint

错

襄 555 16 strokes	丶	亠	产
	亩	审	审
	亩	襄	襄

HUÁI, to hug, to hide

The outer parts (top and bottom) of *huái* form the "gown" rad. (109, above). The rest of *huái* is supposed to represent something hidden in the clothes or hugged against the bosom. Now reclarified with "heart:" 懷. See p. 293a, below.

(四 132)

壞 556 19 strokes	一	十	土
	圹	坮	埫
	塥	壞	壞	坏

HUÀI, bad, rotten, sly

壞人 *huàirén*, evil person
車壞了 *chē huài le*, The car broke down
不壞 *búhuài*, be pretty good

河 557 8 strokes	丶	冫	氵
	沪	沪	沪
	沪	河	

HÉ, river

Kě (77, above) gives the sound; the "water" rad., of course, gives the meaning.

河道 *hédào*, river course, riverbed
河口 *hékǒu*, mouth of a river
河馬 *hémǎ*, hippopotamus

魚 558 11 strokes	丿	勹	仒
	仒	台	角
	鱼	魚	魚	鱼

YÚ, fish; family name. FISH rad. (195) (H210)

飛魚 *fēiyú*, flying fish
魚网 *yúwǎng*, fishnet
金魚 *jīnyú*, goldfish

| 永 559 5 strokes | 丶 | 丁 | 刁 |
| | 永 | 永 | |

YǑNG, eternal

The character is supposed to be a picture of water currents and thus suggests "go on and on" like flowing water: "eternal."

永不 *yǒngbu*, never…
永生 *yǒngshēng*, (religious term) eternal life; immortal

142

巛	く	巛	**CHUĀN, river. RIVER rad. (47)** This character is a picture of flowing water. Compare 442, above, which is another form of this rad. (For the independent form, see p.245b.) This form occurs only as a part of characters.
560 2 strokes (3 strokes)			

羕	⸌⸍	丷	羊	**YÀNG, a long watercourse; ripple, overflow** *Yàng* combines *yáng* (475, above) for sound with "eternal" for meaning. In modern use, reclarified with the "water-dots" 漾.
	羊	羊	羊	
561 11 strokes	羕	羕	羕	

樣	一	十	才	**YÀNG, kind, sort** 一樣 *yíyàng*, be alike 樣子 *yàngzi*, style 怎麼樣 *zěnme yàng*, How about…? How's everything? 這樣 *zhèyàng*, in this way; so; like this
	木	杧	杧	
562 15 strokes	样	样	樣	样

條	丿	亻	亻	**TIÁO, twig; a long, narrow thing, a strip; section; a measure for roads, rivers, fishes, some animals; note (short message)** 一條魚 *yì tiáo yú*, a fish 便條 *biàntiáo*, brief note 條件 *tiáojiàn*, terms, conditions
	仴	仴	修	
563 10 strokes	俇	條	條	条

冫	丶	冫	**BĪNG, ice. ICE rad. (15)(H8)** Note the similarity between the "ice" rad. and the "three-dots-water" form of the "water" rad. The "ice" rad. has two dots instead of three. Often printed ⟫.
564 2 strokes			

143

次	、	㇀	㇑
	㇒	次	次
565 6 strokes			

CÌ, a time; a measure for times or occasions; next (in order); inferior to

下次 *xiàcì*, next time
次要 *cìyào*, second most important
三次 *sān cì*, three times
首次 *shǒucì*, the first time
真次 *zhēncì*, really inferior, terrible

短	㇒	㇀	上
	午	矢	矢
566 12 strokes	矩	短	短

DUĂN, short (opposite of long); lack
The first example below illustrates a favorite Chinese technique of word-formation, putting two contraries together to make an abstract noun: "the long and the short of it" = "length."

長短 *chángduǎn*, length
短少 *duǎnshǎo*, deficient, to lack
短不了 *duǎnbuliǎo*, unable to do without; must

比	一	㇄	上
	比		
567 4 strokes			

BĬ, to set side by side, to compare. COMPARE rad. (81)(H123)

The modern character looks like "ladle" + "ladle" (137, above). The old forms have two men standing side by side. In any case, there are two similar objects side by side, as if for comparison.

亟	一	丁	丂
	百	百	而
568 9 strokes	亟	亟	

JÍ, to hurry

Jí combines meanings, philosophically. The 二 is "heaven and earth, between which men 人 [now the twisty vertical stroke] toil and moil, planning with their mouths 口 and scrabbling with their hands 又, *hurrying* to catch heaven's times and seasons and earth's opportunities so as to get the work done." Not now independent.

極	一	十	才
	札	杯	柯
569 12 strokes	栭	極	極

JÍ, to reach an extreme; extremely; pole (extreme point)

好極了 *hǎojíle*, Superb! Great!
極點 *jídiǎn*, extreme point
極力 *jílì*, with all one's strength

极

144

南	一	十	冖	**NÁN, south: family name**
	内	内	内	南方 *nánfāng*, the South
570	南	南	南	西南 *xīnán*, southwest
9 strokes				南極 *nánjí*, South Pole
				南京 *Nánjīng*, Nanjing (the city)

北	丨	十	爿	**BĚI, north**
	北	北		北方 *běifāng*, the North
571				城北 *chéngběi*, north of the city
5 strokes				東北 *dōngběi*, northeast
				北京 *Běijīng*, Beijing, Peking

左	一	大	左	**ZUǑ, left (opposite of right)**
	左	左		想左了 *xiǎngzuǒle*, to think incorrectly
572				左手 *zuǒshǒu*, left hand
5 strokes				

右	一	大	才	**YÒU, right (opposite of left)**
	右	右		左右 *zuǒyòu*, approximately
				右耳 *yòuěr*, right ear
				左…右… *zuǒ…yòu…*, to do something
573				repeatedly over and over, e.g. 左
5 strokes				思右想, *zuǒ sī yòu xiǎng*, keep
				on thinking about it

穴	丶	八	宀	**XUÉ, cave; lair; acupuncture point; a family name. CAVE rad. (116)(H128)**
	宀	穴		穴位 *xuéwèi*, (Chinese medicine)
574				acupuncture point
5 strokes				

145

邊	冂	自	臬	**BIĀN, side, region; family name** 北邊 *běibiān*, north side, northern region 左邊 *zuǒbiān*, left side 裡邊 *lǐbiān*, inside
	臬	臱	窻	
575 **19 strokes**	邊	邊		(自 515, 放 392)　　边

牙	一	二	亍	**YÁ, tooth; family name, TOOTH rad. (92)(H99)** The "tooth" rad. is a picture. 門牙 *ményá*, incisor 犬牙 *quǎnyá*, canine tooth; dog's fang 牙口 *yákǒu*, the age of an animal according to the appearance of its teeth; the condition of an old person's teeth
	牙			
576 **4 strokes**				

穿	`	八	宀	**CHUĀN, to don, to wear; to thread; to pierce** 看穿 *kànchuān*, to see right through 穿戴 *chuāndài*, clothing, apparel 穿着 *chuānzhuó*, clothing, apparel
	宀	穴	空	
577 **9 strokes**	空	穿	穿	

袁	一	十	土	**YUÁN, robe; family name** Note that in this character, the top part of the "gown" rad. 衣 (109, above) has been corrupted into 土 "earth". *Yuán* is, nevertheless, classified in traditional dictionaries under the "gown" rad., and the relation of its meaning to "gown" is clear enough. In modern use only as a family name.
	吉	吉	声	
578 **10 strokes**	袁	袁	袁	

遠	土	吉	声	**YUǍN, far away; family name** 永遠 *yǒngyuǎn*, forever, always 遠東 *yuǎndōng*, the Far East 遠心力 *yuǎnxīnlì*, centrifugal force 遠見 *yuǎnjiàn*, foresight
	袁	袁	袁	
579 **13 strokes**	遠	遠	遠	远

近	′	厂	斤	**JÌN, near** 斤 (262) gives the sound, "halt" (171) the meaning. 近来 *jìnlái*, recently 遠近 *yuǎnjìn*, distance (cp. 長短 in 566, above); far and near 遠近聞名 *yuǎnjìn wénmíng*, to have one's name heard far and near: famous
	斤	斤	近	
580 7 strokes	近			

凶	ノ	メ	凶	**XIŌNG, cruel, unlucky, calamitous** The "bowl" rad. in this character used to be a pit, and the X shape was a man falling, legs up, into the pit: "calamity." 凶手 *xiōngshǒu*, murderer, butcher (figurative senses) 行凶 *xíngxiōng*, to commit physical assault or murder
	凶			
581 4 strokes				

离	、	亠	宀	**LÍ, hobgoblin** This character is a picture of a hobgoblin. Note that, with the "track" rad. as its lower part, the hobgoblin has hind legs and a tail. The top parts, "lid" + "cruel," have been corrupted from the original picture. In modern usage, this character is only seen as a short form of 583, below.
	文	立	卤	
582 11 strokes	离	离	离	

離	亠	文	卤	**LÍ, to depart from; from** 離開 *líkāi*, to leave 離間 *líjiàn*, to cause a rift between 離奇 *líqí*, strange, weird 離別 *líbié*, bid farewell to, to part from (intending to be gone for some time)
	离	离	劇	
583 19 strokes	離	離	離	离

僉	ノ	人	人	**QIĀN, all, together** Note that the top part of *qiān* — *jí* "get together" (175, above) — gives the meaning. The lower part, "mouth" + "mouth" and "man" + "man," — seems simply to reinforce the idea of getting together or collecting. Not now used as an independent character.
	合	合	僉	
584 13 strokes	僉	僉	僉	佥

147

臉	丿	刀	月	**LIĂN, face**
	刖	肸	脸	The "meat" rad. gives the meaning in this character; the *qiān* part (584, above) suggests the sound.
585 17 strokes	脍	臉	臉	門臉 *ménliǎn*, facade 不要臉 *búyào liǎn*, shameless, to have no conscience 笑臉 *xiàoliǎn*, smiling face 脸

數	丶	口	日	**SHÙ, number; SHŬ, enumerate**
	昌	娄	娄	歲數 *suìshù*, (person's) age 數目 *shùmu*, number, amount 數學 *shùxué*, mathematics 數數兒 *shǔshùr*, to count (literally, to count the numbers)
586 15 strokes	娄	數	數	數字 *shùzì*, numeral, digit; quantity 数

洗	丶	丷	氵	**XĬ, to wash**
	氵	汇	泮	洗臉 *xǐliǎn*, to wash your face 洗手 *xǐshǒu*, (figuratively, as in English) to wash your hands of something; (of a criminal), to go straight 洗禮 *xǐlǐ*, baptism; (figuratively, as in English) a severe test
587 9 strokes	泮	涉	洗	

往	丿	彳	彳	**WĂNG, to go; previous; WĂNG, WÀNG, toward**
	彳	彳	彳	往來 below, (first meaning) is another example of contraries combined to make a word (cf. 長短, in 566, above). 往東 *wǎngdōng*, eastward 往後 *wǎnghòu*, from now on
588 8 strokes	往	往		往往 *wǎngwǎng*, sometimes 往來 *wǎnglái*, (commercial and social) intercourse; to come and go

每	丿	𠂉	亡	**MĚI, each**
	勹	勾	每	每一個 *měi yí ge*, each 每天 *měitiān*, every day 每次 *měicì*, each time
589 7 strokes	每			

但 590 7 strokes	ノ イ 仃 但 但	イ 仃 但	亻 但 但	**DÀN, but; only; family name** 但是 *dànshì*, but 不但 *búdàn*, not only 但願 *dànyuàn*, if only; I wish that
圣 591 5 strokes	フ 圣	又 圣	圣	**KŪ, to work in the fields** The character appears to combine meanings: "right hand" + "earth" = "to work in the fields." In modern Chinese, it is only seen as a part of characters.
怪 592 8 strokes	` 忄 怪	丷 忆 怪	忄 怪	**GUÀI, to blame; to consider weird; to be weird** 奇怪 *qíguài*, peculiar, weird 別怪他 *bié guài tā*, Don't blame him 怪話 *guàihuà*, cynical remark; complaint 怪不得 *guàibude*, no wonder; so *that's* the reason; don't blame…
然 593 12 strokes	ノ 匀 狄	夕 夕 狄	夕 夗 然	**RÁN, right; so, like this** This character originally meant "to roast," and it combined meanings: "meat" (slightly deformed) + "dog" + "fire." "So, like this," comes by sound-loan. 然後 *ránhòu*, afterward 必然 *bìrán*, certainly
午 594 4 strokes	ノ 午	亠	二	**WŬ, noon; the seventh "earthly branch"** The character once meant "to knock against" and was a picture of a battering-ram. Compare the "shield" rad. (87, above). All other meanings are by sound-loan. 下午 *xiàwǔ*, afternoon 正午 *zhèngwǔ*, high noon 午睡 *wǔshuì*, "nooner," nap, siesta; to take a mid-day nap

149

許	、	二	言
	言	訁	訐
595 **11 strokes**	許	許	

XǓ, to permit; to promise; perhaps; family name

許可　*xǔkě*, to permit; permission
許多　*xǔduō*, very many; many things
許願　*xǔyuàn*, to make a vow (to a god); to promise a reward

許

才	一	寸	才
596 **3 strokes**			

CÁI, substance; natural capacity, talent, genius; then (and not till then); only

Distinguish *cái* from "thumb" 寸 (186, above) and from "hand" 扌 (14, above).

天才　*tiāncái*, genius, talent
人才　*réncái*, talented person; (colloquial) handsome man
才能　*cáinéng*, talent, ability

果	、	口	日
	日	旦	甲
597 **8 strokes**	果	果	

GUǑ, fruit; result; really

Guǒ is a picture of fruit on a tree.

水果　*shuǐguǒ*, fruit
果仁　*guǒrén*, nut
果然　*guǒrán*, indeed, certainly

課	、	二	言
	訂	課	課
598 **15 strokes**	課	課	課

KÈ, lesson, course; class section

下課　*xiàkè*, Class dismissed.
課本　*kèběn*, textbook
課文　*kèwén*, text
課時　*kèshí*, class hour

课

世	一	十	廿
	卅	世	
599 **5 strokes**			

SHÌ, world; generation; family name

This character is actually three "ten" rads. 十 (the vertical stroke on the left is bent for the sake of design) written together to suggest "thirty years:" "a generation."

今世　*jīnshì*, this age; contemporary
世上　*shìshang*, in this world, on earth

150

介	ノ	人	介	**JIÈ, between; to regard as important** 介入 *jièrù*, to intervene, get involved 介子 *jièzi*, meson (term from physics: particle of intermediate mass, between baryons 重子 [*zhòngzi*, "heavy ones"] and leptons 輕子 [*qīngzi*, "light ones" — see 1051 for 輕 "be light"])
600 4 strokes	介			

界	ヽ	口	曰	**JIÈ, boundary; world; scope** 世界 *shìjiè*, world 邊界 *biānjiè*, border 新聞界 *xīnwénjiè*, journalistic circles 國界 *guójiè*, national borders, boundaries
	田	田	甼	
601 9 strokes	界	界	界	

海	ヽ	ヾ	氵	**HǍI, sea; family name** 海關 *hǎiguān*, customshouse; Customs 地中海 *Dìzhōnghǎi*, Mediterranean 上海 *Shànghǎi*, Shanghai
	氵	汙	汸	
602 10 strokes	海	海	海	

部	ヽ	二	亠	**BÙ, set, portion, part; department; a measure for vehicles; family name (rare)** 部分 *bùfen*, portion, part 部門 *bùmén*, section, department 部長 *bùzhǎng*, department head 部首 *bùshǒu*, a "radical," that is, an element of the Chinese writing system used to classify characters, as in dictionaries and indexes
	亣	立	音	
603 11 strokes	音ʾ	部ʾ	部	

黃	一	十	廿	**HUÁNG, yellow; family name. YELLOW rad. (201)** 黃豆 *huángdòu*, soybean 黃河 *Huáng hé*, the Yellow River 黃了 *huáng le*, (colloquial) to have fallen through, come to nothing 黃金 *huáng jīn*, "the yellow metal," i.e., gold
	芒	芦	苦	
604 11 strokes	菌	黃	黃	(田 23)

總	㇝	幺	幺	**ZŎNG**, to add together; always; probably, surely
	糸	紀	納	總是 *zŏngshì*, always 總共 *zŏnggòng*, altogether 總數 *zŏngshù*, total, total amount
605 17 strokes	綯	總	總	总

連	一	冂	百	**LIÁN**, to connect; continuously; including; company (military); even; family name
	亘	車	車	連着 *liánzhe*, continuous, continuously 連長 *liánzhǎng*, company commander 連忙 *liánmáng*, right away, promptly
606 10 strokes	連	連		连

只	丶	冂	口	**ZHĬ**, just, only
	尸	只		只得 *zhǐdē*, can do nothing but 只好 *zhǐhǎo*, can do nothing but 只有 *zhǐyǒu*, can do nothing but 只是 *zhǐshì*, but; only
607 5 strokes				

特	丿	㇇	牛	**TÈ**, special
	牜	牜	牰	特別 *tèbié*, special; especially 特點 *tèdiǎn*, special feature 特快 *tèkuài*, express (as in "express train") 特出 *tèchū*, outstanding
608 10 strokes	特	特		

而	一	厂	广	**ÉR**, beard; and, and yet, but. BEARD rad. (126)(H169)
	丙	而	而	*Ér* is a picture of a beard. Distinguish it from "face" 面 (610, below). 而且 *érqiě*, and moreover 而已 *éryǐ*, That's all. 然而 *rán'ér*, but, yet, however
609 6 strokes				

面	一	一	厂	**MIĂN, face. FACE rad. (176)** This character is a picture. 右面 *yòumiàn*, on the right; right side 面子 *miànzi*, face, social standing; width (of textiles) 面目 *miànmù*, facial appearance; behavior 臉面 *liǎnmiàn*, "face," self-respect; a person's feelings
	厉	而	而	
610 9 strokes	面	面	面	
洋	、	ˋ	氵	**YÁNG, ocean; foreign** 大西洋 *Dàxīyáng*, the Atlantic 太平洋 *Tàipíngyáng*, the Pacific 洋鬼子 *yángguǐzi*, "foreign devil," foreigner (derogatory)
	氵	氵	氵	
611 9 strokes	氵	汫	洋	
于	一	二	于	**YÚ, on, to, at; family name** In traditional texts, this *yú* is often replaced by 於 (656, below); but in mainland Chinese texts, this *yú* (612) seems to be preferred. 等于 *děngyú*, equal to, virtually the same as, tantamount to 于是 *yúshì*, consequently; thereupon 于今 *yújīn*, since, from then till now; nowadays
612 3 strokes				
余	ノ	人	公	**YÚ, (bookish) I, me; family name** Note that this character is now commonly seen as the short form of 872, below.
	今	仐	余	
613 7 strokes	余			
除	ˋ	了	阝	**CHÚ, except; to divide (arithmetic); to remove** 除去 *chúqù*, in addition to; to remove 除了…以外 *chú le…yǐwài*, in addition to 除夕 *chúxī*, (on) New Year's Eve
	阝	阞	队	
614 10 strokes	阹	除	除	

153

江	、	٠	氵	**JIĀNG, river; family name**
	氵	江	江	長江 Chángjiāng, the "long river," i.e., the Yangtse
615 **6 strokes**				江西 *Jiāngxī*, Kiangsi (province) 江山 jiāngshān, rivers and mountains; landscape; (by metonymy) nation

全	丿	入	人	**QUÁN, complete, completely; all, the whole; family name**
	亼	全	全	The student should distinguish this from the "gold" rad. 金 (94, above).
616 **6 strokes**				完全 *wánquán*, complete; completely, perfectly 全部 *quánbù*, whole thing; completely

乾	一	十	古	**GĀN, dry; unadorned; used up; in name only; QIÁN, male; sky; first symbol in the _I Ching_ (_Yi Jing_): "the Creative;" family name**
	古	直	卓	One authority explains: "The sun 日 as it rises 早 draws up vapors" (乞, 322), so releasing natural energies: "buds open, seeds germinate, etc." Evaporation also = "to dry."
617 **11 strokes**	乾	乾	乾	乾洗 *gānxǐ*, to dry clean 干

爭	⺈	⺈	⺈	**ZHĒNG, to argue, to fight**
	爫	马	马	The character shows two hands struggling over an object.
618 **8 strokes**	争	爭		爭取 *zhēngqǔ*, to work hard for 爭氣 *zhēngqì*, determined; to prove one's ability 争

淨	、	٠	氵	**JÌNG, to clean, clean; net (as opposed to gross); everywhere**
	氵	氵	氵	Now often seen in the form 净.
619 **11 strokes**	淨	淨	淨	乾淨 *gānjìng*, clean 淨得 *jìngdé*, net profit 淨重 *jìngzhòng* net weight

154

胡	一	十	古
620 9 strokes	古	却	胡
	胡	胡	

HÚ, Tartars; Mongols; foolish; family name

胡説 *húshuō*, to talk nonsense; "Nonsense!" "Bunkum!"
胡來 *húlái*, not know what you are doing, "to mess around"

湖	丶	丶	氵
621 12 strokes	汁	沽	浿
	湖	湖	湖

HÚ, lake

湖北 *Húběi*, Hubei (province)
湖南 *Húnán*, Hunan (province)
江湖 *jiānghú*, rivers and lakes; all over the country
江湖 *jiānghu*, traveling con artists (entertainers, fake doctors, and the like) or their professions

商	丶	亠	亠
622 11 strokes	六	广	肖
	肖	商	商

SHĀNG, quotient; commerce; merchant; family name

商人 *shāngrén*, businessman
商船 *shāngchuán*, merchant ship
進口商 *jìnkǒushāng*, importer
商會 *shānghuì*, chamber of commerce

業	丶	丷	川
623 13 strokes	业	业	业
	芈	芈	業

YÈ, business, profession, course of study; property; family name (the short form is H rad. 140)

業 has a tree, flourishing (the thick foliage at the top): productive activities and the prosperity they create.
商業 *shāngyè*, business
業主 *yèzhǔ*, property owner
重工業 *zhòng gōngyè*, heavy industry 业

| 民 | ⁷ | ⁷ | ⁷ |
| 624 5 strokes | 民 | 民 | |

MÍN, folk, people

人民 *rénmín*, the common people
民法 *mínfǎ*, civil law
民主 *mínzhǔ*, democracy, democratic; "people power"
回民 *Huímín*, the Muslim people of China

155

黨	ノ	⺌	⺍
	尚	尚	常
625 20 strokes	堂	堂	黨

DĂNG, association; political party; family name

國民黨 *Guómíndǎng*, Chinese Nationalist Party, Kuomintang
民主黨 *Mínzhǔdǎng*, Democratic Party
入黨 *rùdǎng*, join or be admitted to a political party (or to the Party)
黨報 dǎngbào, party newspaper

党

産	丶	二	亠
	文	立	产
626 11 strokes	产	彦	産

CHĂN, to produce, product; property

出産 *chūchǎn*, to produce; production output
共産黨 *Gòngchǎndǎng*, Communist Party
産業 *chǎnyè*, property (real estate)

产

斬	一	匚	冂
	百	亘	車
627 11 strokes	軒	斬	斬

ZHĂN, to behead; to cut to pieces

The character is explained as "a chariot with axes in it."
斬首 *zhǎnshǒu*, to behead

斬

暫	一	冂	百
	車	斬	斬
628 15 strokes	斬	暫	暫

ZÀN, ZHÀN, temporarily

暫時 *zànshí, zhànshí*, temporarily
暫且 *zànqiě, zhànqiě*, for a short time
短暫 *duǎnzàn, duǎnzhàn*, brief, transient
暫定 *zàndìng, zhàndìng*, provisional temporary

暫

淮	丶	冫	氵
	氵	汀	汀
629 11 strokes	洴	淮	淮

HUÁI; the name of the Huai River

Distinguish from 准 *zhǔn* "to permit" (p. 261a, below). Clue: is it "water" or "ice" at the left?

淮河 *Huáihé*, the Huai River
淮南 *Huáinán*, Huainan (Anhui Province)

156

準	`	氵	氵
630 13 strokes	沪	泮	淮
	淮	準	

ZHǓN, water-level; standard; to regulate; accurate

As to the short form of 準, see also p. 261a.

準時 *zhǔnshí*, on time
水準 *shǔizhǔn*, standard, level
準保 *zhǔnbǎo*, for sure

准

| 久 | ノ | ⺈ | 久 |
| 631
3 strokes | | | |

JIǓ, to last for a long time

The student should distinguish this character from "slow" and "follow" (337 and 319, above).

永久 *yǒngjiǔ*, eternally, permanently
長久 *chángjiǔ*, be long (in time)

| 癶 | ⼃ | ⺈ | ⺈' |
| 632
5 strokes | ⺈⺈ | 癶 | |

BÒ, back-to-back, opposed. BACK rad. (105)(H154)

The character shows two feet — the "toe" rad. 止 (195, above) — faced away from each other, that is, back to back. Hence the idea "back." Not seen now as an independent character.

發	⼃	⺈'	癶
	癶	癶	癶
633 12 strokes	發	發	發

FĀ, to send out, to bring out, to shoot

The bow 弓 may help with the idea "to shoot;" 殳 was once an arrow 矢.

發行 *fāxíng*, to issue (bonds, banknotes); to publish
發現 *fāxiàn*, to discover
發作 *fāzuò*, to begin to have an effect; to have a temper fit
發信 *fāxìn*, to mail a letter

发

冓	一	二	㐄
	廾	丗	丼
634 10 strokes	冓	冓	冓

GÒU, webwork, interlacery

The character is supposed originally to have been a picture of a webwork fishtrap. It sometimes meant "inner rooms," perhaps by sound-loan. Not now used as an independent character.

157

講	、	言	言	**JIĂNG, to speak; conscientious about**
	言	訐	諆	講話 *jiǎnghuà*, talk, to make a speech 講學 *jiǎngxué*, an academic subject 聽講 *tīngjiǎng*, to attend a lecture 講明 *jiǎngmíng*, to explain, to clarify
635 17 strokes	講	講	講	讲

種	ニ	千	禾	**ZHŎNG, kind, sort, species; ZHÒNG, to plant, to sow, to grow; CHÓNG, family name (rare)**
	禾	秆	稻	種子 *zhŏngzi*, seed 種地 *zhòngdì*, to farm 種種 *zhŏngzhŏng*, all kinds 種馬 *zhŏngmǎ*, stud
636 14 strokes	稻	種	種	种

四	丨	冂	冊	**WĂNG, net, NET rad. (122)(H145)**
	冊	四		This form of "net" occurs only as a part of characters. (The independent form is 446, above). Note that this form of the "net" rad. is identical to a form of the "eye" rad. (132, above) — but in traditional dictionaries *as a classifier for characters*, this form is almost always "net," and in H as a classifier is always so.
637 5 strokes (6 strokes)				

傅	丿	亻	亻	**FÙ, to teach; a teacher; family name**
	仁	信	伸	The student should distinguish this character from *chuán* "transmit" 傳 (640, below). 傅粉 *fūfěn*, to make up, to put on face powder
. 638 12 strokes	傅	傅	傅	

專	一	亐	直	**ZHUĀN, solely, family name (rare)**
	車	車	車	專門 *zhuānmén*, specialized, specialty 專車 *zhuānche*, special car
639 11 strokes	車	專	專	专

傳

640
13 strokes

ノ	イ	イ
侟	俥	俥
俥	傳	傳

CHUÁN, to transmit; ZHUÀN, record, biography

傳説 *chuánshuō*, to spread a rumor; rumor; legend
傳教 *chuánjiào*, to proselytize
自傳 *zìzhuàn*, autobiography

传

虫

641
6 strokes

| 丶 | 口 | 口 |
| 中 | 虫 | 虫 |

CHÓNG, bug. BUG rad. (142)(H174)

This character is a picture of a bug. The traditional form, presumably twice "reclarified," has two more bugs: 蟲 (see p. 299b, below).

雖

642
17 strokes

丶	口	口
吕	吊	虽
虽	虽	雖

SUĪ, although

雖然 *suīrán*, although
雖説 *suīshuō*, (colloquial) although

虽

象

643
12 strokes

ノ	⺈	⺈
臽	各	争
象	象	象

XIÀNG, elephant; image

The character is a picture of an elephant.

現象 *xiànxiàng*, phenomenon
象牙 *xiàngyá*, elephant tusk; ivory
象話 *xiànghuà*, reasonable, appropriate, seemly

像

644
14 strokes

ノ	イ	イ
伫	伄	俙
傄	像	像

XIÀNG, to present an image of, look like; picture, portrait, statue; such as…

When the use of 象 would create an ambiguity, 象 is not used as a short form for 像.

畫像 *huàxiàng*, to portray; portrait
人像 *rénxiàng*, portrait, image

象

159

凡	丿	凡	
645 2 strokes			

JĪ, table. TABLE rad. (16)(H30)

Jī is a picture of a table. The student should distinguish it from "legs" 儿 and from "man with amputated foot" 兀 (57 and 58, above). Reading pronunciation *jǐ*. Nowadays, *jī* is most likely to be encountered as the short form for 幾 "how many" (419, above).

茶几 *chájī*, tea table

歹	丶	丆	广
646 5 strokes (4 strokes)	歺	歹	

DǍI, chip. CHIP rad. (78)

The character is supposed to be a picture of bone chips. The student should distinguish it from the "dusk" rad. 夕 (117, above). This form of "chip" occurs only as a part of characters. (Its independent form is 727, below).

亮	丶	二	亠
	六	古	卢
647 9 strokes	卢	疒	亮

LIÀNG, bright; to show

亮相 *liàngxiāng*, (Beijing opera) strike a pose; state your views
天亮了 *tiān liàng le*. It's already daylight.
明亮 *míngliàng*, well-lit; bright and shining; become clear

佔	丿	亻	仃
	什	佧	佔
648 7 strokes	佔		

ZHÀN, to occupy, to constitute
This character is often written 占 in modern texts

佔多數 *zhàn duōshù*, to constitute a majority
佔先 *zhànxiān*, take the lead, get ahead of
佔有 *zhànyǒu*, to own; to occupy
佔便宜 *zhàn piányi*, to take unfair advantage; advantageous

軍	丶	冖	冖
	冖	宁	宫
649 9 strokes	宣	軍	

JŪN, military, army; army corps

軍人 *jūnrén*, soldier
軍官 *jūnguān*, military officer
軍長 *jūnzhǎng*, corps commander
軍事 *jūnshì*, military affairs
軍容 *jūnróng*, military discipline and bearing

军

160

運	ノ	一	一	**YÙN, to transport; fate, luck**
	冒	冝	軍	運河 *yùnhé*, canal 運用 *yùnyòng*, to utilize 運氣 *yùnqì*, luck 運行 *yùnxíng*, to move, to be in motion
650 12 strokes	軍	渾	運	运

越	土	丰	丰	**YUÈ, to pass over, to exceed; (if repeated) the more… the more…; family name**
	走	走	走	越界 *yuèjiè*, to encroach 越發 *yuèfā*, more than before 越來越 *yuè lái yuè…*, to become more and more…
651 12 strokes	赺	越	越	越南 *Yuènán*, Vietnam

敢	一	工	干	**GǍN, dare**
	产	首	肯	敢情 *gǎnqíng*, of course; after all; Oh, so…! 不敢當 *bùgǎndāng*, You flatter me. 敢於 *gǎnyú*, to dare to
652 12 strokes	耴	耴	敢	

並	丶	丷	业	**BÌNG, side by side; and; actually; moreover** Usual modern form: 并, Classical form: 幷.
	并	并	並	並不 *bìng bu*, actually not; certainly not 並且 *bìngqiě*, moreover 並行 *bìngxíng*, to implement (two things) at the same time
653 8 strokes	並	並		合並 *hébìng*, to merge

非	ノ	ﾉ	刁	**FĒI, wrong, false; not. WRONG rad. (175)(H205).** Distinguish from the "leeks" rad. 韭 (p. 268a).
	扌	扌	非	是非 *shìfēi*, right and wrong 並非 *bìngfēi*, It's not that… 非常 *fēicháng*, exceptionally
654 8 strokes	非	非		胡作非為 *hú zuò fēi wéi*, to act barbarously and behave wrongly; to commit many outrages

161

	ノ	⺊	牛
造	牛	牛	告
655 10 strokes	告	浩	造

ZÀO, to manufacture, to build; party to a lawsuit

原造 *yuánzào*, plaintiff
造汽車 *zào qìchē*, to manufacture cars
造反 *zàofǎn*, to rebel
造愛 *zàoài*, to make love

	丶	亠	方
於	方	扩	於
656 8 strokes	於	於	

YÚ, with reference to; than; family name

Now often written 于.

於是 *yúshì*, thereupon
於我 *yú wǒ*, the way I see it…, with reference to me
多於 *duōyú*, more than

	一	冖	二
束	三	申	束
657 7 strokes	束		

SHÙ, bundle; to bind; family name (H192)

Shù is a picture of a bundle. It should be distinguished from *cì* "thorn" 束 (p. 261a).

束手 *shùshǒu*, "to have your hands tied," i.e., be helpless
束身 *shùshēn*, to control yourself

	申	束	束
敕	剌	剌	剌
658 11 strokes	敕		

CHÌ, to correct; imperial orders

	一	三	束
整	剌	敕	敕
659 16 strokes	整	整	整

ZHĚNG, to tinker with; to give trouble; whole; exactly

兩點整 *liǎng diǎn zhěng*, 2:00 sharp
整天 *zhěngtiān*, all day
整容 *zhěngróng*, get a shave and a haircut, get spiffed up
整個 *zhěnggè*, whole, entire

JÌ, record; year; discipline; JǏ, to order; a family name

紀念 *jìniàn*, to commemorate
年紀 *niánjì*, age
世紀 *shìjì*, century
軍紀 *jūnjì*, military discipline

660
9 strokes

SHÙ, a tree; to plant, cultivate; to set up

果樹 *guǒshù*, fruit tree
樹枝 *shùzhī*, tree branch
樹立 *shùlì*, to set up, establish
樹林 *shùlín*, a grove, woods

661
16 strokes

(木 64)

**PÍ, bark, leather, skin, fur; a family name.
SKIN rad. (107)(H153)**

The character is supposed to show a hand flaying off pieces of hide. Note the "right hand" rad. 又 in *pí*.

皮帶 *pídài*, leather belt
皮包 *píbāo*, leather bag
皮鞋 *píxié*, leather shoes

662
5 strokes

HUÓ, alive; movable; work (usually, manual work)

生活 *shēnghuó*, life; to live
活力 *huólì*, vitality
活字 *huózì*, movable type

663
9 strokes

**SHÍ, rock; DÀN, a picul (133–1/3 pounds).
ROCK rad. (112)(H136)**

The "mouth" is supposed to be a rock that has rolled to the foot of the cliff.

石頭 *shítóu*, stone, rock
石頭子兒 *shítóuzǐr*, (colloquial) pebble
石像 *shíxiàng*, stone statue
石英 *shíyīng*, quartz

664
5 strokes

絲	㇖	ㄠ	ㄠ	**SĪ, silk; trace, a bit; a unit of weight (0.0005 gram)** This character is composed of two "silk" rads. side by side. 真絲 *zhēnsī*, pure silk 粉絲 *fěnsī*, vermicelli 一絲不差 *yì sī bú chā*, no difference whatsoever
	ㄠ	ㄠ	糸	
665 **12 strokes**	絲			丝

艸	㇖	屮	少	**CǍO, grass. GRASS rad. (140)** This form of the "grass" rad. is composed of two "sprout" rads. (465, above), side by side, to suggest "grass" sprouting up. The student has learned another form of "grass" (192, above). The form here is the independent form. The commonly used form, however, is 草 : 992 below.
	屮	艸	艸	
666 **6 strokes**				

變	亠	言	言	**BIÀN, change** 變成 *biànchéng*, to change into 事變 *shìbiàn*, incident; emergency; the course of events 變臉 *biànliǎn*, suddenly become hostile
	綰	綰	綜	
667 **23 strokes**	綜	變	變	(ㄠ 25)　　変

步	㇑	ㅏ	止	**BÙ, step, pace; on foot; a family name** *Bù* used to be a picture of two feet or of a foot in two successive positions to suggest motion. In the modern form, one of these feet is corrupted into "few." 步行 *bùxíng*, go on foot 步子 *bùzi*, pace, step
	止	牛	井	
668 **7 strokes**	步			

庀	㇑	ㅏ	ㅳ	**HŪ, tiger. TIGER rad. (141)(H173)** This character is a picture of a tiger. Dictionaries often call this form "top of the character *hū* 'tiger' 虎" (see 688, below). This form does not appear now as an independent character.
	卢	卢	庀	
669 **6 strokes**				

164

豦 670 13 strokes	丶	广	庐
	虍	虏	虍
	虏	虏	豦

JÙ, wild boar

Jù combines meanings: "tiger" + "pig" = "tiger-pig, a pig fierce as a tiger." Thus: "wild boar." Not in modern use as an independent character.

據 671 16 strokes	一	扌	扌
	扩	护	护
	捛	據	據

JÙ, according to; to take in your hand; evidence, proof

Jù (670, above) gives the sound; "hand" gives the meaning "to take in the hand." Other meanings are derivative.

據説 *jùshuō*, People say…
佔據 *zhànjù*, to occupy (by force)

据

炎 672 8 strokes	丶	丶	少
	火	火	火
	炑	炎	

YÁN, to blaze; very hot; inflammation

Yán combines meanings: "fire" over "fire" = "to blaze." As a part of characters, this character usually indicates the sound *dan* or *tan*.

發炎 *fāyán*, to become inflamed; inflammation

談 673 15 strokes	丶	二	言
	言	言	言
	訫	談	談

TÁN, to chat, to talk about; a family name

The "word" rad. gives the meaning; *yán* (672) here has the sound value *tan*.

談話 *tánhuà*, to talk; statement
談心 *tánxīn*, have a heart-to-heart talk; heart-to-heart talk
談到 *tándào*, to talk about

谈

淡 674 11 strokes	丶	丶	氵
	氵	汸	沙
	沙	淡	

DÀN, weak, thin, insipid, pale

看得很淡 *kànde hěn dàn*, indifferent to
生意很淡 *shēngyì hěn dàn*, Business is bad.
淡水 *dàn shuǐ*, fresh water

165

坴

675
8 strokes

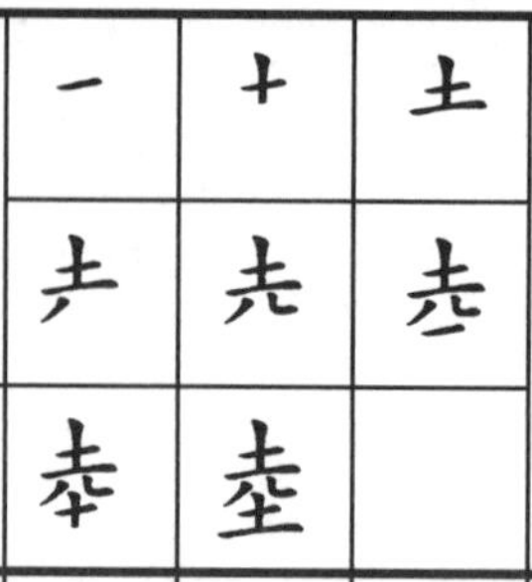

LÙ, clod, lump of earth

The "earth" rad. at the bottom gives the meaning; the sound is suggested by the rest of the character, which has been corrupted from *liù* (149, above). Not in modern use as an independent character.

陸

676
11 strokes

LÙ, land; family name

This word is likely cognate with *lù* "clod" (675, above). The character is reclarified with the "mound" rad.

大陸 *dàlù*, continent, mainland
陸軍 *lùjūn*, army
陸地 *lùdī*, land, dry land

陆

丸

677
3 strokes

WÁN, bullet, BB, pill, ball (H rad. 66)

The student should distinguish *wán* from 凡 (682, below) and from 刃 (522, above).

丸子 *wánzi*, pill, small ball
魚丸 *yǔwán*, fish-ball (food)

熱

678
15 strokes

RÈ, hot, to heat

Distinguish 熱 (1042, below) — compare the upper left-hand corners.

熱心 *rèxīn*, enthusiastic
熱情 *rèqíng*, passionate
熱力學 *rèlìxué*, thermodynamics
炎熱 *yánrè*, blazing hot
(灬 34)

热

鬥

679
10 strokes

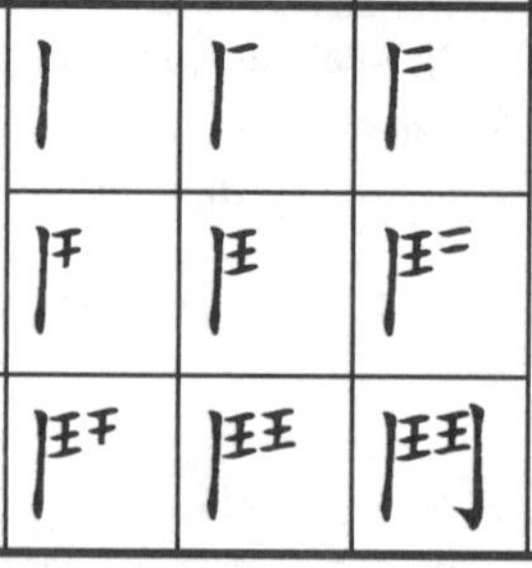

DÒU, to fight. FIGHT rad. (191)

The old form of this character was a picture of two men struggling with each other. Some scholars explain the modern form as "two kings confined in a small space, whence 'to fight.'" Distinguish from *mén* "gate" 門 (45, above).

鬥牛 *dòuniú*, bullfighter

斗

市	`丶`	`二`	`广`	**SHÌ, market, marketplace; municipality; standard system of weights and measures**
	`市`	`市`		市長 *shìzhǎng*, mayor 市寸 *shìcùn*, Chinese standard inch 黑市 *hēishì*, black market 市容 *shìróng*, the look of a city
680 5 strokes				

鬧	`｜`	`⻆`	`⻆`	**NÀO, to make a disturbance; disturbed by; to get (perhaps with difficulty)**
	`⻆`	`⻆王`	`鬥`	*Nào* combines meanings: "to fight in the marketplace" = "to make a disturbance." 鬧鐘 *nàozhōng*, alarm clock 打鬧 *dǎ nào*, to raise a ruckus 熱鬧 *rènào*, bustling; have a
681 15 strokes	`鬥`	`鬧`	`鬧`	lively time 闹

凡	`丿`	`几`	`凡`	**FÁN, common, all**
				Fán is said to combine meanings: an object (the dot) thrown under a table may be any old thing you would leave under the table. 凡是 *fánshì*, all those who are 平凡 *píngfán*, be ordinary 凡人 *fánrén*, an ordinary fellow, a bloke
682 3 strokes				

恐	`一`	`丁`	`工`	**KǑNG, to fear**
	`㣺`	`巩`	`巩`	恐怕 *kǒngpà*, be afraid that; "probably" 恐水病 *kǒngshuǐbìng*, hydrophobia
683 10 strokes	`恐`	`恐`	`恐`	

云	`一`	`二`	`云`	**YÚN, to say; family name**
	`云`			*Yún* originally was a picture and meant "cloud." It came to mean "to say" by sound-loan. Often seen in modern texts for 雲 *yún* "cloud" (p. 256a, below).
684 4 strokes				

陰	⼁	⼃	阝
	阝	阝人	阝人
685 11 strokes	阷	阷	陰

YĪN, shady, dark; "yin" in "yin and yang;" be cloudy; be crafty; secret; lunar; negative; incised; to deceive; family name

陰天 *yīntiān*, be overcast
樹陰 *shùyīn*, shade of a tree
陰部 *yīnbù*, private parts
陰門 *yīnmén*, vaginal opening

阴

昜	⼁	冂	日
	旦	旵	号
686 9 strokes	昜	昜	

YÁNG, bright, brilliance

This character originally meant "south slope of a hill" or "north side of a riverbank", i.e., the side that gets the sun (cp. 687, below). The student should distinguish this character from *yì* "to change; be easy" 易 (376, above). In modern use, replaced by 687, below.

陽	⼃	⼃	阝
	阝冂	阝旦	阝旵
687 12 strokes	阷	陽	陽

YÁNG, sun, solar; "yang" in "yin and yang;" open; positive; male organ; to cut in relief; family name

This character is 686 above, reclarified with "mound."

太陽 *tàiyáng*, sun
陽極 *yángjí*, (term from electricity) positive pole, anode

阳

虎	⼁	⼘	上
	广	卢	虍
688 8 strokes	虏	虎	

HǓ, tiger; family name

老虎 *lǎohǔ*, tiger
馬馬虎虎 *mǎmǎhūhū*, be careless, be sloppy (note change of tone on *hǔ*)
虎口 *hǔkǒu*, dangerous situation
虎穴 *hǔxué*, tiger's lair

丂	一	丂
689 2 strokes		

KǍO, sigh, breath (especially one taken with difficulty)

The character is explained as "breath (the bottom part) trying to escape but being blocked (blockage indicated by the horizontal stroke across the top)." Some commentators see in the bottom part a similarity to 乞 (322, above). Not in modern use as an independent character.

号	﹨	口	口	**HÀO, to call, to cry out**
	马	号		The character combines meanings: *kǎo* "sigh, breath" + "mouth" is used to suggest the idea "to call, to cry out." Compare 691, below.

690
5 strokes

號	口	马	号	**HÁO, to cry out; HÀO, appellations, means of identification; name, size, number, sign, mark; order; bugle**
	号ʳ	驴	驴	號頭 *hàotóu*, (colloquial) number 問號 *wènhào*, question mark 號令 *hàolìng*, order

691
13 strokes 號 號 號   号

予	フ	マ	予	**YǓ, to give; YÚ, I**
	予			The student should learn to tell *yǔ* from the "child" rad. 子 (18, above) and the "spear" rad. 矛 (840, below). 予以 *yǔyǐ*, to grant, give

692
4 strokes

預	フ	マ	予	**YÙ, beforehand; to anticipate**
	予ʳ	预	預	The "head" rad. here suggests the meaning "to anticipate;" *yǔ* (692, above) gives the sound. 預算 *yùsuàn*, to make advance plans 預先 *yùxiān*, beforehand

693
13 strokes 預 預 預   预

備	丿	亻	亻	**BÈI, to prepare, to get ready for**
	亻	伊	伊	預備 *yùbèi*, to get ready, to plan; preparation 準備 *zhǔnbèi*, to get ready; to intend to 備馬 *bèimǎ*, to saddle a horse

694
12 strokes 伊 備 備   备

希	ノ	メ	乄
	产	斉	希
695 7 strokes	希		

XĪ, loose; rare; to hope

The "crisscross" rad. is supposed to show the loose mesh of a cloth; the "cloth" rad. is there to help develop this meaning. The meaning "hope" (the most common modern use of this character) is by sound-loan.

望	丶	亠	亡
	切	切	胡
696 11 strokes	胡	望	望

WÀNG, to look for; to expect; towards; family name

希望 *xīwàng*, hope, to hope for
名望 *míngwàng*, reputation
看望 *kànwàng*, to pay a visit to, call on

紅	ㄑ	幺	幺
	糸	糸	糹
697 9 strokes	紅	紅	紅

HÓNG, red

紅茶 *hóngchá*, "black" tea
紅人 *hóngrén*, favorite of an important person
紅十字會 *hóng shí zì huì*, Red Cross
臉紅 *liǎnhóng*, to blush; get red-faced with anger or other excitement

紅

切	一	土	切
	切		
698 4 strokes			

QIĒ, to slice, to carve; tangent in geometry; QIÈ, sure to; close to

親切 *qīnqiè*, closely related to
切身 *qièshēn*, personal; of importance to a person
切合 *qièhé*, to suit, to go well with

代	ノ	イ	仁
	代	代	
699 5 strokes			

DÀI, to take the place of; an age

代表 *dàibiǎo*, to represent; representative
代數學 *dàishùxué*, algebra
古代 *gǔdài*, ancient times
現代 *xiàndài*, contemporary; modern times

袋	イ	代	代	**DÀI, bag, pocket**
	代	伐	伐	The "gown" rad. gives the meaning in this character; *dài* (699, above) gives the sound.
				口袋 *kǒudài*, bag, pocket 麻袋 *mádài*, gunny sack 睡袋 *shuìdài*, sleeping bag
700 11 strokes	袋	袋	袋	

妾	丶	二	宀	**QIÈ, wife of inferior rank, concubine**
	立	立	立	*Qiè* is explained: "to stand" + "woman" = a woman who stands when her husband or wives of superior status are present; therefore, "concubine." This explanation, historically not accurate, can help you remember the character in any case.
701 8 strokes	妾	妾		

接	一	十	扌	**JIĒ, to receive; to connect; to meet; to catch; to take over**
	扩	护	护	接着 *jiēzhe*, to catch; to follow closely 接頭 *jiētóu*, to connect; (colloquial) to contact (somebody); know about 接頭兒 *jiētóur*, joint, junction 接受 *jiēshòu*, to accept
702 11 strokes	挓	挓	接	

化	丿	亻	化	**HUÀ, to change, to melt; to evaporate; works like English suffixes -ize, -ify**
	化			If "man" + "ladle" suggests "alchemy" to you, you can use that as a mnemonic for *huà*. "Alchemy" = "to transmute, to change."
703 4 strokes				化學 *huàxué*, chemistry 工業化 *gōngyèhuà*, to industrialize

花	一	十	十一	**HUĀ, flower, blossom; flowery; design; cotton; to spend; fireworks**
	艹	艹	花	花樣 *huāyàng*, design, pattern 花生 *huāshēng*, peanut 一束花 *yí shù huā*, a bunch of flowers 放花 *fànghuā*, to set off fireworks
704 8 strokes	花	花		

171

聲	士	吉	吉	**SHĒNG, sound, tone; to declare; reputation**
	吉	声	殸	The "ear" gives part of the meaning. The top part is an old meaning-meaning compound itself; a musical instrument + "club" = "to strike the musical instrument with a stick," "to make sounds."
705 17 strokes	殸	聲	聲	聲音 *shēngyīn*, sound 声

襄	、	亠	亠	**XIĀNG, to take off (clothes), to disrobe**
	吂	亗	審	Note that the "gown" rad. occurs as part of this character to give the meaning. The significance of the rest of *xiāng* is not known. Not in modern use as an independent character.
706 17 strokes	窜	襄	襄	

讓	二	言	言	**RÀNG, to yield, to allow; to lower (in price); to offer; to step aside; to cause, to make; by**
	言	諝	諝	讓步 *ràngbù*, to concede, to compromise 讓位 *ràngwèi*, to abdicate; give way to 讓茶 *ràngchá*, to offer somebody tea
707 24 strokes	諲	讓	讓	让

類	丶	半	米	**LÈI, class, species, kind**
	类	类	类	人類 *rénlèi*, mankind 分類 *fēnlèi*, to classify 同類 *tónglèi*, the same kind 類別 *lèibié*, class (resulting from a classification); category
708 19 strokes	类	類	類	(米 101, 頁 333)　　类

休	ノ	イ	仁	**XIŪ, to rest; to cease; to divorce**
	什	休	休	休 combines meanings and is supposed to show a man resting under a tree, whence "to rest." 休學 *xiūxué*, to drop out (of school) 休業 *xiūyè*, to close a business (for a holiday or vacation)
709 6 strokes				

息	′	亻	竹	**XĪ, to breathe; to rest; to stop; to cease; a family name** 息 is supposed to combine "nose" + "heart" to suggest "to breathe." (The significance of "heart" is, perhaps, obscure.) 休息 *xiūxi*, to rest 信息 *xìnxī*, information, news
	自	自	自	
710 10 strokes	息	息	息	

式	一	二	〒	**SHÌ, form, fashion, model, style** 新式 *xīnshì*, new style 式樣 *shìyàng*, style, type
	王	式	式	
711 6 strokes				

登	丿	夕	癶	**DĒNG, to go up; to press down on with the foot; to publish** The "flask" used to be a pedestal; the "back-to-back" showed two feet that had climbed onto it. 登報 *dēngbào*, to publish (in a newspaper or magazine) 登山 *dēngshān*, mountain-climbing
	癶	癶	癶	
712 12 strokes	咎	登	登	

燈	′	″	丷	**DĒNG, lantern, lamp** The "fire" rad. gives the meaning here; *dēng* (712, above) gives the sound. 點燈 *diǎndēng*, to light a lamp 花燈 *huādēng*, colored lantern
	火	炒	炒	
713 16 strokes	燃	燈	燈	灯

普	′	丷	丷	**PǓ, general, universal; a family name** 普 combines the meanings "side by side" (653, above) + "sun" to suggest "all the places the sun shines:" "universal, general." 普天下 *pǔtiānxià*, all over the world, everywhere 普希金 *Pǔxījīn*, Pushkin (the Russian poet)
	半	并	並	
714 12 strokes	並	並	普	

173

	715 7 strokes	⁼	⁼	⁼	**YǑNG**, bulk measure: ten "pecks;" name of a river in Zhejiang (Chekiang) province; short for Ningbo (the city — which is on the Yong River)
甬		甬	甬	甬	甬 originally meant "a big bell" and was a picture, with a hook at the top by which the bell could be hung. "Ten pecks" is by sound-loan. 甬道 *yǒngdào*, covered passage, corridor

TŌNG, to go through; thoroughgoing, universal

通

716
10 strokes

普通 *pǔtōng*, be universal; be widespread or common
普通話 *Pǔtōnghuà*, "Mandarin" Chinese
通過 *tōngguò*, to go through; to pass in a parliamentary meeting
通知 *tōngzhī*, to inform; a notice

DIÀN, electricity; lightning

電

717
13 strokes

The character shows a streak of lightning falling under the rain.

電燈 *diàndēng*, electric light
電話 *diànhuà*, telephone
電氣 *diànqì*, electricity

电

SHŌU, to put away; to receive; to collect

收

718
6 strokes

收起來 *shōuqǐlái*, to put away
收入 *shōurù*, income; to earn
收成 *shōuchéng*, harvest
收工 *shōugōng*, to knock off work

CHŪN, spring (the season); a family name

春

719
9 strokes

春 is supposed to show vegetation burgeoning in the sun.

春天 *chūntiān*, springtime
青春 *qīngchūn*, youth
春意 *chūnyì*, the feeling of early spring; thoughts of love

| 兆 720 6 strokes | 、 | ⺀ | ⺍ |
| | 兆 | 兆 | 兆 |

ZHÀO, omen; a family name

兆 shows the cracks on the heated tortoise shell which were anciently used in China for divination. (Read the note in 118, above).

兆頭　zhàotou, omen
預兆　yùzhào, signs of the times
吉兆　jízhào, a good omen

跳 721 13 strokes	丶	⼝	⼝
	𠯢	𧾷	𧾷
	𧾷	跳	跳

TIÀO, to leap

The "foot" rad. gives the meaning; zhào (720, above) is supposed to give the sound.

跳遠　tiàoyuǎn, broad jump
跳行　tiàoháng, to skip a line; to change your job
心跳　xīntiào, heart palpitations

殺 722 10 strokes	丿	メ	乄
	羊	羊	杀
	殺	殺	殺

SHĀ, to kill; to tighten (a belt); to add up; to sting; to hurt; to reduce; to brake, to stop

自殺　zìshā, to commit suicide
殺氣　shāqì, to look or act like you wanted to kill somebody
殺人　shārén, to commit murder

杀

| 処 723 5 strokes | 丿 | 勹 | 夂 |
| | 処 | 処 | |

CHÙ, place; CHǓ, to dwell

Chù, chǔ is composed of the "slow" rad. + the "table" rad. Originally "slow" was a picture of a man, and "table" was a small stool. "Man" + "stool" is a good way to suggest "dwell:" folk sitting outside their homes on little stools (often seen). Not now used independently. Cp. 724, short form.

處 724 11 strokes	丶	⼘	上
	广	庐	虍
	虏	處	處

CHÙ, place; CHǓ, to dwell

處 is the same word as 723, above. The character was reclarified with "tiger," but nobody is quite sure why.

處世　chùshì, chǔshì, to get along in the world, especially with other people
處女　chùnǚ, chǔnǚ, virgin

処

175

| 風 725 9 strokes | ノ 凡 凡 凡 凨 凨 凬 風 風 風 | **FĒNG**, wind; news; custom; rumor; desire. WIND rad. (182)(the short form = H rad. 121) The dictionaries say that *fǎn* (682, above) gives the sound; the "bug" gives the meaning "because when the wind stirs, the bugs breed." 風聞 *fēngwén*, The rumor is… 风 |

| 俗 726 9 strokes | ノ 亻 亻 亻 尒 伀 佟 俗 俗 | **SÚ**, vulgar, common The "valley" rad. is supposed to suggest "ravines, mountain country;" with the addition of "man," we get "hillbilly," hence "uncultivated, vulgar." 風俗 *fēngsú*, custom 俗氣 *súqì*, be in poor taste |

| 歹 727 4 strokes | 一 厂 歹 歹 | **DǍI**, chip. CHIP rad. (78)(H97) This character is supposed to be a picture of bone chips. Compare 歹 to the form of this rad. you have already learned (646, above). The form here may occur as an independent character. Distinguish "chip" from "dusk" 夕 (117, above). |

| 死 728 6 strokes | 一 厂 歹 歹 死 死 | **SǏ**, to die; dead; stubbornly *Sǐ* combines meanings. The "ladle" rad. is corrupted from an earlier "man" rad., and "man" + "bone chips" is supposed to suggest death. 死亡 *sǐwáng*, to die; death 死尸 *sǐshī*, corpse 死黨 *sǐdǎng*, diehards, sworn followers |

| 題 729 18 strokes | 口 旦 早 是 是 是 題 題 題 | **TÍ**, theme, subject 問題 *wèntí*, question, problem 題目 *tímù*, topic, title, heading; problem, exercise 出題 *chūtí*, to set questions (for an exam) (日 160, 頁 333) 題 |

176

QIŪ, autumn

In China, after the grain is threshed, it is common to stack and burn the unusable stalks. These "grain fires" are a part of the autumn scene; whence, perhaps, this character.

秋天 *qiūtiān*, autumn

730
9 strokes

LIÁNG, be cool, be cold; LIÀNG, to make or become cool

Alternate form: 凉.

涼快 *liángkuai*, be cool
着涼 *zhāoliáng*, to catch cold
涼水 *liángshuǐ*, cold water, unboiled water

731
11 strokes

YUÁN, be round; person with certain duties, member

"Mouth" + "cowrie" is supposed to suggest roundness. The meaning "member, etc." is by sound-loan.

教員 *jiàoyuán*, teacher
會員 *huìyuán*, member
海員 *hǎiyuán*, sailor

员

732
10 strokes

YUÁN, be round; to make excuses; currency; to interpret

This character is now used rather than 732, above, to mean "be round;" the character is reclarified with "surround."

美圓 *Měiyuán*, American currency

圆

733
13 strokes

GǍI, to change

改變 *gǎibiàn*, to change, change
改革 *gǎigé*, to reform, to improve
改良 *gǎiliáng*, to improve, improvement
改正 *gǎizhèng*, to correct (as, an error)

734
7 strokes

177

理	一	二	干	**LǏ, principle; to set in order; to speak to; to pay attention to**
	王	玑	玑	理 originally meant "veins in jade" and was a sound-meaning compound.
735 11 strokes	玾	理	理	道理 *dàolǐ*, reason, logical basis; doctrine 理想 *lǐxiǎng*, ideal, be ideal

清	丶	冫	氵	**QĪNG, be clear; to clear**
	汀	汢	沣	"Water" gives the meaning; *qing* (198, above) gives the sound. 清理 *qīnglǐ*, to clean up (literally or figuratively)
736 11 strokes	清	清	清	说不清 *shuōbuqīng*, be unable to express clearly 清白 *qīngbái*, be unsullied

楚	一	十	才	**CHǓ, be distinct; a family name** 清楚 *qīngchǔ*, be clear 一清二楚 *yì qīng èr chǔ*, be *very* clear
	木	林	梺	楚楚 *chǔchǔ*, be clear; be neat
737 13 strokes	梺	梺	楚	

記	丶	二	言	**JÌ, to remember; to record; mark, sign** The "word" rad. gives the meaning; *jǐ* (273, above) gives the sound.
	言	訂	記	记得 *jìdé*, to remember 记住 *jìzhù*, to fix in the mind 记者 *jìzhě*, reporter
738 10 strokes	記			记

留	丿	乀	乀	**LIÚ, to keep; to stay; to ask someone to stay; to leave behind; family name** 留声机 *liúshēngjī*, record player
	幻	切	留	留心 *liúxīn*, to be careful 留学生 *liúxuéshēng*, student studying abroad; someone who has returned from studying abroad
739 10 strokes	留	留	留	

178

召	フ	フ	刀
	刀	召	召
740 5 strokes			

ZHÀO, to summon; SHÀO, a place name; a family name

The meaning "to summon" comes by combining "mouth" for meaning with *dāo* (102, above) for sound.

紹	ㄥ	ㄠ	ㄠ
	ㄠ	糹	幻
741 11 strokes	紒	紹	紹

SHÀO, to join together

The "silk" rad. suggests the meaning; *zhào, shào* (740, above) gives the sound.

介紹 *jièshào*, to introduce

绍

管	ノ	ト	上
	竹	竹	竺
742 14 strokes	竿	管	管

GUǍN, reed, pipe; to manage; to guarantee; family name

For the basic meaning, "pipe," the "bamboo" rad. gives the meaning; *guǎn* (407, above) gives the sound. Other meanings are by sound-loan.

管理 *guǎnlǐ*, to manage

勸	一	艹	艹
	苗	苹	萑
743 20 strokes	萑	雚	勸

QUÀN, to exhort

The "strength" rad. gives the meaning in this character; *guàn* (193, above) suggests the sound.

勸告 *quàngào*, to urge
勸説 *quànshuō*, to advise

(力 206)

劝

安	丶	八	宀
	宀	安	安
744 6 strokes			

ĀN, be peaceful, be at ease; peace; to install; family name

安 is a famous meaning-meaning character: "one woman under your roof means peace."

安全 *ānquán*, be safe; safety
安全第一 *ānquán dìyī*, Safety first!
安定 *āndìng*, be secure, be steady

案	、	宀	宀	**ÀN, table; case at law; bill (legislative); legal record** *Ān* (744, above) suggests the sound; the "tree" rad. suggests "table."
	安	安	安	辦案子 *bàn ànzi*, to handle a legal case 方案 *fāng'àn*, plan, program
745 10 strokes	宰	穽	案	案件 *ànjiàn*, law case
求	一	十	寸	**QIÚ, to reach for; to beg** 求乞 *qiúqǐ*, to beg 求親 *qiúqīn*, to seek a marriage alliance; to propose
	扌	求	求	乞求 *qǐqiú*, to beg for, to implore
746 7 strokes	求			
救	一	十	寸	**JIÙ, to rescue, to save** 求救 *qiújiù*, to ask for help 救生 *jiùshēng*, to save a life
	求	求	求	救火車 *jiùhuǒchē*, fire engine 救世軍 *Jiùshìjūn*, the Salvation Army
747 11 strokes	救	救	救	
光	丨	小	小	**GUĀNG, light, brightness; to make bare; be used up; only; family name (rare) (H rad. 172)**
	业	兴	光	用光了 *yòngguāng le*, be used up 陽光 *yángguāng*, sunlight 光陰 *guāngyīn*, time
748 6 strokes				春光 *chūnguāng*, spring scene
無	丿	丿	仁	**WÚ, to lack, not to have; not…** 無非 *wúfēi*, only 無法 *wúfǎ*, be unable to…
	仁	血	血	無名 *wúmíng*, be nameless; be indescribable, ineffable 無用 *wúyòng*, be useless
749 12 strokes	無	無	無	无

750 — 8 strokes

侖

ノ 人 人
个 合 侖
侖 侖

LÚN, to arrange

This character combines meanings. The bottom part means "documents." The top part means "to get together." Combined, "to get together, to collect" and "documents" are supposed to suggest "to arrange." Not in modern use as an independent character.

751 — 15 strokes

論

丶 二 言
言 訇 訟
訟 論 論

LÙN, to discuss; theory; works like English suffix -ism to form words meaning "theory of" or "doctrine of," e.g. "materialism," "evolutionism," etc.; LÚN, first syllable in *Analects* (a Confucian book)

論文 *lùnwén*, dissertation, essay
無論 *wúlùn*, no matter; regardless of
論理 *lùnlǐ*, logic

论

752 — 9 strokes

亭

丶 二 亠
声 古 古
亮 高 亭

TÍNG, kiosk

The top part is a slightly abbreviated "tall" rad. (75, above), which, as the student will remember, is a picture of a tower. *Dīng* (519, above) gives the sound.

亭子 *tíngzi*, kiosk, pavilion
書亭 *shūtíng*, bookstall

753 — 11 strokes

停

ノ 亻 亻
亻 仵 仵
仵 停 停

TÍNG, to stop

停止 *tíngzhǐ*, to stop (doing something)
停車 *tíngchē*, to park
停火 *tínghuǒ*, cease-fire
暫停 *zhàntíng, zàntíng*, to suspend; (sports) a time-out

754 — 12 strokes

隋

⻖ ⻖ ⻖
⻖ 阣 阣
阣 隋 隋

DUÒ, mincemeat; SUÍ, the name of a dynasty; a family name

In the case of *duò*, the "meat" rad. gives the meaning. The rest of the character once gave the sound. In modern times, only read *suí* (for the dynasty or the family name).

181

隨

755
15 strokes

SUÍ, to follow; any, all; family name

隨便 *suíbiàn*, at your convenience; Do as you please.
隨時 *suíshí*, at any time
隨員 *suíyuán*, attaché

随

量

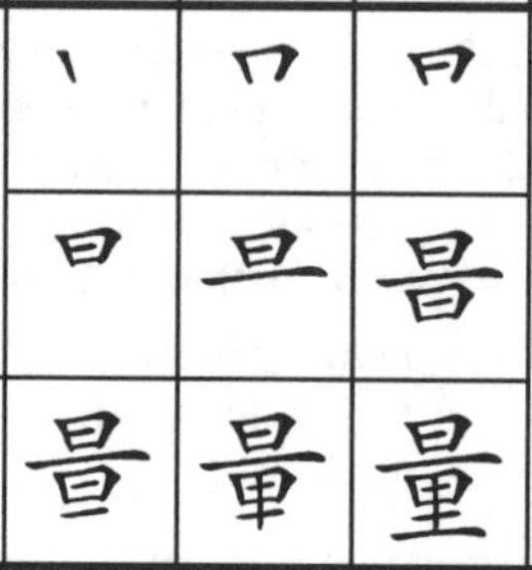

756
12 strokes

LIÁNG, to consider carefully; to weigh, to measure; LIÀNG, quantity, volume, capacity; to weigh; to estimate

The bottom part of this character used to be *zhòng* "be heavy" 重 (242, above). It has been corrupted into "village" in the modern form. The sun used to be merely an object being weighed.

倍

757
10 strokes

BÈI, times, fold

The student should distinguish *bèi* from *bù* "a set, etc." 部 (603, above).

三倍 *sān bèi*, three times as much
倍數 *bèishù*, a multiple
成倍 *chéngbèi*, to double, be doubled
加倍 *jiābèi*, to double

賤

758
15 strokes

JIÀN, be cheap; be humble; be unresponsive

The "cowrie" rad. gives the meaning; *jiān* (166, above) suggests the sound.

賤賣 *jiànmài*, to sell at a low price
下賤 *xiàjiàn*, be low-life
賤骨頭 *jiàngǔtou*, (insulting) "rat", low-life

贱

剛

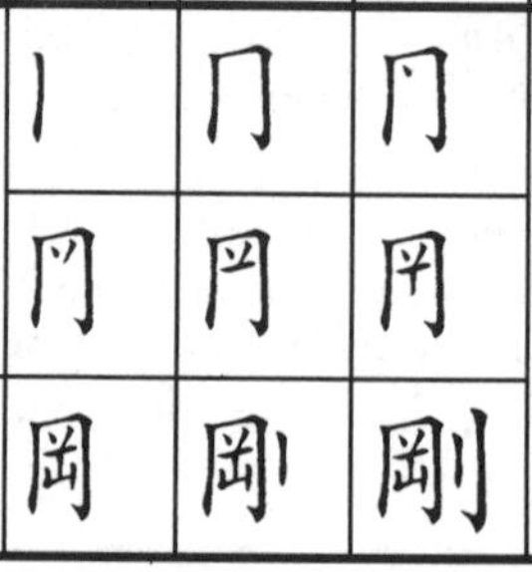

759
10 strokes

GĀNG, just now; exactly; only; be firm, be hard

剛才 *gāngcái*, just now
剛直 *gāngzhí*, be firm in one's purpose
剛好 *gānghǎo*, Perfect!
剛剛 *gānggang*, be exactly…; just now

刚

巳 **760** 2 strokes	乛	巳		**JIÉ, seal. SEAL rad. (26)** The student has learned the independent form of the "seal" rad. already (84, above). The form here only occurs as a part of characters. Distinguish "seal" from "self" 己, "already" 已, and *sì* 巳 (273–275, above).
危 **761** 6 strokes	丿 户	𠂊 夯	厃 危	**WĒI, danger; be lofty; family name** The character is explained as "a man at the top of a cliff, looking down at something that has fallen off." 危樓 *wēilóu*, tall building 危機 *wēijī*, crisis 病危 *bìngwēi*, be critically ill
險 **762** 16 strokes	乛 阝 险	阝 阶 险	阝 阭 險	**XIĂN, be dangerous; be difficult to get through or to** 危險 *wēixiǎn*, be dangerous, danger 險些 *xiǎnxiē*, nearly, almost 天險 *tiānxiǎn*, natural barrier (e.g., a mountain) 冒險 *màoxiǎn*, to forge ahead despite the danger 险
厚 **763** 9 strokes	一 厎 厚	厂 厚 厚	厂 厚 厚	**HÒU, be thick; be generous; family name** 厚實 *hòushí*, be thick 厚道 *hòudào*, be generous 厚意 *hòuyì*, kindness, thoughtfulness 厚臉皮 *hòuliǎnpí*, "have thick skin on your face," i.e., be brazen
舛 **764** 6 strokes	丿 夕 舛	夕 夗	夕 夗	**CHUĂN, to face away, to oppose, be discordant. DISCORD rad. (136)** The original form of this character was two men facing away from each other. From "face away," of course, come the other ideas of "oppose, be discordant." It is counted here as 6 strokes, but is often actually written, as here, in 7 strokes.

183

既 765 11 strokes	亻	勹	白
	皀	皀	皀
	皀	飰	既

JÌ, be finished; since, now that; already; a family name.

Usually written 既.

既然 *jìrán*, this being the case…
既是 *jìshì*, this being the case…
既而 *jì'ér*, (bookish) afterwards

辰 766 7 strokes	一	厂	厂
	厏	辰	辰
	辰		

CHÉN, be early; the fifth "earthly branch." EARLY rad. (161)(H187)

辰 can mean "early" in the sense "early in the day" or "early in the year." One modern scholar (Guo Moruo) thinks it is a picture of a stone tool used in ancient times to break the soil for cultivation.

研 767 9 strokes	一	丆	兂
	石	石	石
	矸	研	研

YÁN, to grind fine; to do research, to investigate thoroughly

The "stone" rad. suggests the meaning "to grind." *Jiān* (502, above) is supposed to help with the sound.

究 768 7 strokes	丶	丷	宀
	宀	宍	空
	究		

JIŪ, to look into

研究 *yánjiū*, research, to do research; knowledge
究辦 *jiūbàn*, to prosecute and settle a case
究問 *jiūwèn*, to investigate in detail; to try a case

貫 769 11 strokes	㇄	口	毌
	毌	毌	毌
	貫	貫	貫

GUÀN, to string together; to pierce

貫 is a picture of two cowries strung together on a string, the way cash (Chinese coins) were later. The form of the top cowrie is slightly corrupted.

一貫 *yíguàn*, consistent; all along

貫

實

770
14 strokes

SHÍ, fruit; be solid; true, real

實在 *shízài*, truly
實現 *shíxiàn*, to come true
實得 *shídé*, net income
切實 *qièshí*, be feasible; earnestly

实

簡

771
18 strokes

JIǍN, to abridge; be simple; letter

Variant 简.

簡直 *jiǎnzhí*, simply, frankly
簡寫 *jiǎnxiě*, write a character in simplified form; write a simplified version (as of a book) for beginners

(竹 54, 日 160)

简

單

772
12 strokes

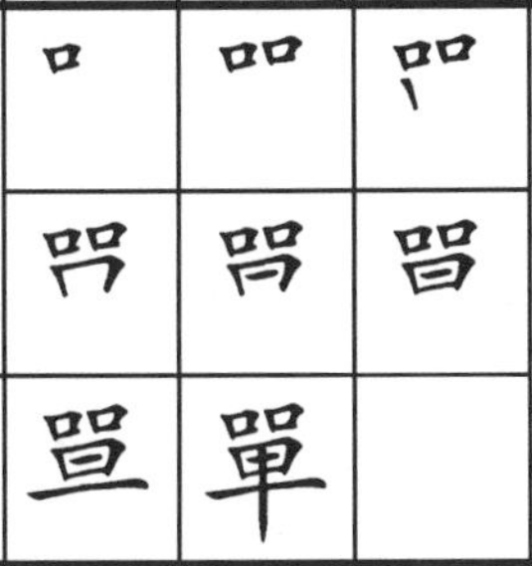

DĀN, be odd (numbered); be single, be simple; list; SHÀN, family name

簡單 *jiǎndān*, be simple
開單子 *kāi dānzi*, to make a list
單位 *dānwèi*, unit

单

背

773
9 strokes

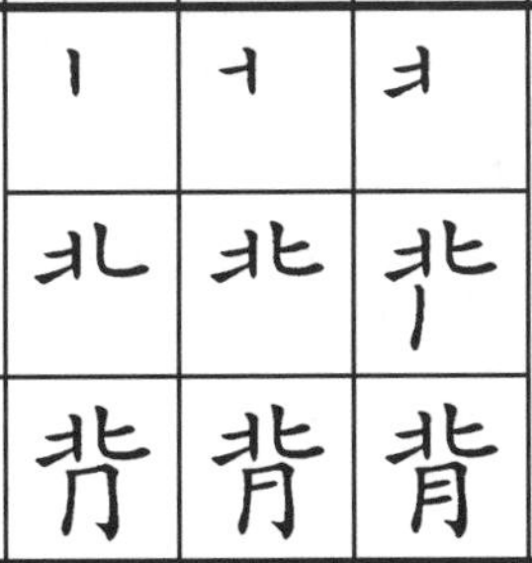

BÈI, back; to turn one's back on; be bad; to memorize; to recite; BĒI, to carry on the back

手背 *shǒubèi*, back of the hand
背後 *bèihòu*, in back of; behind someone's back
背包 *bēibāo*, knapsack

景

774
12 strokes

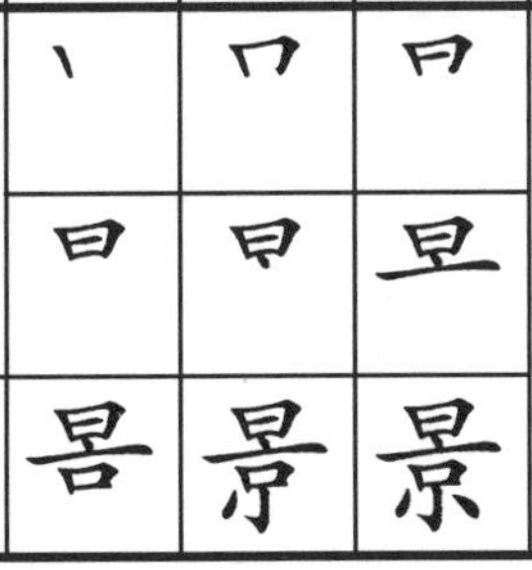

JǏNG, scene, scenery; outlook; family name

背景 *bèijǐng*, background
景象 *jǐngxiàng*, scene, sight
風景 *fēngjǐng*, scenery, landscape

同	丨	冂	冂	**TÓNG, be the same; with, together**
	冋	同	同	同意 *tóngyì*, to agree 同學 *tóngxué*, classmate 同樣 *tóngyàng*, all the same, nevertheless 胡同 *hútòng*, lane, alley (note pronunciation of 同)
775 6 strokes				

巽	㇇	㇇	巳	**XÙN, to yield, be yielding**
	巳ʼ	吧	巴	Not in modern use as an independent character.
776 12 strokes	毘	毘	巽	

選	㇇	㇇	巳	**XUǍN, to choose; brief**
	巴	毘	毘	選民 *xuǎnmín*, the enfranchised, those who can vote 文選 *wénxuǎn*, anthology 普選 *pǔxuǎn*, general election
777 15 strokes	巽	選	選	选

結	㇀	幺	幺	**JIÉ, to tie together; JIÉ, JIĚ, knot; JIĒ, to bear fruit**
	幺	糸	糹	結果 *jiéguǒ*, result; The outcome was… 結論 *jiélùn*, conclusion, deduction 吧結 *bājie*, to fawn on, "kiss ass" 結實 *jiēshí*, to bear fruit 結實 *jiēshi*, to be strong
778 12 strokes	糺	結	結	结

昏	㇀	𠂉	丘	**HŪN, dusk, darkness**
	氏	氐	昏	The top of this character used to be *dǐ* "foundation; bottom; to go down" (528, above), and the character was a meaning-meaning compound: "go down" + "sun" = "darkness, dusk." The dot has dropped out of *dǐ* in this form.
779 8 strokes	昏	昏		

婚	く	夕	女	**HŪN, marriage**
	女	奶	奶	結婚 *jiéhūn*, to marry, marriage 離婚 *líhūn*, to divorce 婚禮 *hūnlǐ*, wedding, marriage ceremony
780 11 strokes	妪	婚	婚	

羽	]	]	习	**YǓ, wings. WINGS rad. (124)(H183)** The character is a picture. Printed 羽.
	习	羽	羽	羽毛 *yǔmáo*, feather 黨羽 *dǎngyǔ*, member of a clique (pejorative)
781 6 strokes				

習	]	]	∃	**XÍ, to practice; practice, habit**
	羽	羽	羿	學習 *xuéxí*, to study 習氣 *xíqì*, habits (good or bad) 習題 *xítí*, school exercise, academic problem 研習 *yánxí*, to study, to do research in
782 11 strokes	習	習	習	习

加	]	力	加	**JIĀ, to add, to increase, plus…**
	加	加		加一倍 *jiā yí bèi*, to double 加入 *jiārù*, to join an organization 加快 *jiākuài*, to speed up
783 5 strokes				

稱	二	千	禾	**CHĒNG, to weigh; name; CHÈN, to own; to suit**
	禾	秆	稻	名稱 *míngchēng*, name 稱道 *chēngdào*, to praise 稱心 *chènxīn*, accord with one's wishes
784 14 strokes	稻	稱	稱	称

旁	丶	亠	亠	**PÁNG, other; side; beside**
	亠	亠	立	旁邊 *pángbiān*, beside; the area near 旁人 *pángrén*, other people 旁聽 *pángtīng*, to audit (a course) 旁白 *pángbái*, an aside (side remark in a play)
785 10 strokes	立	旁	旁	

按	一	扌	扌	**ÀN, to press with the finger or thumb; according to**
	扌	扩	护	按着 *ànzhe*, according to 按月 *ànyuè*, by the month 按理 *ànlǐ*, Logically… 按時 *ànshí*, be on time
786 9 strokes	抡	按	按	

如	く	乂	女	**RÚ, be like; be as good as; according to; if**
	女	如	如	如意 *rúyì*, be satisfied 如今 *rújīn*, nowadays 如果 *rúguǒ*, if 如同 *rútóng*, like, as
787 6 strokes				

決	丶	冫	氵	**JUÉ, to decide; decidedly; to execute (a person); to burst**
	汇	江	决	Now often written 决. 決定 *juédìng*, to decide, decision 決不 *juébù*, be determined not to (do something) 決心 *juéxīn*, determination
788 7 strokes	決			

華	一	十	艹	**HUÁ, flowers; glory; Chinese; HUÀ, family name**
	艹	苎	苎	中華民國 *Zhōnghuá Mínguó*, The Republic of China 華北 *Huá běi*, North China 華而不實 *huá ér bù shí*, to flower but bear no fruit, to make a big show and produce nothing 华
789 10 strokes (12 strokes)	苎	苹	華	

790 性 8 strokes

性 性 忄 忄 忄 忄 忄 性 性

XÌNG, nature, temperament; sex

"Heart" is for meaning, *shēng* "birth" for sound; or 性 and 生 stand for cognate words; or 性 combines meanings: what's in you at birth, "temperament, disposition."

人性 *rénxìng*, human nature
性情 *xìngqíng*, temperament, disposition
性別 *xìngbié*, sexual difference, sex
性交 *xìngjiāo*, sexual relations

791 呆 7 strokes

呆 口 口 口 口 早 呆 呆

ÁI, DĀI, be stupid, be idiotic; to stay, to remain

呆子 *dāizi*, stupid person, fool; enthusiast (see next item)
書呆子 *shū dāizi*, "bookworm"
發呆 *fādāi*, to stare like a fool, be in a daze
呆在家裡 *dāi zài jiālǐ*, to stay at home

792 保 9 strokes

保 丿 亻 个 伊 伊 伊 伊 保 保

BĂO, to protect; guarantee, surety

保險 *bǎoxiǎn*, to insure, insurance
保管 *bǎoguǎn*, to hold in trust, to take care of (legally)
保全 *bǎoquán*, to keep intact, to preserve

793 向 6 strokes

向 丿 亻 白 向 向 向 向 向

XIÀNG, toward, to face; habitually in the past; family name

向來 *xiànglái*, always; up till now
向着 *xiàngzhe*, toward, facing
一向 *yíxiàng*, up to now
不知去向 *bù zhī qùxiàng*, I don't know where (he/she/it/they) went

794 借 10 strokes

借 丿 亻 仁 什 伊 供 供 借 借

JIÈ, to lend; to borrow

Context or other words distinguish "to lend" from "to borrow."

借入 *jièrù*, to borrow
借出 *jièchū*, to lend
借給 *jiègěi*, to lend
借據 *jièjù*, notes (receipts for loans)
借光 *jièguāng*, Excuse me (polite)
借口 *jièkǒu*, to use as an excuse; excuse

規 795 11 strokes	一 夫 相	二 刲 規	丰 刦 規	**GUĪ, (drawing) compasses; rule, regulation; to correct (a fault); fee** 規勸 *guīquàn*, reprimand 規定 *guīdìng*, to make a regulation 校規 *xiàoguī*, school regulations 規
觀 796 24 strokes (25 strokes)	一 茁 雚	艹 萉 雚	苫 華 觀	**GUĀN, to look at, view** 觀念 *guānniàn*, concept 觀點 *guāndiǎn*, viewpoint 旁觀 *pángguān*, be a spectator 觀光 *guānguāng*, visit a place as a tourist 观
社 797 7 strokes	、 礻 社	冫 礻	礻 社	**SHÈ, society** This character combines meanings: "sign" + "earth" = "altar to the spirits of the land" (original meaning), "tutelary diety, village, society." 社會 *shèhuì*, society 社交 *shèjiāo*, social relations
度 798 9 strokes	、 广 庐	亠 庐 庎	广 庐 度	**DÙ, to pass through; degree, rule, extent; family name** 度過 *dùguò*, to pass through (a period of time) 度數 *dùshù*, degree 高度 *gāodù*, altitude 度日如年 *dù rì rú niǎn*, to pass days like years (i.e., time creeps by)
由 799 5 strokes	丨 由	冂 由	日	**YÓU, to rest with, be up to (someone), from, by; cause; family name (H.rad.143)** 自由 *zìyóu*, freedom 由於 *yóuyú*, due to 理由 *lǐyóu*, reason 由此 *yóucǐ*, hence, from this point

命	ノ	人	스	**MÌNG, destiny, fate; life; order**
	亼	合	合	生命 *shēngmìng*, life 革命 *gémìng*, to carry out a revolution, revolution 命令 *mìnglìng*, order, command 算命 *suànmìng*, to tell a person's fortune
800 8 strokes	合	命		

注	﹅	﹅	氵	**ZHÙ, to comment on; to concentrate on; note, commentary; to pour into; bet**
	氵	泹	汢	注重 *zhùzhòng*, to emphasize 貫注 *guànzhù*, to pay sharp attention to 下注 *xiàzhù*, to get down a bet 注意 *zhùyì*, to pay attention to
801 8 strokes	汢	注		

展	﹁	﹁	尸	**ZHĂN, to unroll; to postpone; family name**
	尸	屏	屈	發展 *fāzhǎn*, to develop, development 展開 *zhǎnkāi*, to open out 展出 *zhǎnchū*, to unfold, open out 畫展 *huàzhǎn*, a show (of paintings)
802 10 strokes	屏	展	展	

替	一	二	丰	**TÌ, for, in place of, to substitute**
	夫	扶	扶	替工 *tìgōng*, susbtitute workman 代替 *dàitì*, to represent; representing… (i.e., in place of…) 替死鬼 *tìsǐguǐ*, scapegoat 替身 *tìshēn*, substitute; scapegoat
803 12 strokes	替	替	替	

祖	﹅	﹅	礻	**ZŬ, ancestor; family name**
	礻	礼	初	祖先 *zǔxiān*, ancestor(s) 祖父 *zǔfù*, ancestor 祖國 *zǔguó*, fatherland 祖傳 *zǔchuán*, be handed down from one's ancestors
804 9 strokes	祖	祖	祖	

191

丢	一	二	千	**DIŪ, to lose**
				Note that this character is simply *qù* "to go" with a "left" rad. over it.
	王	丢	丢	丢臉 *diūliǎn*, "to lose face" 丢人 *diūrén*, "to lose face"
805 **6 strokes**				

體	冂	日	且	**TǏ, body**
				身體 *shēntǐ*, body 體重 *tǐzhòng*, weight (of human beings)
	骨	骨	骨	體面 *tǐmiàn*, be pretty, be in good taste; honor
806 **23 strokes**	體	體	體	(骨 511, 曲 478)　　　　体

示	一	二	丁	**SHÌ, sign. SIGN rad. (113) (H132)**
				Compare this to the form of the "sign" rad. already learned: 礻 (480, above).
	示	示		示意 *shìyì*, to show what you mean or intend 展示 *zhǎnshì*, to show, to lay bare
807 **5 strokes**				

宗	丶	八	宀	**ZŌNG, ancestor; law case; batch; family name**
				Zōng combines meanings. "Roof" over the "sign" rad. (for spiritual manifestations) suggests the altar to the ancestors which every traditional family has in the home.
	宀	宀	宁	
808 **8 strokes**	宗	宗		祖宗 *zǔzōng*, ancestor 宗教 *zōngjiào*, religion

鹿	丶	广	户	**LÙ, deer; family name. DEER rad. (198)(H222)**
				The character is a picture of a deer.
	户	庐	庐	小鹿 *xiǎolù*, fawn 鹿皮 *lùpí*, deerskin
809 **11 strokes**	鹿	鹿	鹿	鹿死誰手 *lù sǐ shéi shǒu*, the deer will die by whose hand? (i.e, who'll win?)

印	´	⼷	幻
	印		
810 4 strokes			

ÁNG, to lift up; to hold high office

The right half of this character, the "seal" rad., suggests the high office of which the seal was a symbol; the left half of the character is a "man" rad., slightly distorted. The two halves combine to give the meaning. Not in modern use as an independent character.

迎	´	⼷	幻
	卬	卬	迎
811 7 strokes	迎		

YÍNG, to face; toward; to meet

歡迎 *huānyíng*, to welcome
迎接 *yíngjiē*, to receive or welcome someone
迎面 *yíngmiàn*, facing each other; the space opposite

申	⼂	冂	曰
	曰	申	
812 5 strokes			

SHĒN, to stretch; to state, to inform; Shanghai; the ninth "earthly branch;" family name (H rad. 144)

The old character was two hands stretching an object (the "down" rad.). In traditional dictionaries, 申 is classified under the "field" rad.; in H, it is itself a rad.
申請 *shēnqǐng*, to apply for
申報 *shēnbào*, report (to a superior)

神	丶	⼀	礻
	礻	礻	初
813 9 strokes	神	神	神

SHÉN, spirit, god; family name

神話 *shénhuà*, myth
留神 *liúshén*, be careful
神經 *shénjīng*, nerve, nerves
神經病 *shénjīngbìng*, disease of the nervous system; mental disorder

政	一	丁	下
	正	正	正
814 9 strokes	政	政	政

ZHÈNG, government; political; administration

政體 *zhèngtǐ*, system of government
政界 *zhèngjiè*, government circles
政客 *zhèngkè*, politician (pejorative)

193

付	ノ	イ	仁	**FÙ, to hand over; set** The "thumb" (representing a hand) hands over something to the "man." 付清 *fùqīng*, to clear, to pay off (an account, a debt) 對付 *duìfu*, to deal with; to make do with
	付	付		
815 5 strokes				

府	丶	亠	广	**FǓ, prefecture; palace** 政府 *zhèngfǔ*, government 府上 *fǔshàng*, (your) residence (polite expression) 王府 *wángfǔ*, royal palace
	广	斤	斥	
816 8 strokes	府	府		

賈	一	丆	两	**JIǍ, family name; GǓ, merchant; to sell** The "cowrie" rad. (for "money") gives the meaning here; *xià* "cover" (122, above) suggests the sound. 賈人 *gǔrén*, merchant
	両	西	西	
817 13 strokes	罥	曹	賈	(貝 123)　　　　　　　賈

價	ノ	イ	仁	**JIÀ, price** This is the same word as 817, above. The character is reclarified with "man." 價錢 *jiàqián*, price 原價 *yuánjià*, original price 講價 *jiǎngjià*, to haggle, to discuss price
	仨	価	価	
818 15 strokes	僴	僧	價	价

彡	ノ	ク	彡	**SHĀN, streaks. STREAKS rad. (59)(H63)** The character is a picture. Not in modern use as an independent character.
819 3 strokes				

194

影	丶	口	日	**YǏNG, shadow, image, photograph**
	日	旦	昌	電影 *diànyǐng*, movie 陰影 *yīnyǐng*, shadow, shade 影射 *yǐngshè*, to counterfeit
820 15 strokes	룾	景	影	(京 299)

壬	一	二	千	**RÉN, to carry on the shoulder; great; the ninth "heavenly stem;" family name**
	壬			The character seems to show the "knight" rad. carrying some object (the "left" rad.) thrown over his shoulder. Originally the character was a picture of the standard carrying pole with an object fixed to each end for balance; at the center was the carrier.
821 4 strokes				

任	丿	亻	亻	**RÈN, to allow; term of office; responsibility; to employ; to endure; RÉN, family name**
	仁	任	任	任用 *rènyòng*, to appoint 任免 *rènmiǎn*, hiring and firing 任命 *rènmìng*, appointment; nomination
822 6 strokes				

何	丿	亻	亻	**HÉ, what; family name**
	仃	何	何	任何 *rènhé*, any 何必 *hébì*, Why must…? 如何 *rúhé*, how? in what way? How about…? 幾何學 *jǐhéxué*, geometry
823 7 strokes	何			

詳	丶	二	言	**XIÁNG, in detail; to know**
	言	言	言	*Xiáng* is supposed to be a sound-meaning compound, "words" 言 giving the meaning, *yáng* 羊 suggesting — imperfectly — the sound.
824 13 strokes	訐	詳	詳	詳談 *xiángtán*, discuss in detail 詳情 *xiángqíng*, detailed information 不詳 *bùxiáng*, be unknown 　　詳

XÌ, be fine, be thin

Note that the rads. in *xì* are the same as in *lèi* 累 (29, above), but the position is different. Originally *xì* had "silk" + "head" = "hair;" therefore, "fine." Head was corrupted.

詳細 *xiángxì*, be in detail

825
11 strokes

XĪ, to pity

可惜 *kěxī*, unfortunately; Alas!
愛惜 *àixī*, to love and take care of
惜別 *xībié*, be reluctant to part
不惜工本 *bùxī gōngběn*, not to spare labor or capital, i.e., go for it with everything you've got

826
11 strokes

GĒN, root; square root; a measure for long, thin things

根本 *gēnběn*, be basic, fundamental; from the beginning
根據 *gēnjù*, to base something on; according to; basis
方根 *fānggēn*, square root

827
10 strokes

SHǏ, history; historian; family name

In old forms, the bottom part of *shǐ* was a right hand (still discernible) holding "a case containing the bamboo slips on which history is written." The character now is classified in dictionaries under "mouth" (33, above).

828
5 strokes

LÌ, civil servant

Lì was originally just a variant of *shǐ* (828, above). But 史 and 吏 are now different characters, and the student should learn to tell them apart.

829
6 strokes

使 830 8 strokes	ノ	イ	仁
	仨	佢	佢
	伊	使	

SHǏ, envoy; to use; to cause; with

使得 *shǐdé*, to make; to cause; be able to use; be all right
大使 *dàshǐ*, ambassador
大使館 *dàshǐguǎn*, embassy
使命 *shǐmìng*, mission, assignment

味 831 8 strokes	⎸	⼝	口
	口一	口二	吽
	味	味	

WÈI, flavor; odor; a measure for medicines and for courses (of a meal)

味覺 *wèijué*, sense of taste
氣味 *qìwèi*, smell, flavor
味道 *wèidào*, flavor
玩味 *wánwèi*, to think over, to ponder

亂 832 13 strokes	一	⼃	𠬠
	吾	肙	肙
	甮	甮	亂

LUÀN, be disorderly, disorder

內亂 *nèiluàn*, civil war
亂説 *luànshuō*, to speak recklessly; to gossip
亂真 *luànzhēn*, be a good imitation (of a painting or sculpture)

乱

| 辰 833
6 strokes | 一 | 厂 | 厂 |
| | 斤 | 斤 | 辰 |

PÀI, branch off

The character is a picture of a stream dividing, from which comes the meaning "to branch off." The character 834, below, is now usually used in this sense.

派 834 9 strokes	丶	丶丶	氵
	氵	氵	氵
	汦	派	派

PÀI, to branch off; to appoint; school or sect; to levy; to distribute

黨派 *dǎngpài*, political party
派出所 *pàichūsuǒ*, precinct house
氣派 *qìpài*, manner, style
派頭 *pàitóu*, style, manner

助	｜	冂	月	**ZHÙ, to help**
	月	且	助	幫助 *bāngzhù*, to help, help 助手 *zhùshǒu*, assistant 助教 *zhùjiào*, teaching assistant 助理 *zhùlǐ*, assistant
835 7 strokes	助			

設	丶	亠	二	**SHÈ, to establish; if**
	言	言	言	設備 *shèbèi*, equipment 設立 *shèlì*, to set up 設法 *shèfǎ*, to figure out a way; to try to 設想 *shèxiǎng*, to imagine; to take into account, have consideration for; rough plan, preliminary idea
836 11 strokes	訊	設	設	设

醫	一	三	矢	**YĪ, to heal**
	医	殴	殹	醫生 *yīsheng*, medical doctor 醫學 *yīxué*, medical science 中醫 *Zhōng yī*, Chinese traditional medicine
837 18 strokes	醫	醫	醫	医

院	⺈	⻖	⻖	**YUÀN, public building; courtyard**
	⻖	⻖	阮	電影院 *diànyǐngyuàn*, movie theater 法院 *fǎyuàn*, court of law 醫院 *yīyuàn*, hospital
838 10 strokes	阼	陀	院	

服	｜	刀	月	**FÚ, to serve; to swallow; to be used to; clothes**
	月	刖	肌	衣服 *yīfú*, clothes (note change from *fú* to *fù*) 說服 *shuōfú*, to convince 服從 *fúcóng*, to obey
839 8 strokes	那	服		

矛	⌐	⌐	卫	**MÁO, spear. SPEAR rad. (110)(H155)**
	予	矛		This character is a picture of a spear. The student should learn to distinguish the "spear" rad. from *yǔ* "to give;" 予 (692, above).
840 5 strokes				矛頭 *máotóu*, spearhead (literal and figurative)

務	⌐	予	矛	**WÙ, affairs; must**
	矛	矜	豸	務必 *wùbì*, without fail 服務 *fúwù*, to serve, service 外務 *wàiwù*, foreign affairs 業務 *yèwù*, business, professional work
841 11 strokes	敄	務	務	务

精	ヽヽ	⸌⸝	⺌	**JĪNG, essence, spirit, sperm; very; to be skillful; be essential, pure; be smart**
	米	米゠	米゠	精神 *jīngshén*, spirit, vitality 精神病 *jīngshénbìng*, mental illness, psychosis 精明 *jīngmíng*, be shrewd
842 14 strokes	精	精	精	精通 *jīngtōng*, to know very well 精華 *jīnghuá*, essence, best part

奴	⟨	乄	女	**NÚ, handmaiden, slave**
	如	奴		The character combines meanings. 奴才 *núcái*, slave 奴性 *núxìng*, be servile, servile disposition
843 5 strokes				

努	⟨	乄	女	**NǓ, to strive, to work hard at**
	如	奴	努	努力 *nǔlì*, "put your back into it," effort
844 7 strokes	努			

199

動	一	二	亏
	亐	盲	重
845 11 strokes	重	動	動

DÒNG, to move

活動 *huódòng*, be active, activity
動機 *dòngjī*, motive, intention
動員 *dòngyuán*, to mobilize, call up (troops); mobilization
運動 *yùndòng*, movement (physical), exercise; campaign, movement (political)
五四運動 *Wǔ Sì Yùndòng*, the May Fourth Movement (1919)

动

靠	㇒	牛	牛
	牛	告	告
846 15 strokes	靠	靠	靠

KÀO, to lean on, to depend on

可靠 *kěkào*, be reliable
靠近 *kàojìn*, be near to
靠背 *kàobèi*, chair back

(非 654)

夂	彡	夂	
847 3 strokes			

YǏN, to march. MARCH rad. (54)(H36)

Yǐn is a picture of a man marching out. The student should be careful to distinguish "march" from the form ⻌ of the "halt" rad. (171, above). *Yǐn* is not in modern use as an independent character.

建	㇕	㇕	⺕
	⺕	⺕	聿
848 9 strokes	建	建	

JIÀN, to set up; Fujian (old style: "Fukien")

建設 *jiànshè*, to build, to build up
建立 *jiànlì*, to establish
建造 *jiànzào*, to build, to make

爿	㇄	㇉	㇉
	爿		
849 4 strokes			

QIĀNG, bed. BED rad. (90)(H rad. 42 is forms 丬 and 爿)

This rad. is a picture of a bed. The student should distinguish it from the "slice" rad. (927, below). "Bed" is now written 牀 or 床, pronounced *chuáng* (p. 250a); *qiāng* is now seen independently only as the character for a dialect word, *pán*, a measure for shops.

200

牆	㇄	㇉	爿	**QIÁNG, wall**
	爿	爿	牁	*Qiáng* (849, above) gives the sound. The right half of this character used to be "wheat" (cp. 431, above) over a picture of "a double wall for storing grain." The
850	牁	牆	牆	character 墙 — with the "earth" rad. rather than the "bed" rad. — is now often used for this word.
17 strokes				城牆 *chéngqiáng*, city wall　　墙

蒦	一	十	艹	**HUÒ, to grab, to catch in hunting; to measure**
	疒	芢	芢	The character shows a hand catching a bird. The bird either has a crest or is hidden in the grass. The meaning "to measure" is by sound-loan. In modern times, *huò* has been
851	萑	蒦	蒦	reclarified by the "dog" rad. and replaced by 獲 (p. 265a).
13 strokes (14 strokes)				(隹 39)

護	丶	二	言	**HÙ, to protect**
				保護 *bǎohù*, to protect
	言	許	評	護士 *hùshì*, nurse
				救護 *jiùhù*, to rescue, to save
852	謢	護	護	
20 strokes				(言 38)　　　　护

莫	一	十	艹	**MÙ, evening; MÒ, don't; no one; family name**
	艹	苩	苩	The old form had "grass-sun-grass:" the sun in the grass; therefore, "evening, late." The bottom "grass" was corrupted into "big." "Don't" and "no one" are by sound-loan.
853	莒	莫	莫	For "evening," *mu* gets reclarified with another "sun" and is written 暮.
10 strokes				莫非 *mòfēi*, is it possible that…?

模	一	十	才	**MÓ, pattern (pronounced MÚ in some compounds)**
				模子 *múzi*, mold, die
	木	杧	枋	模樣 *múyàng*, facial appearance, face
854	椲	模	模	模特兒 *mótèr*, model
14 strokes (15 strokes)				

修	ノ	イ	彳
	彳	伩	攸
855 9 strokes (10 strokes)	修	修	修

XIŪ, to repair, to build; be long; to study

This character is also seen as 修, whence its alternative count of 9 strokes.

修理 *xiūlǐ*, to fix
修改 *xiūgǎi*, to revise
自修 *zìxiū*, to educate oneself; study period (in school)

省	ノ	小	小
	少	屮	省
856 9 strokes	省	省	省

SHĚNG, province; to save

省錢 *shěngqián*, be economical (saving of money)
省得 *shěngde*, lest
河北省 *Héběi shěng*, Hebei (Hopei) Province

尺	コ	コ	尸
	尺		
857 4 strokes			

CHĬ, a Chinese "foot" (about 14 English inches); pronounced CHÍ in some compounds); ruler (H rad. 117)

尺寸 *chǐcun*, size (in feet and inches)
市尺 *shìchǐ*, Chinese standard foot
尺子 *chǐzi*, ruler

萑	一	十	艹
	产	芦	苩
858 11 strokes (12 strokes)	首	萑	萑

HUÁN, mountain sheep with horns

Huán undoubtedly was a picture of the animal to which it refers. Not in modern use as an independent character.

(見 214)

寬	丶	八	宀
	宀	宇	宵
859 14 strokes (15 strokes)	宮	宵	寬

KUĀN, be broad

The dot is sometimes omitted when this character is written by hand.

寬大 *kuāndà*, be spacious; to fit loosely; be lenient
寬厚 *kuānhòu*, be generous
寬容 *kuānróng*, to tolerate

寛

系	ノ	ㄠ	幺	**XÌ, to tie; department (of a college); system**
	幺	彑	糸	社會學系 *shèhuìxué xì*, sociology department
860 7 strokes	系			太陽系 *tàiyáng xì*, the solar system 系數 *xìshù*, coefficient

縣	l	Π	目	**XIÀN, a *xian* ("*hsien*") (administrative district, similar to a U.S. county)**
	目	目	県	縣長 *xiànzhǎng*, magistrate of a *xian* 縣城 *xiànchéng*, county seat
861 16 strokes	縣	縣	縣	(目 120)　　　　　　　県

公	ノ	八	公	**GŌNG, public; male; equitable; metric; "Mr."; grandfather**
	公			公尺 *gōngchǐ*, meter (measure of length) 公社 *gōngshè*, commune
862 4 strokes				公使 *gōngshǐ*, minister (diplomatic) 公鹿 *gōnglù*, stag 花花公子 *huāhuā gōngzǐ*, a dandy, "dude"

哉	一	十	土	**ZĀI, (bookish) a sentence-final particle, expressing doubt or regret; Alas!**
	士	吉	吉	何哉 *hé zāi*, Why? 有何難哉 *yǒu hé nán zāi*, Why is it
863 9 strokes	哉	哉	哉	difficult? What's the problem?

鐵	ノ	人	仁	**TIĚ, iron; be strong; family name**
	牟	余	釒	鐵路 *tiělù*, railroad 鐵定 *tiědìng*, to decide definitely 鐵絲 *tiěsī*, wire
864 21 strokes	鐼	鐼	鐵	手無寸鐵 *shǒu wú cùn tiě*, be completely unarmed; be defenceless 铁

203

台	ㄥ	ㄙ	台	**YÍ, I, me; TÁI; the name of a group of stars; platform, terrace; desk; stand, base; broadcasting station**
	台	台		There is no helpful explanation of this character. It occurs in other characters to suggest the sound — sometimes for a *tai* sound, sometimes a *zhi* or *shi* sound. Not in modern use as *yí*, "I, me."
865 **5 strokes**				

治	丶	冫	氵	**ZHÌ, to govern; to heal, to treat**
	汋	治	治	政治 *zhèngzhì*, politics 治理 *zhìlǐ*, to govern 治病 *zhìbìng*, to treat an illness
866 **8 strokes**	治	治		

吾	一	丆	五	**WÚ, (bookish) I, me; a surname**
	五	五	吾	吾人 *wúrén*, we, us 吾愛 *wúài*, address to someone held in affection (translation of English "my dear") 吾兄 *wúxiōng*, "you" (polite: to a male friend)
867 **7 strokes**	吾			

語	丶	亠	言	**YǓ, language, speech**
	言	言	訂	語言 *yǔyán*, language 語法 *yǔfǎ*, grammar 語系 *yǔxì*, language family 成語 *chéngyǔ*, set expression, idiom 四字成語 *sì zì chéngyǔ*, four-character set expression (= a common feature of Chinese rhetoric) 语
868 **14 strokes**	訝	語	語	

弗	ㄱ	⼁	弓	**FÚ, (bookish) not; not willing**
	弗	弗		This character originally meant "rope" and was a picture of a piece of rope (the "bow" rad.) tying two things — now "left" and "down" — together. The meaning "not, not willing" comes by sound-loan.
869 **5 strokes**				

費	一	二	弓	**FÈI, to waste; expense, fee; family name**
	弗	弗	弗	學費 *xuéfèi*, tuition (fees for education) 費用 *fèiyòng*, expense 費力 *fèilì*, require great effort, be strenuous 費心 *fèixīn*, take trouble over; (polite) Would you mind to…
870 12 strokes	費	費	費	(貝 123)　　　　　　　　　　　費

其	一	十	廿	**QÍ, his, her, its, their**
	廿	甘	並	其實 *qíshí*, The fact is… 尤其 *yóuqí*, especially 其次 *qícì*, next in order; second 其他 *qítā*, other (also written 其它 when it means "other *thing*;" for 它, see p. 247a)
871 8 strokes	其	其		

餘	丿	丿	𠂉	**YÚ, surplus, remainder**
	今	今	食	其餘 *qíyú*, the rest of it 餘數 *yúshù*, balance, remainder; complement of a number 餘閑 *yúxián*, spare time, leisure
872 15 strokes	飲	飰	餘	(余 613)　　　　　　　　　　余

勢	土	圭	夫	**SHÌ, power; momentum; tendency; outward appearance; gesture**
	幸	執	執	勢力 *shìlì*, influence 時勢 *shíshì*, current situation 手勢 *shǒushì*, gesture, (hand) signal
873 13 strokes	執	勢	勢	(坴 675)　　　　　　　　　　勢

範	丿	⺮	⺮	**FÀN, pattern, rule; family name**
		竻	笛	模範 *mófàn*, model 範本 *fànběn*, textbook of examples or models 示範 *shìfàn*, to demonstrate, set an example
874 15 strokes	範	範	範	(車 412)　　　　　　　　　　范

205

韋	ㄱ	九	五	**WÉI**, (bookish) to walk off, to walk off in opposite directions; soft leather; family name. WALK OFF rad. (178). The short form is H. rad. 91.
	土	吉	吾	韋 used to have "foot" at top and bottom, with a circle in between, to suggest two feet walking off in opposite directions.
875 9 strokes	音	韋	韋	The short form = *wéi*, leather; a family name. 韦

圍	|	冂	冂	**WÉI**, to go around; circumference
	冂	闬	圊	範圍 *fànwéi*, scope, sphere 圍牆 *wéiqiáng*, enclosing wall 包圍 *bāowéi*, to surround
876 12 strokes	圊	圍	圍	围

彼	ノ	㇒	彳	**BǏ**, the other; he, she
	彳	彷	彷	彼此 *bǐcǐ*, each other, mutually 彼處 *bǐchù*, (in) that place 要知己知彼 *yào zhī jǐ zhī bǐ*, you should know yourself and know your enemy
877 8 strokes	彼	彼		

允	ㄥ	ㄙ	㇆	**YǓN**, to consent; true, sincere
	允			允許 *yǔnxǔ*, to permit, permission 允從 *yǔncóng*, to assent 允當 *yǔndàng*, be suitable, satisfactory
878 4 strokes				

充	、	二	亠	**CHŌNG**, to fill up; to pretend to be
	云	产	充	The student should distinguish this character from *kàng* "be high" 亢 (952, below). 充分 *chōngfèn*, be adequate 冒充 *màochōng*, to act falsely as, to impersonate 充足 *chōngzú*, be sufficient
879 6 strokes				

206

880
12 strokes

TŎNG, to control; all; succession

總統 *zŏngtŏng*, president (of a country)
傳統 *chuántŏng*, tradition
統一 *tŏngyī*, to unify, unity

统

881
11 strokes

TUĪ, to push; to elect; to make excuses; to cut, to clip; to deduce

推行 *tuīxíng*, to carry into operation
推動 *tuī dòng*, to put into action; to promote; to propel
推子 *tuīzi*, barber's clippers

882
12 strokes

DÁ, to answer; DĀ, answer

回答 *huídá*, to answer, answer
答應 *dáyìng*, to answer, to agree to
答案 *dáàn*, answer, solution
答非所問 *dá fēi suǒ wèn*, to give an irrelevant answer; irrelevant or evasive answer

883
11 strokes

HUÒ, goods; currency

國貨 *guóhuò*, domestic goods (i.e., not imports)
洋貨 *yáng huò*, imports ("foreign goods")
通貨 *tōnghuò*, legal tender

货

884
9 strokes

XIÁN, (bookish) all; a family name

In modern texts, this character is usually seen as the short form for 鹹 (p. 245b), e.g., 咸魚 for 鹹魚 *xiányú*, salted fish.

				JIǍN, decrease; "minus"
減	丶	氵	汇	Now often written 减, i.e., with the "ice" rad. rather than "three-dots-water."
	汇	汇	泻	減少 *jiǎnshǎo*, to decrease; to subtract 減價 *jiǎnjià*, to cut prices; to hold a sale 五減三 *wǔ jiǎn sān*, five minus three
885 **12 strokes**	減	減	減	

				XÍNG, form
形	一	二	干	形勢 *xíngshì*, appearance, condition of things; pertain to topography, be topographical
	开	开	形	形容 *xíngróng*, to describe 情形 *qíngxíng*, circumstances of a matter
886 **7 strokes**	形			(口 33)

				SHĒNG, to ascend, to raise; Chinese dry quart (31.6 cubic inches); quart box
升	丿	二	壬	升學 *shēngxué*, be promoted to a higher school
	升			一升米 *yī shēng mǐ*, quart of rice 升平 *shēngpíng*, be peaceful, peace
887 **4 strokes**				

				DĪ, be low, to lower
低	丿	亻	亻	低頭 *dītóu*, to bow the head 低聲下氣 *dī shēng xià qì*, be meek, be submissive (literally, "lower your voice and keep down your energy")
	仁	仟	低	
888 **7 strokes**	低			低三下四 *dī sān xià sì*, be humble, lowly, servile

				CHǍNG, be long. LONG rad. (168)
镸	一	厂	ᶫ	This form of the "long" rad. does not occur as an independent character; it occurs only as a part of characters. The student should be prepared, however, to recognize this form in characters as the "long" rad. The independent form has already been given: 長 (226, above).
	ᶫ	镸	镸	
889 **7 strokes** **(8 strokes)**	镸			

208

降

890
10 strokes

JIÀNG, to descend; to lower; to demote; XIÁNG, to surrender; to control

降低 *jiàngdī*, to drop, to lower
升降機 *shēngjiàngjī*, an elevator (literally, an ascend-and-descend machine)
下降 *xiàjiàng*, to descend

昭

891
9 strokes

ZHĀO, to shine

Rì "sun" 日 is for meaning, *zhào* 召 (740, above) for sound.

昭然 *zhāorán*, be clear, be evident
昭示 *zhāoshì*, publicly declare, make public

照

892
13 strokes

ZHÀO, to reflect; to shine on; according

This appears to be *zhāo* (891, above), reclarified with the "fire-dots" (34, above).

按照 *ànzhào*, according to…
照相 *zhàoxiàng*, to take a photograph
護照 *hùzhào*, passport
照常 *zhàocháng*, as usual

忽

893
8 strokes

HŪ, suddenly; to neglect

忽然 *hūrán*, all of a sudden
忽而…忽而… *hū ér…, hū ér…*, do one thing one minute and another thing the next minute (e.g., 忽而哭忽而笑 *hū ér kū hū ér xiào*, to weep one minute and laugh the next)

樂

894
15 strokes

YUÈ, music; family name; LÈ, happiness; family name

The character is a picture of musical paraphernalia — bells and so on — on a wooden stand (the "tree" rad.).

音樂 *yīnyuè*, music
快樂 *kuàilè*, be happy; happiness

乐

泉	′	′′	白
	白	㝵	㝵
895 9 strokes	㝵	泉	

QUÁN, a spring; family name

This character is usually explained: "white" (for "pure") + "water" = "spring."

泉水　*quánshuǐ*, spring water
甘泉　*gān quán*, sweet spring water
黃泉　*Huáng Quán*, "The Yellow Springs" (land of the dead)

線	＿	＿	幺
	幺	糸	紀
896 15 strokes	絤	綿	線

XIÀN, thread, wire; clue

An alternate character for this word, now often seen, is 綫 (of which the short form is now used for 線).

線人　*xiànrén*, stool pigeon, "fink"
平行線　*píngxíngxiàn*, parallel lines
毛線　*máoxiàn*, knitting wool

线

郵	′	＝	千
	千	垂	垂
897 11 strokes	垂	郵	郵

YÓU, postal

郵費　*yóufèi*, postage
郵差　*yóuchāi*, postman (archaic)
郵件　*yóujiàn*, mail
郵包　*yóubāo*, parcel

邮

局	＇	＝	尸
	尸	局	局
898 7 strokes	局		

JÚ, office; situation

郵政局　*yóuzhèngjú*, post office
電報局　*diànbàojú*, telegraph office
電話局　*diànhuàjú*, telephone office
局勢　*júshì*, situation

證	＇	′′	言
	言	言	訂
899 19 strokes	訝	證	證

ZHÈNG, proof, to prove; permit

證據　*zhèngjù*, proof
通行證　*tōngxíngzhèng*, travel permit
證婚　*zhènghūn*, to perform a wedding ceremony

(登 712)

证

210

空	丶	八	宀
	宀	穴	空
900 8 strokes	空	空	

KŌNG, be empty; sky, air; for nothing, in vain; **KÒNG**, be empty, leave empty; empty space; free time

The "cave" rad. gives the idea "be empty;" *gōng* (443, above) suggests the sound.

空氣 *kōngqì*, air
太空員 *tàikōngyuán*, astronaut
空白 *kòngbái*, blank space

色	丿	勹	夕
	夕	刍	色
901 6 strokes			

SÈ, color; looks; kind; desire; **SHǍI**, color. COLOR rad. (139)

氣色 *qìsè*, complexion
好色 *hàosè*, be lustful
臉色 *liǎnsè*, complexion; facial expression
春色 *chūnsè*, spring scenery

困	丨	冂	冂
	因	困	困
902 7 strokes	困		

KÙN, difficulty, hardship; to trap; to maroon; to beseige; be sleepy

The character is supposed to show a tree in a box, whence "difficulty."

困難 *kùnnán*, be difficult, difficulty
圍困 *wéikùn*, to surround, hem in, besiege

滿	氵	氵	汁
	汁	浩	滿
903 14 strokes	滿	滿	滿

MǍN, be full

不滿 *bùmǎn*, be dissatisfied
滿足 *mǎnzú*, to satisfy
滿意 *mǎnyì*, be satisfied

(氵 181)   满

角	丿	丷	宀
	角	角	角
904 7 strokes	角		

JIǍO, horn; angle; corner; a measure for dimes; role; **JUÉ**, role. HORN rad. (148)(H201)

The character is a picture of an animal's horn. Now usually written 角.

直角 *zhíjiǎo*, right angle
牛角 *niújiǎo*, oxhorn

解	ク	角	角	**JIĚ, to loosen, to untie**
	角	角	角	解決 *jiějué*, to solve; to kill; solution 了解 *liǎojiě*, to understand 解放 *jiěfàng*, to liberate 講解 *jiǎngjiě*, to explain
905 **13 strokes**	解	解	解	(刀 102)

組	ㄥ	ㄠ	ㄠ	**ZǓ, to organize; section, department**
	幺	糸	糸	人事組 *rénshìzǔ*, personnel department 組長 *zǔzhǎng*, section chief 組合 *zǔhé*, to consolidate; (mathematical) combinations
906 **11 strokes**	紀	組	組	组

織	糸	糸	糸	**ZHĪ, to weave**
	紵	綷	繕	組織 *zǔzhī*, to organize, organization 織毛衣 *zhī máoyī*, knit a sweater 織造 *zhīzào*, weaving
907 **18 strokes**	織	織	織	(戠 525) 织

复	ノ	宀	亇	**FÚ, to return**
	乍	白	自	The "slow" rad. at the bottom is supposed to suggest the meaning of this character. The top part — now "left-one-sun" — once was a character that gave the sound. In use now as the short form for 909, below.
908 **9 strokes**	戸	复	复	

復	ノ	ノ	彳	**FÙ, to return; to repeat; to reply**
	彳	彳	徊	This is the same word as 908, above. The character is reclarified with the "step" rad. Distinguish from 911, below. 復原 *fùyuán*, to recover, to get better 復員 *fùyuán*, to demobilize 復活 *fùhuó*, to resuscitate, to revive
909 **12 strokes**	徉	復	復	复

212

衤 910 5 strokes (6 strokes)	丶	㇇	㇋
	㇏	㇋	

YĪ, gown. GOWN rad. (145)(H129)

This form of the "gown" rad. occurs only as a part of characters. The student already has learned the independent form of "gown" (109, above). The student should distinguish this form of "gown" from the form of the "sign" rad. ㇈ (480, above).

複 911 14 strokes (15 strokes)	㇇	㇋	衤
	衤	衤	衵
	衴	褚	複

FÙ, be complex; to repeat

Distinguish this character from 909, above (909 has the "step" rad. as its left side; 911, here, has the "gown" rad.) Note also that *both* characters have the same short form.

重複 *chóngfù*, to duplicate
複寫紙 *fùxiězhǐ*, carbon paper
複習 *fùxí*, to review
(e.g., school work)

复

雜 912 18 strokes	丶	亠	广
	六	衆	宗
	剁	雜	雜

ZÁ, be mixed; be miscellaneous

複雜 *fùzá*, be complex
雜貨 *záhuò*, sundries
雜亂 *záluàn*, be mixed up, be in disorder

(木 64, 隹 39)

杂

典 913 8 strokes	丶	冂	曰
	曲	曲	典
	典	典	

DIǍN, canon, be canonic; to borrow or lend money on security of land or house

字典 *zìdiǎn*, dictionary of characters
典故 *diǎngù*, classical allusion; historical background
典範 *diǎnfàn*, model, example

查 914 9 strokes	一	十	才
	木	术	杳
	杳	查	查

CHÁ, to investigate

查字典 *cházìdiǎn*, to look up in the dictionary
查點 *chádiǎn*, to check a list of goods
查對 *cháduì*, to verify

限	`	了	阝
	阝7	阝7	阝ヨ
915 9 strokes	限	限	限

XIÀN, limit

限定 *xiàndìng*, to set a limit
限量 *xiànliàng*, limit; to estimate
有限 *yǒuxiàn*, be limited; "Ltd."
無限 *wúxiàn*, be infinite, unlimited

提	一	十	才
	扌?	担	担
916 12 strokes	捍	捉	提

TÍ, to raise; to lift in the hand; rising stroke (in writing); DĪ in some compounds (as 提防 *dīfáng*, to defend against (防: p. 263a)

提案 *tí'àn*, to move (in a meeting); proposal
提出 *tíchū*, bring up; to withdraw money
提前 *tíqián*, to move up (the date of an event)

肯	↓	⊢	止
	止	广	肯
917 8 strokes	肯	肯	

KĚN, be willing

肯定 *kěndìng*, to accept; to recognize (e.g., another nation)

冬	ノ	ク	夂
	冬	冬	
918 5 strokes			

DŌNG, winter; family name

冬天 *dōngtiān*, winter
冬至 *dōngzhì*, winter solstice
冬菜 *dōngcài*, preserved, dried cabbage

夏	一	一	厂
	丆	百	百
919 10 strokes	頁	夏	夏

XIÀ, summer; family name

夏天 *xiàtiān*, summer
夏至 *xiàzhì*, summer solstice
夏收 *xiàshōu*, summer harvest

214

冷	丶	冫	⺀	**LĚNG, be cold; family name**
	冸	冸	冷	冷清 *lěngqīng*, be lonely; be quiet and peaceful
920	冷			冷貨 *lěnghuò*, unsalable goods
7 strokes				乾冷 *gānlěng*, be dry and cold (of the weather)

皿	丶	冂	皿	**MǏN, dish. DISH rad. (108)(H146)**
	皿	皿		The character is a picture. The student should be careful to distinguish "dish" from the "blood" rad. (922, below), from "net" 罒 (637, above), and from "eye," 罒 (132, above).
921				
5 strokes				

血	丿	亻	仐	**XUĒ, XIĚ, blood. BLOOD rad. (143)(H181)**
	血	血	血	*Xuē* is a dish with something in it (the "left" rad.). See 921, above, about look-alike rads.
922				殺人不見血 *shārén bù jiàn xiě*, to kill by subtle means (literally, "to kill a person [so that people] don't see the blood")
6 strokes				血親 *xiěqīn*, blood relations

囚	丨	冂	冂	**QIÚ, prisoner**
	囚	囚		This character is a picture of a man in an enclosure, whence "prisoner." The student should compare 囚 to the bottom part of *hé* "what?" 曷 (387, above) and note that they are not the same.
923				死囚 *sǐqiú*, prisoner under sentence of death
5 strokes				

盈	丶	冂	冂	**WĒN, be kind**
	囚	囚	囚	*Wēn* is "prisoner" over "dish," and the character is explained: "to feed a prisoner to be kind." Usually written 昷. Not in modern use as an independent character.
924	昷	昷	盈	
10 strokes				

溫	`	`:`	`氵`
	氵	汈	汩
925 13 strokes	淠	溫	溫

WĒN, be warm; review; family name

Note that this character appears to be 924, above, reclarified with "three-dots water." Usually written 温.

溫度 *wēndù*, temperature
溫習 *wēnxí*, review, study
溫泉 *wēnquán*, hot spring

該	`	`二`	`言`
	言	訁	訁
926 13 strokes	訬	該	該

GĀI, to owe; to be someone's turn; ought to; the said (aforementionted)…

應該 *yīnggāi*, ought
該死 *gāi sǐ*, What a crime! Disgusting!
該我 *gāi wǒ*, It's my turn!

該

片	丿	丿'	片
	片		
927 4 strokes			

PIÀN, slice, to slice, piece; an expanse; PIÀN, PIĀN, card. SLICE rad. (91)(H114)

The student should distinguish the "slice" rad. from the "bed" rad. 爿 (849, above).

照片 *zhàopiàn*, photograph
明信片 *míngxìnpiàn*, postcard

肉	丨	冂	内
	内	肉	肉
928 6 strokes			

RÒU, meat; fruit pulp; be sluggish. MEAT rad. (130)

This is the form of the "meat" rad. that can occur as an independent character. The student has learned the form which may occur as a part of characters (326, above). 肉 is a picture of dried meat.

牛肉 *niúròu*, beef

星	丶	冂	日
	日	尸	旦
929 9 strokes	昰	晜	星

XĪNG, star, planet; a bit

火星 *huǒxīng*, a spark; Mars
星星 *xīngxīng*, star
明星 *míngxīng*, star as in "movie star," etc.

216

期	一	十	廿	**QĪ, period; issue (of a magazine); to expect**
	甘	其	其	星期 *xīngqī*, week 期滿 *qīmǎn*, to expire 期望 *qīwàng*, to look forward to 日期 *rìqī*, date
930 12 strokes	其	期	期	

段	ㄱ	ㄱ	ㄸ	**JIǍ, to borrow; fake**
	ㄸ	ㄸ	ㄸ	Note that the right side of this character is not the "club" rad. (183, above). *Jiǎ* is classified in traditional dictionaries under the "right hand" rad. 又. In modern use, this *jiǎ* has been replaced by 932, below.
931 9 strokes	ㄸ	ㄸ	段	

假	ノ	亻	亻	**JIǍ, to borrow; fake; JIÀ, vacation**
	亻	亻	作	This is 931, above, reclarified with the "man" rad. 假意 *jiǎyì*, with false intent 假如 *jiǎrú*, if
932 11 strokes	作	假	假	放假 *fàngjià*, to have a vacation 假牙 *jiǎyá*, false tooth, denture

與	ㄅ	ㄅ	ㄅ	**YǓ, to hand over; with**
	臼	臼	臼	與其 *yǔqí*, rather than 與世無爭 *yǔ shì wú zhēng*, to get out of the "rat race," not to "fight the world"
933 13 strokes	臼	與	與	与

舉	ㄅ	ㄅ	ㄅ	**JǓ, to lift; to begin; behavior; all**
	臼	臼	與	選舉 *xuǎnjǔ*, to elect, election 舉動 *jǔdòng*, behavior 舉行 *jǔxíng*, to hold (e.g., a meeting) 舉頭望明月，低頭思故鄉 *jǔ tóu wàng míng yuè, dī tóu sī gù xiāng*, (I) raise (my) head and look at the bright moon, Lower (my) head and think of home. (李白)
934 16 strokes	與	舉	舉	举

217

義 935 13 strokes	丶	丷	丷
	半	羊	羊
	羊	義	義

YÌ, meaning; right conduct; public; free

主義 zhǔyì, doctrine; -ism
義務 yìwù, duty; without pay; open to all
望文生義 wàng wén shēng yì, glance at the words and conceive the meaning; i.e., take a text too literally
社會主義 shèhuìzhǔyì, socialism

义

被 936 10 strokes	丶	丆	衤
	衤	衤	衤
	衤	衤	被

BÈI, quilt; by (sign of agent in passive construction); to be (sign of passive construction)

被子 bèizi, quilt
被告 bèigào, the accused; defendant
被動 bèidòng, be passive

利 937 7 strokes	一	二	千
	禾	禾	利
	利		

LÌ, interest (on money); profit; be sharp; family name

淨利 jìnglì, net profit
複利 fùlì, compound interest
利用 lìyòng, to make use of
吉利 jílì, be lucky, be auspicious

| 存 938 6 strokes | 一 | 尢 | 才 |
| | 存 | 存 | 存 |

CÚN, to keep, to store; deposit

存在 cúnzài, to exist, existence
存在主義 cúnzàizhǔyì, existentialism
保存 bǎocún, to preserve
存放 cúnfàng, to entrust to somebody; to deposit

肖 939 7 strokes	丨	丷	丷
	丬	肖	肖
	肖		

XIÀO, to look like; XIĀO, family name. Printed 肖.

肖像 xiàoxiàng, photograph, portrait (painted or carved)
生肖 shēngxiào, any of the twelve symbolical animals, each associated with one of the Earthly Branches and with years in the duodecimal cycle ("Year of the Rat," "Year of the Cock," etc.)

218

消	`	``	氵	**XIĀO, to consume, to abolish; be necessary**
				取消 *qǔxiāo*, to abolish
	氵	氵	氵	消化 *xiāohuà*, to digest, digestion
940				消息 *xiāoxi*, news, information
10 strokes	氵	消	消	

制	ノ	ー	⸢	**ZHÌ, to measure, to regulate; institution, system**
				限制 *xiànzhì*, to limit, restrict
	午	乍	制	專制 *zhuānzhì*, be despotic
941				制度 *zhìdù*, system
8 strokes	制	制		

考	一	十	土	**KǍO, to test; be tested; exam**
				大考 *dàkǎo*, final exam
	耂	耂	考	考查 *kǎochá*, to investigate
942				考古 *kǎogǔ*, to do archaeological research
6 strokes				

試	`	二	言	**SHÌ, to try**
				考試 *kǎoshì*, to take or give an exam; exam
	言	訁	訁	口試 *kǒushì*, oral exam
943				筆試 *bǐshì*, written exam
13 strokes	訂	試	試	(口 33) 试

参	ノ	人	仌	**ZHĚN, thick hair**
				The character shows a "man" rad. over the "streaks" rad. It is supposed to be a picture of a man with thick, heavy hair. Not in modern use as an independent character.
	参	参		
944				
5 strokes				

219

參

945
11 strokes

CĀN, to take part in; to refer; to consult; SHĒN, ginseng

參加 *cānjiā*, to take part in
參考 *cānkǎo*, to consult, to consider
參觀 *cānguān*, to sightsee at

参

髟

946
10 strokes

BIĀO, long hair. HAIR rad. (190)(H220)

The "streaks" rad. stands for the hair; the "long" rad. gives the rest of the meaning.

將

947
11 strokes

JIĀNG, to take hold of; be about to, just; to nurture; JIÀNG, a general

將就 *jiāngjiu*, to make do with; to compromise
將來 *jiānglái*. in the future

将

蜀

948
13 strokes

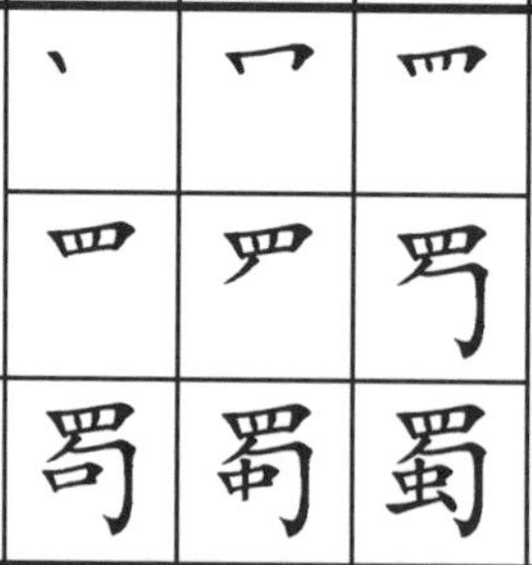

SHǓ, caterpillar

The oldest form of this character did not have the "bug" rad. in it and was a simple picture of a caterpillar. Some scribe reclarified it with a "bug," and then, later on, another reclarified it with another bug, so the traditional form became 蠋.

(虫 641)

屬

949
21 strokes

SHǓ, to belong to; genus, family; be subordinate

屬於 *shǔyú*, to belong to, be tantamount to
屬國 *shǔguó*, dependent territories; colonies
屬性 *shǔxìng*, qualities, attributes

属

畢	丶	口	日	**BÌ, to finish; family name**
	旦	旦	异	畢業 *bìyè*, to graduate 畢生 *bìshēng*, all one's life
950 11 strokes	艮	艮	畢	毕

拾	一	丁	扌	**SHÍ, to pick up; to find; ten**
	扌	払	扒	This is a form of 十 used in accounting (to minimize the possibility of error or fraud). 拾取 *shíqǔ*, to pick up, collect
951 9 strokes	拎	拾	拾	

亢	丶	二	亠	**KÀNG, be high, to go high; be haughty**
	亢			The student should distinguish this character from *yǔn* "to consent; sincere" 允 (878, above) and from *chōng* "fill up" 充 (879, above). 高亢 *gāokàng*, be sonorous, resounding 亢進 *kàngjìn*, be hyperactive (of a bodily organ — a medical term)
952 4 strokes				

航	丿	丿	力	**HÁNG, to sail, to navigate**
	舟	舟	舟	航空 *hángkōng*, aviation; air-, aerial 航行 *hángxíng*, to sail, to fly, to navigate 航線 *hángxiàn*, shipping route, flight route
953 10 strokes	舟	舟	航	

旅	亠	宀	方	**LǙ, to travel; troops, brigade**
	方	方	扩	旅社 *lǚshè*, inn 旅館 *lǚguǎn*, hotel 旅行 *lǚxíng*, to take a trip, to travel 旅長 *lǚzhǎng*, brigade commander
954 10 strokes	旅	旅	旅	

急	ノ	ク	⺈
	⺈	刍	刍
955 9 strokes	急	急	急

JÍ, be hurried; be upset; be urgent

急忙 *jímáng*, be hassled, busy
急救 *jíjiù*, first aid
着急 *zháojí*, to worry, feel anxious
急性子 *jíxìngzi*, to be an impatient type; an impatient type

寄	ˋ	ˊ	宀
	宀	宇	宎
956 11 strokes	宭	寄	寄

JÌ, to mail; to entrust; to dwell

寄信 *jìxìn*, to mail a letter
寄存 *jìcún*, to deposit; deposits
寄件人 *jìjiànrén*, sender
寄賣 *jìmài*, to consign (goods)

票	一	ˋ	二
	西	西	西
957 11 strokes	覀	票	票

PIÀO, ticket, stamp, bank note, check, document; vote

支票 *zhīpiào*, check
郵票 *yóupiào*, postage stamp
傳票 *chuánpiào*, summons (legal)
票房 *piàofáng*, a place to buy tickets; booking office, box office

布	一	ナ	才
	右	布	
958 5 strokes			

BÙ, cotton cloth; to publish; to spread, lay out; to announce

In the senses "to spread, to announce," the character 佈 is often used (see p. 265b).

一疋布 *yì pǐ bù*, a bolt of cloth (now usually written 一匹布)
布景 *bùjǐng*, stage scenery
布告 *bùgào*, notice, bulletin

奐	ノ	⺈	⺈
	刍	刍	刍
959 9 strokes	奐	奐	奐

HUÀN, be lively, be elegant

Not in modern use as an independent character, *huàn* serves to indicate the sound in some common characters (see, for example, 960 and 961, below).

				HUÀN, to call out
喚	丶	口	口	In this character, *huàn* (959, above) gives the sound; the "mouth" rad. gives the meaning.
	口⺊	吟	吟	喚起 *huànqǐ*, to incite, to stir up
960 12 strokes	呐	呬	喚	叫喚 *jiàohuàn*, to cry out, to shout

				HUÀN, to exchange
換	一	十	扌	換錢 *huànqián*, to change money 改換 *gǎihuàn*, to change
	扩	扩	抣	換取 *huànqǔ*, to get something by exchange, to barter for something
961 12 strokes	换	搀	換	換句話説 *huàn jù huà shuō*, in other words

				DĪ, stem, base
商	丶	亠	亠	Distinguish this character from *shāng* "merchant" 商 (622, above). The key is: what's above "mouth"? If "legs," then the character or part of a character is "merchant;" but if "ten" is above "mouth," then it's "stem, base." *Dī* does not now appear independently; it gives the sound in several characters. (口 33)
	亠	产	产	
962 11 strokes	产	商	商	

				SHÌ, to follow, chase; be suitable
適	亠	亠	产	適當 *shìdàng*, be proper, be suitable 合適 *héshì*, be appropriate
	产	商	商	適宜 *shìyí*, be suitable, to fit 適時 *shìshí*, be timely
963 14 strokes	滴	滴	適	适

				XIÉ, shoe
鞋	一	卄	卄	布鞋 *bùxié*, cloth shoes 皮鞋 *píxié*, leather shoes
	苎	莒	革	鞋底 *xiédǐ*, shoe sole 鞋跟 *xiégēn*, heel of a shoe
964 15 strokes	靯	靯	鞋	(口 33, 土 86)

223

德 965 15 strokes	ノ 什 德	ク 待 德	イ 待 德	**DÉ, virtue; personal energy; family name** Scholars say: the upper right part of *dé* is 真, "be real, be true" (302, above), distorted. With "heart" and "step" (for "action"), *dé* combines meanings: "true-heartedness in action," i.e. virtue. 德國 *Déguó*, Germany 同心同德 *tóng xīn tóng dé*, be of one heart and one mind (四 132)
彦 966 9 strokes	、 玄 彦	亠 产 彦	文 户	**YÀN, decoration** In *yàn* we see the "pattern" rad., the "slope" rad., and the "streaks" rad. The relevance of "pattern" and "streaks" to "decoration" is clear enough; the "slope" rad. originally was part of the decoration and did not mean "slope." Not in modern use independently.
顔 967 18 strokes	文 彦 顔	户 顔 顔	彦 顔 顔	**YÁN, color; face; family name** The "head" rad. gives the meaning; *yàn* (966, above) suggests the sound. 容顔 *róngyán*, looks, appearance 顔色 *yánsè*, color; countenance 顔面 *yánmiàn*, face; prestige, respect 颜
係 968 9 strokes	ノ 仁 係	イ 伾 係	イ 係 係	**XÌ, to connect; be related; to be** 關係 *guānxi*, relationship, relevance 係數 *xìshù*, coefficient (mathematics) 系
烟 969 10 strokes	、 火 炯	` ` 炯 炯	⺌ 炯 烟	**YĀN, smoke; tobacco, cigarette** For this word, the character 煙 is now often used. 烟袋 *yāndài*, pipe (for tobacco) 烟鬼 *yānguǐ*, opium addict; nicotine fiend 烟火 *yānhuǒ*, fireworks 香烟 *xiāngyān*, cigarette; smoke from incense

224

ZŪ, rent, to rent

In China, rent traditionally was land rent and was paid in grain, hence the "grain" rad. in *zū*.

租借 *zūjiè*, to lease
租户 *zūhù*, tenant; lessee
租金 *zūjīn*, amount of rent, rental

970
10 strokes

XŪ, to need

需要 *xūyào*, to need, need
必需 *bìxū*, be essential, be indispensable
需求 *xūqiú*, to require, to demand

(雨 283)

971
14 strokes

GUĂNG, be broad; family name

廣東 *Guǎngdōng*, Guangdong (old style "Canton") Province
廣告 *guǎnggào*, advertisement
廣大 *guǎngdà*, be big, numerous, extensive

(黃 604)

972
15 strokes

广

ZHÍ, be worth, to have a (certain) value

Usually printed 值.

值錢 *zhíqián*, be worth some money, be valuable
值得 *zhíde*, be worth…; be worthwhile
价值 *jiàzhí*, price

973
10 strokes

YÚ, to say "yes;" a family name

Usually printed 俞.

974
9 strokes

225

偷	ノ	イ	伫	**TŌU, to steal** 偷偷的 *tōutōude*, stealthily, on the sly 偷看 *tōukàn*, to steal a look at; to peep, look at surreptitiously 偷閒 *tōuxián*, to loaf, to shirk 偷稅 *tōushuì*, to evade tax
	伫	伶	价	
975 11 strokes	偷	偷	偷	

戎	一	二	于	**RÓNG, weapons of war, arms; family name** This character is a meaning-meaning compound. The student will recognize the right half, of course, as the "lance" rad. The other part — "one" + "left" in the modern character — is supposed to be armor: "armor" + "lance" = "weapons of war, arms."
	尢	戎	戎	
976 6 strokes				

賊	｜	冂	目	**ZÉI, thief; extremely** It is said that "one" + "left" in 賊 was 刀 "knife" (102, above) and that the combination of meanings is: the guy that gets his cowries (貝 , "money") with knife and lance: a thief. 有賊 *yǒu zéi*, Thief! 賣國賊 *màiguózéi*, traitor 工賊 *gōngzéi*, scab, strike-breaker 賊冷 *zéilěng*, (slang) be very cold
	貝	貝	貝	
977 13 strokes	財	賊	賊	賊

苟	一	十	艹	**GǑU, (bookish), negligent; if** This character used to mean "grass," and the "grass" rad. gave the meaning; the rest of the character, *jù* (289, above), gave the sound. Now the character is used by sound-loan for "negligent" and "if." 苟和 *gǒuhé*, illicit sex (literally, "negligent joining, negligent coupling")
	艹	艿	芍	
978 9 strokes	芍	苟	苟	

敬	一	丶	艹	**JÌNG, to revere; family name** 敬重 *jìngzhòng*, to respect a person 敬愛 *jìngài*, to honor 敬禮 *jìnglǐ*, to salute; salutation, formal greeting
	北	芍	苟	
979 13 strokes	苟攵	敬攵	敬	

226

警	﹀	﹀﹀	芍	**JĬNG, to warn**
	苟	苟攵	敬	*Jĭng* combines meanings: use "words" to induce "reverence, caution" = "warn."
980 20 strokes	敬攵	警	警	警告 *jĭnggào*, to warn, warning 警報 *jĭngbào*, warning signal 火警 *huǒjĭng*, fire alarm (言 38)

察	丶	八	宀	**CHÁ, to investigate**
	宀	罗	罗	警察 *jĭngchá*, policeman 警察局 *jĭngchájú*, police station 察看 *chákàn*, to look into
981 14 strokes	窛	窛	察	

銀	丿	𠂉	𠂋	**YÍN, silver; family name**
	午	金	釒	銀子 *yínzi*, silver 銀行 *yínháng*, bank (financial institution) 白銀 *báiyín*, silver 銀河 *yínhé*, the Milky Way
982 14 strokes	釕	銀	銀	银

辵	一	二	三	**CHUÒ, halt. HALT rad. (162)**
	辛	辛	乔	The "halt" rad. originally was a picture of a foot halted at a crossroads. Compare the form of "halt" which you have already learned (171, above). The form here is the form once used as an independent character (but not now in use independently).
983 7 strokes	辵			

銅	丿	𠂉	𠂋	**TÓNG, brass, copper, bronze**
	午	金	金	黃銅 *huángtóng*, bronze 紅銅 *hóngtóng*, copper 銅像 *tóngxiàng*, bronze statue
984 14 strokes	釘	銅	銅	铜

| | | | | (口 33) |

苦	一	十	艹	**KǓ, be bitter**
	芏	艼	芊	吃苦 *chīkǔ*, to suffer 苦處 *kǔchù*, hardship 甘苦 *gānkǔ*, "the sweet and the bitter," weal and woe
985 8 strokes (9 strokes)	苦	苦		叫苦 *jiàokǔ*, to complain, whine, "piss and moan"

約	ㄥ	纟	幺	**YUĒ, to agree**
	纟	纟	纟	約會 *yuēhuì*, appointment, engagement 條約 *tiáoyuē*, treaty 約定 *yuēdìng*, to agree to
986 9 strokes	糸	約	約	约

堂	㇑	ㅛ	ㅛ	**TÁNG, hall; a measure for classes**
	丷	屮	峃	講堂 *jiǎngtáng*, lecture hall 教堂 *jiàotáng*, church 一堂中文課 *yì táng Zhōngwén kè*, Chinese
987 11 strokes	堂	堂	堂	language class

躬	㇓	㇓	勹	**GŌNG, (bookish) the body; personally; to bend, to bow**
	身	身	身	The "torso" rad. (185, above) gives the meaning in this character; *gōng* (218) gives the sound.
988 10 strokes	躬	躬	躬	躬身 *gōngshēn*, to bend at the waist, to bow 躬親 *gōngqīn*, personally, in person

窮	㇔	八	宀	**QIÓNG, be poor, be impoverished**
	宊	宊	穷	窮苦 *qióngkǔ*, be very poor 窮忙 *qióngmáng*, be busy without purpose 哭窮 *kūqióng*, to complain about being
989 15 strokes	窮	窮	窮	poor; to go about pleading poverty 穷

228

静	二	丰	主	**JÌNG, be quiet; family name**
				安静 *ānjìng*, be quiet
				静電 *jìngdiàn*, static electricity
	青	青	青	静止 *jìngzhǐ*, be motionless, be static
990 16 strokes	靗	静	静	(青 198, 争 618)

興	⺈	⺈	目	**XĪNG, be happy; XÌNG, to begin; family name**
				高興 *gāoxìng*, be happy
	印	印	同	興建 *xīngjiàn*, to rebuild
				復興 *fùxīng*, be revived, to resurge
				紹興酒 *Shàoxīng jiǔ*, wine from Shaoxing
991 16 strokes	同	興	興	(widely recognized as very good Chinese wine) 兴

草	一	十	艹	**CǍO, grass**
				The "grass" rad. gives the meaning; *zǎo* (438, above) suggests the sound.
	艹	节	节	草地 *cǎodì*, lawn
				草帽 *cǎomào*, straw hat
				草字 *cǎozì*, cursive script
992 9 strokes (10 strokes)	苩	莗	草	斬草除根 *zhǎncǎo chúgēn*, to "slash the grass and remove the roots," to destroy thoroughly, to extirpate

雪	一	⺁	二	**XUĚ, snow; family name**
				下雪 *xiàxuě*, It's snowing; snowfall
	平	帚	帚	雪花 *xuěhuā*, snowflake
				雪人 (兒) *xuěrén(r)*, snowman
				昭雪 *zhāoxuě*, to right a wrong, to rehabilitate somebody (after unjust
993 11 strokes	雪	雪	雪	conviction or punishment)

鳥	⼂	⼂	⼽	**NIǍO, bird. BIRD rad. (196)(H152)**
				The "bird" rad. is a picture of a bird.
	自	自	鸟	鳥叫 *niǎojiào*, bird cries, birdsong
				鳥 *diǎo*, penis; used as an insult in old novels (note pronunciation)
994 11 strokes	鳥	鳥	鳥	鸟

229

場	一	十	土	**CHĂNG, field; a 'field,' of human activity or experience; a measure for events; CHÁNG; a measure for spells or periods of things**
	圤	坦	坦	一場大雨 *yì cháng dà yǔ*, a cloudburst 廣場 *guăngchăng*, public square 情場殺手 *qíngchăng shāshŏu*, a 'killer' in the area of emotion, lady-killer
995 12 strokes	垻	場	場	飛機場 *fēijīchăng*, airfield (場 686)　　場

圖	丨	冂	冋	**TÚ, picture, map, diagram**
	冋	昌	昌	圖書館 *túshūguăn*, library 地圖 *dìtú*, map 草圖 *căotú*, rough sketch or diagram 圖畫 *túhùa*, drawing, painting
996 14 strokes	冒	圖	圖	(囗 33)　　图

彑	ㄥ	ㄅ	彑	**JÌ, pig's head. PIG'S HEAD rad. (58)(H70)** The student already has learned one form of this rad. (80, above). Here, the horizontal stroke across the bottom is supposed to be the ground; the pig's head rises above it. Compare 緣 *yuán* (p.259a). In H, the forms ヨ and 彑 are also classified
997 3 strokes				as rad. 70.

彔	ㄥ	ㄅ	彑	**LÙ, prosperity** The explanations we have of this character are not helpful. The student will simply have to remember that "pig's head" over "water" = *lù* "prosperity." The character is now used only as a part of characters to give the sound.
	彐	彐	彐	
998 8 strokes	录	彔		

綠	ㄥ	乡	幺	**LÙ, be green** 草綠 *căolù*, grass green 綠豆 *lùdòu*, mung beans 綠燈 *lùdēng*, green light (as in traffic) 青山綠水 *qīngshān lùshuǐ*, (dark) green hills and green waters (i.e., lovely scenery)
	糸	糸	絲	
999 14 strokes	綧	綧	綠	绿

俄	ノ	イ	亻	**É; used to write foreign words**
1000 9 strokes	仁	仟	俟	俄國 *Éguó*, Russia 俄語 *Éyǔ*, Russian language 俄國革命 *Éguó gémìng*, Russian Revolution
	俄	俄	俄	

害	、	丷	宀	**HÀI, to harm; be harmed by, 'catch' (i.e., a disease); evil, calamity**
1001 10 strokes	宀	宇	宔	害病 *hàibìng*, to get sick 害怕 *hàipà*, to get scared 殺害 *shāhài*, to murder, to kill (someone) 害蟲 *hàichóng*, pests, harmful bugs
	宔	害	害	

柬	一	丆	帀	**JIĂN, to select**
1002 9 strokes	帀	帀	両	The character combines meanings. It is composed of "bundle" 束 (657, above) + two dots resembling the "eight" rad. (88, above). The two dots mean "to divide," and the character is explained: "to divide a bundle; therefore, 'to select.'" In modern Chinese, it means "a note, a card." Cf. 揀, p. 291a.
	帀	柬	柬	

練	㇜	纟	幺	**LIÀN, to practice; family name**
1003 15 strokes	幺	糸	糹	練習 *liànxí*, practice; to practice 練字 *liànzì*, to study Chinese characters 老練 *lǎoliàn*, be seasoned, be experienced
	絅	紳	練	练

秝	丿	二	千	**LÌ, to set up at regular intervals; to set up and space out**
1004 10 strokes	禾	禾	禾	The character's two "grain" rads. are intended to suggest the regular spacing of the plants in a field of grain. Not in modern use as an independent character.
	秝	秝	秝	

231

麻	一	厂	厂
	𠂆	厈	厈
1005 12 strokes	厈	厡	麻

LÌ, to pass through

In rural China, the main routes of passage in many places are roads or paths on the dikes that crisscross the paddies. It is perhaps for this reason that the "slope" rad. is in *lì* "to pass through," while the two grain rads. suggest the paddy. Not in modern use as an independent character.

曆	一	厂	𠂆
	厈	厈	麻
1006 16 strokes	曆	曆	曆

LÌ, to calculate the course of heavenly bodies as they pass through the Zodiac; to make a calendar; to calculate

陽曆 *yánglì*, solar calendar
陰曆 *yīnlì*, lunar calendar

历

歷	一	厂	𠂆
	厈	麻	麻
1007 16 strokes	厤	歷	歷

LÌ, to pass through

Compare 1005, above. The character is reclarified with the "toe" rad.

歷史 *lìshǐ*, history
經歷 *jīnglì*, experience, to experience
歷來 *lìlái*, always; through the years

历

私	一	二	千
	禾	禾	私
1008 7 strokes	私		

SĪ, private; selfish

私事 *sīshì*, personal affair
私立 *sīlì*, be privately run (like a private school or hospital)
自私 *zìsī*, be selfish
私生活 *sīshēnghuó*, private life

斗	丶	丷	三
	斗		
1009 4 strokes			

DǑU, unit of volume equal to 316 cubic inches, usually translated as "peck." PECK rad. (68)(H82)

This character is a picture of the old scoop or measure which was used to measure out "pecks." *Dǒu* is now primarily seen in use as the short form for 鬥 (679, above).

KĒ, category

The student should distinguish 科 from *liào* "material" 料 (p. 256a).

科學 *kēxué*, science
科長 *kēzhǎng*, department chief (in a government office)
文科 *wénkē*, liberal arts

1010
9 strokes

TÒNG, to ache

頭痛 *tóutòng*, to have a headache
痛苦 *tòngkǔ*, be unhappy
痛快 *tòngkuài*, be happy
痛處 *tòngchù*, sore spot, tender spot

1011
12 strokes

(甬 715)

YÁO, be high

It may help the student to remember this character if he thinks of it as "earth piled on earth" to suggest "high." The character is most often seen as the name of the Emperor Yao (traditional dates of reign, 2357–2255 B.C.), a Chinese culture hero.

尧

1012
12 strokes

SHĀO, to burn

燒飯 *shāofàn*, to cook a meal
發燒 *fāshāo*, to have a fever
燒開水 *shāokāi shuǐ*, to boil water
紅燒肉 *hóngshāoròu*, pork stewed in soy sauce

烧

1013
16 strokes

XIĂO, be clear; dawn; to understand

曉得 *xiǎode*, to know, to know of
曉示 *xiǎoshì*, to proclaim
通曉 *tōngxiǎo*, to know quite well, to be proficient in

晓

1014
16 strokes

233

檢	一	十	才
	术	朴	柃
1015 **17 strokes**	柃	検	檢

JIǍN, to look into

檢查 *jiǎnchá*, to examine
檢查官 *jiǎncháguān*, district attorney
檢點 *jiǎndiǎn*, to check; to speak or act cautiously (literally, to look into [even] the dots)

检

藥	一	十	艹
	艻	苩	茒
1016 **18 strokes** **(19 strokes)**	滋	藥	藥

YÀO, medicine; (some) chemicals

吃藥 *chīyào*, to take medicine
藥房 *yàofáng*, drugstore
西藥 *xīyào*, Western (non-Chinese) medicine
火藥 *huǒyào*, gunpowder
殺蟲藥 *shāchóngyào*, bug-killing chemical (i.e., insecticide)
(白 231, 幺 25)

药

球	二	干	王
	王'	刲	珇
1017 **11 strokes**	珇	球	球

QIÚ, ball, orb, round thing

打球 *dǎqiú*, to play ball
球場 *qiúchǎng*, ball field
地球 *dìqiú*, the earth, the globe
足球 *zúqiú*, soccer; (American) football; the ball used in either of those sports
网球 *wǎngqiú*, tennis; tennis ball

園	丨	冂	門
	周	周	周
1018 **13 strokes**	周	園	

YUÁN, garden, park

公園 *gōngyuán*, public park
花園 *huāyuán*, flower garden
園丁 *yuándīng*, gardener

(土 86, 口 33)

园

虘	丶	卜	上
	卢	卢	虍
1019 **13 strokes**	虘	虘	虘

XĪ, crockery dish

The "flask" rad. is in this character for meaning; the significance of the "tiger" rad. is uncertain. Traditional art includes many dishes in animal shapes, so a *xī* may have been a tiger-shaped crockery dish. Not in modern use as an independent character.

(豆 453)

戲	卜	广	虍
	虗	虘	虘
1020 17 strokes	戲	戲	戲

XÌ, (theater) play

Popular variant 戯.

京戲 *jīngxì*, Beijing opera
看戲 *kànxì*, to attend a play
戲院 *xìyuàn*, theater
馬戲 *mǎxì*, circus

戏

拉	一	十	扌
	扌	扩	扩
1021 8 strokes	扩	拉	

LĀ, to pull; used for foreign words

拉手 *lāshǒu*, to shake hands; to hold hands
拉皮條 *lāpítiáo*, to pimp, to act as a
　　　　procurer
拉丁文 *Lādīngwén*, Latin language

隻	丿	亻	亻
	仁	佳	隹
1022 10 strokes	隻	隻	

ZHĪ, a measure for animals, birds, boats; single

Cp. 1023, below. The student should
distinguish 隻 from 集, "to get together"
(1025, below).

隻言片語 *zhīyán piànyǔ*, a word or two; a
　　　　　smattering of conversation
一隻鳥 *yī zhī niǎo*, a bird
一隻船 *yī zhī chuán*, a boat
隻身 *zhīshēn*, oneself, alone

只

雙	丿	亻	亻
	仁	佳	隹
1023 18 strokes	雔	雙	雙

SHUĀNG, pair; even (opposite of "odd")

雙數 *shuāngshù*, an even number
雙關語 *shuāngguānyǔ*, paronomasia, a pun
一雙 *yī shuāng*, a pair

双

邑	丶	口	口
	吕	吕	吕
1024 7 strokes	邑		

YÌ, city. CITY rad. (163)

The student already has learned the form of
"city" which occurs as a part of characters
(136, above). The form here is the
independent form of the rad.

城邑 *chéngyì*, city

JÍ, to get together; family name

The student should distinguish this character from 隻, the measure for animals, birds, boats (1022, above).

全集 *quánjí*, complete works (of an author)
集會 *jíhuì*, to gather, to assemble
集中 *jízhōng*, to concentrate

1025
12 strokes

DÀN, egg

下蛋 *xiàdàn*, to lay an egg
壞蛋 *huàidàn*, a "bad egg" (that is, a bad person)
蛋白石 *dànbáishí*, opal
王八蛋 *wángbādàn*, bastard (insulting expression)

1026
11 strokes

CHÉNG, be sincere

誠實 *chéngshí*, be sincere, be honest
誠心 *chéngxīn*, sincerity, wholeheartedness
誠意 *chéngyì*, good faith, sincerity
真誠 *zhēnchéng*, be sincere, be true

诚

1027
13 strokes
(14 strokes)

QÙ, be interesting, be pleasant

有興趣 *yǒuxìngqù*, be interested in
有趣 *yǒuqù*, be interesting
趣味 *qùwèi*, interest

(耳 201)

1028
15 strokes

LĚI, plow. PLOW rad. (127)(H176)

The character is a picture. Note that it appears to include the "tree" rad. The extra horizontal strokes are supposed to represent the blades of the plow.

1029
6 strokes

負	刁	刀	刀	**FÙ, back; to carry on the back; negative; to turn one's back on, be ungrateful**
	刍	刍	刍	Distinguish *fù* from *pín* "be poor" 貧 (p. 260). Variant 负. 負號 *fùhào*, minus sign 負約 *fùyuē*, to break an agreement
1030 9 strokes	負	負		负

賴	一	一	一	**LÀI, to hang about (too long); to attempt to deny responsibility; to blame others; family name**
	曰	束	束	賴婚 *làihūn*, break a marriage promise 別總賴我 *bié zǒng lài wǒ*, How come I get blamed for everything? 賴不了了，只好走 *làibuliǎo le, zhǐ hǎo zǒu*, We can't stay here, let's go!
1031 16 strokes	束	賴	賴	賴學 *làixué*, to cut classes 賴皮 *làipí*, to have no honor 赖

懶	'	∣	ㅑ	**LǍN, be lazy**
	忄	忄	忄	偷懶 *tōulǎn*, to dodge work, be lazy 懶洋洋 *lǎnyángyáng*, be languid, take your own sweet time (to do something)
1032 19 strokes	懶	懶	懶	懒

奚	′	⺌	⺌	**XĪ, (bookish) "big belly;" used as a sound-loan; family name**
	爫	爫	爫	The "big" rad. at the bottom gives the meaning of this character. The rest of the character, "claws" + "coil," once gave the sound. *Xī* is now used as a sound-loan for various words: "who? what? why?" the name of an old Tartar tribe; etc.
1033 10 strokes	奚	奚	奚	

鷄	⺌	乑	奚	**JĪ, chicken**
	奚	奚	奚	*Xī* is supposed to give the sound in this character; the "bird" rad. gives the meaning. The student may also see *jī* "chicken" written with the "dove" rad. (39, above) instead of the "bird" rad. for meaning: 雞
1034 21 strokes	鷄	鷄	鷄	公鷄 *gōngjī*, rooster 鷄蛋 *jīdàn*, egg (鳥 994) 鸡

237

				JÌ, to calculate, to reckon; strategem, plan; family name
計	丶	二	三	計算 *jìsuàn*, to compute
	言	言	言	計算機 *jìsuànjī*, calculator, computer (computers are commonly called *diànnǎo* "電腦" "electric brains;" for 腦, see p. 250a).
1035 **9 strokes**	言	言	計	百年大計 *bǎinián dàjì*, a (very) long-range plan; a project of lasting importance 計

				YÈ, foliage
枼	一	十	卅	*Yè* is a picture of a tree; the strokes at the top represent its foliage.
	卅	世	世	
1036 **9 strokes**	芔	枼	枼	

				YÈ, a leaf; a surname
葉	一	十	艹	This is the same word as 1036, above. The character is reclarified with the "grass" rad. This form is the form in common use today; 1036 is seldom seen.
	艹	芊	芷	綠葉 *lǜyè*, green leaves
1037 **12 strokes** **(13 strokes)**	莊	葉	葉	叶

				HUÀ, to mark; to cut, to engrave; **HUÁ**, to row (a boat); to pay off, be profitable; to scratch
劃	ㄱ	ㄱ	刁	計劃 *jìhuà*, to plan, plan
	聿	聿	書	劃分 *huàfēn*, to cut apart; to dissociate 劃定 *huàdìng*, to delimit
1038 **14 strokes**	畫	畫	劃	劃算 *huásuàn*, to calculate; to pay off (be profitable) 划

				TUÁN, corps, club; a measure for round things
團	丨	冂	冂	團體 *tuántǐ*, organization
	同	同	同	團結 *tuánjié*, to unite 一團線 *yì tuán xiàn*, ball of string
1039 **14 strokes**	團	團	團	团

享	、	亠	宀

XIĂNG, to offer a sacrifice; to receive

This character is a picture of "a dish on which cooked food was offered as a sacrifice; the lid is on." This character is very much like the "flask" rad. 豆 (453, above).

享受 *xiǎngshòu*, to receive; to enjoy
享樂 *xiǎnglè*, to lead a lazy, pleasure-seeking life

1040
8 strokes

孰	、	亠	宀

SHÚ, (bookish) be cooked; be done; who? which?

The basic meaning of this character is "be cooked, be done." The meaning "who? which?" occurs by sound-loan.

孰是孰非 *shú shì shú fēi*, Which is right? Which is wrong?

1041
11 strokes

熟	亠	亩	享

SHÚ, be cooked, be done; be ripe; be very familiar with (also SHÓU)

熟 and 孰, above, originally stood for the same word; 熟 here is reclarified with "fire dots." Distinguish 熱 (678) — look at the upper left-hand corners.

熟人 *shúrén*, acquaintance, friend, "buddy"
熟手 *shúshǒu*, skilled person, "old hand"

1042
15 strokes

油	、	丶	氵

YÓU, oil

石油 *shíyóu*, petroleum
牛油 *niúyóu*, butter
汽油 *qìyóu*, gasoline
鞋油 *xiéyóu*, shoe polish

1043
8 strokes

香	一	二	千

XIĀNG, smell sweet, be fragrant; incense, scent. SCENT rad. (186)

Xiāng once had "grain" over "sweet" and was a meaning-meaning compound. Now the "sweet" rad. 甘 is 日 "sun."

香水 *xiāngshuǐ*, perfume
鳥語花香 *niǎoyǔ huāxiāng*, "The birds chatter and the flowers smell sweet" (used to evoke a fine spring day).

1044
9 strokes

239

齊	亠	㐄	亣	**QÍ, to line up, to arrange; be even, be uniform; family name. LINE-UP rad. (210) (the short form is H rad. 160)**
	亦	厺	㐂	This rad. is supposed to be a picture of neatly arranged hairpins in a lady's coiffure.
1045 14 strokes	㐃	齊	齊	齊全 *qíquán*, complete; ready to go 百花齊放 *bǎi huā qí fàng*, "Let a hundred flowers bloom!" 齐

濟	丶	冫	氵	**JÌ, to help out; to complete**
	汇	沪	泲	經濟 *jīngjì*, economy; be economical 經濟學 *jīngjìxué*, economics 經濟學家 *jīngjìxuéjiā*, economist
1046 17 strokes	濟	濟	濟	济

較	一	冖	百	**JIÀO, to compare**
	亘	車	車	比較 *bǐjiào*, to compare 較量 *jiàoliàng*, to compare, to match; to contrast
1047 13 strokes	車	車	較	较

壯	L	丩	丬	**ZHUÀNG, be strong**
	爿	爿	壯	壯丁 *zhuàngdīng*, (archaic) able-bodied man; man subject to the draft 壯年 *zhuàngnián*, the prime of life 壯大 *zhuàngdà*, get stronger, expand; strengthen
1048 7 strokes	壯			壯

裝	丩	爿	壯	**ZHUĀNG, to load up**
	壯	壯	芺	裝運 *zhuāngyùn*, to load up and transport 裝門面 *zhuāngménmiàn*, be pretentious, put up a front 服裝 *fúzhuāng*, dress, attire, costume
1049 13 strokes	裝	裝	裝	装

240

慣	ヽ	忄	忄	**GUÀN, be used to**
	忄	忄	忄	習慣 xíguàn, habits 慣性 guànxìng, inertia 慣用 guànyòng, use habitually; be customary, habitual
1050 14 strokes	忄	慣	慣	惯

輕	一	亓	百	**QĪNG, be light (in weight)**
	車	車	軒	輕重 qīngzhòng, weight 輕工業 qīng gōngyè, light industry 輕而易舉 qīng ér yì jǔ, be easy to do
1051 14 strokes	車	輕	輕	轻

器	ヽ	口	口	**QÌ, dish, implement**
	叩	叩	罗	Why should four mouths and a dog mean "dish"? Scholars have different explanations, some fanciful. All agree that the mouths stand for people. Dishes for people and for the dog: all kinds of dishes?
1052 16 strokes	哭	哭	器	機器 jīqì, machine, engine 鐵器 tiěqì, hardware, iron tools 器官 qìguān, organ (of the body)

架	フ	力	加	**JIÀ, frame; a measure for airplanes**
	加	加	加	架子 jiàzi, frame 書架 shūjià, bookshelf 一架飛機 yī jià fēijī, an airplane 打架 dǎjià, get into a fight (with)
1053 9 strokes	架	架	架	

基	一	十	廿	**JĪ, base**
	甘	其	其	基本 jīběn, be basic, be fundamental 基地 jīdì, base (military) 基金 jījīn, a fund
1054 11 strokes	其	基	基	

241

洛	`	`	⺡
	⺡	沙	汐
1055 **9 strokes**	洛	洛	洛

LUÒ; the name of a river; a family name; used to write foreign words

洛陽 *Luòyáng*, Luoyang (old style "Loyang" — famous ancient capital of China)

落	一	十	艹
	艹	艹	艹
1056 **12 strokes**	莎	茨	落

LUÒ, to fall, to come down; to let fall, to drop; LÀ, to leave out, be left out; to leave behind; to lag

落下來 *luòxiàlái*, to fall (leaves)
降落 *jiàngluò*, to land (airplanes)
落第 *luòdì*, to fail an exam
丟三落四 *diū sān là sì*, be absent-minded, be scatter-brained (literally, "to lose three [things] and leave behind four")

志	一	十	士
	士	志	志
1057 **7 strokes**	志		

ZHÌ, will, volition

See 1058, below, for a note on *zhì*.

壯志 *zhuàngzhì*, be determined, resolute
志向 *zhìxiàng*, one's intention, aspiration
志願 *zhìyuàn*, ambitions, "heart's desire"
同志 *tóngzhì*, "Comrade"

誌	`	⺀	言
	言	言	計
1058 **14 strokes**	計	誌	誌

ZHÌ, to remember; to record, record

In modern use, 誌 is often replaced by 志 — 1057, above.

雜誌 *zázhì*, magazine (publication)
誌喜 *zhìxǐ*, to express one's joy

志

聯	一	丌	耳
	耳	耴	聯
1059 **17 strokes**	聯	聯	聯

LIÁN, to unite

聯和國 *Liánhéguó*, United Nations
聯想 *liánxiǎng*, association of ideas (psychological term)
聯貫 *liánguàn*, to string together

(幺 25)

联

穌

1060
16 strokes

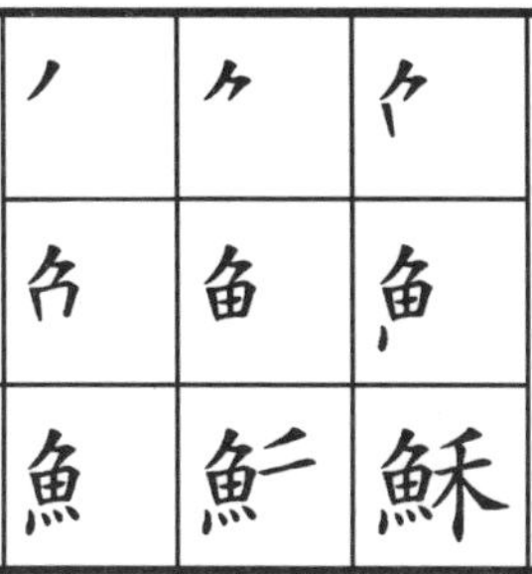

SŪ, to revive

Sū is supposed to suggest "to revive" by means of suggesting a good meal: "fish" + "grain" = "a good meal."

(魚 558, 禾 65) 稣

蘇

1061
19 strokes
(20 strokes)

SŪ, Suzhou (old style "Soochow" — city famous for its scenery, canals, and gardens); used to write foreign words

Originally this character, like 1060, above, meant "to revive" and was 1060 reclarified with the "grass" rad. (for vegetables, perhaps).

蘇聯 *Sūlián*, Soviet Union

復蘇 *fùsū*, to revive, to be revived

苏

司

1062
5 strokes

SĪ, to control; company

公司 *gōngsī*, company, corporation

司機 *sījī*, chauffeur, driver

司令 *sīlìng*, (military) commander

REMAINING CHARACTERS

of the "1,020 List" and the "2,000 List"

和	HÉ, and, with; to make peace; HUÒ, to mix; HUO; a verb-suffix: "comfortably"	破	PÒ, be broken 破壞 *pòhuài*, to wreck; to change drastically
章	ZHĀNG, chapter, section, paragraph; a measure	須	XŪ, must; be necessary 須要 *xūyào*, must 须
初	CHŪ, the beginning, the first	川	CHUĀN, river. RIVER rad. (47) Compare 442, above.
段	DUÀN, paragraph, section, passage (of writing); a measure	順	SHÙN, to move with; to agree with; favorable; prosperous 顺
辭	CÍ, word or expression; to decline; to resign, to fire 辞	訓	XÙN, to give advice 訓練 *xùnliàn*, to drill 训
疲	PÍ, be worn out	煩	FÁN, to pester, to annoy 麻煩 *máfan*, be troublesome 烦
波	BŌ, a wave; to flow 波動 *bōdòng*, to undulate	絕	JUÉ, to break off; (before a negative) very 绝
坡	PŌ, slope, bank 坡度 *pōdù*, gradient	暖	NUĂN, be warm 暖和 *nuǎnhuo*, be warm
婆	PÓ, old woman; mother-in-law; stepmother	援	YUÁN, to pull along; to give a hand to, to aid

緩	HUǍN, be slack; to goof off; be late 緩	似	SÌ, to resemble (also pronounced *shì* in some combinations)
啦	LA; a sentence-final particle = 了 + 啊	罪	ZUÌ, crime; suffering, to suffer
倒	DÀO, on the contrary; be flipped, be upside down; DǍO, to fall, topple	野	YĚ, be wild, uncivilized 野心 *yěxīn*, be overly ambitious
舒	SHŪ, to relax, to stretch out 舒展 *shūzhǎn*, fold out; limber up	印	YÌN, to print; to tally, agree; family name
責	ZÉ, responsibility 責任 *zérèn*, responsibility 责	功	GŌNG, achievement; effectiveness; hard work
積	JĪ, to accumulate 積極 *jījí*, be energetic, positive 积	攻	GŌNG, to attack 攻破 *gōngpò*, to break through
績	JĪ, to join threads; to finish; accomplishment 绩	貢	GÒNG, tax, to tax; contribution; to announce 贡
債	ZHÀI, to owe money; debt 借債 *jièzhài*, to borrow money 债	項	XIÀNG, nape of the neck; a measure for articles in documents or for items 项
轉	ZHUǍN, to turn 轉變 *zhuǎnbiàn*, to transform 转	散	SÀN, to scatter, to disperse 散布 *sànbù*, to spread
確	QUÈ, be true, be definite 确	繼	JÌ, to continue, to succeed to 继
吹	CHUĪ, to blow 吹牛 *chuīniú*, to boast	斷	DUÀN, to break into segments; to stop (doing something); to decide a law case 断

246

續	XÙ, to add to; to prolong; to follow 续
讀	DÚ, to recite; to study 讀本 *dúběn*, text-book 读
贖	SHÚ, to redeem, to ransom; to atone for 赎
致	ZHÌ, to send; to cause 致意 *zhìyì*, pay respects to
肝	GĀN, the liver 肝炎 *gānyán*, hepatitis
幹	GÀN, to do 幹活 *gànhuó*, work, to work 干
旱	HÀN, drought; dry land 旱年 *hànnián*, year of drought
桿	GĀN, pole; GǍN; a measure for rifles, pistols, spears 杆
稈	GǍN, grain stalk; straw 秆
趕	GǍN, to rush after, to rush at; to chase off; by the time that… 赶
刊	KĀN, to carve, to engrave. Printed 刊.

岸	ÀN, high cliff, high riverbank
奸	JIĀN, be crafty, be treacherous; traitor; illicit sex
訂	DÌNG, to investigate; to decide; to revise for publication 订
釘	DĪNG, nail 釘帽 *dīngmào*, nailhead 钉
頂	DǏNG, top of the head; to carry on the head; be lofty; to oppose; very 顶
若	RUÒ, if 若是 *ruòshì*, if
偶	OǓ, be accidental; be even (numbers); image (of a person); spouse
遇	YÙ, to run into 遇事 *yùshì*, when something happens, as, 如遇火警, if there's a fire
列	LIÈ, line, rank, to line up, to rank; each; a measure for trains
例	LÌ, example 例如 *lìrú*, for example
烈	LIÈ, to blaze; be brilliant or famous

裂	LIÈ, to split 分裂 *fēnliè*, to split	鄰	LÍN, neighbor 鄰近 *línjìn*, to adjoin
劇	JÙ, stage play; be severe; be intense 剧	憐	LIÁN, to pity 憐愛 *liánài*, to love tenderly 怜
祕	MÌ, be secret, be private	眼	YǍN, eye; hole; a measure for glances, wells, and musical beats
密	MÌ, be secluded; be deep; be secret, be mysterious; be still	班	BĀN; a measure for classes (students), squads, and trips (flights, trains); shift, troupe
蜜	MÌ, honey 蜜月 *mìyuè*, honeymoon	小	XĪN, HEART rad. (61). Compare 70, above. This form occurs only as a part of characters.
退	TUÌ, to back off; to give back; to fade	添	TIĀN, to add on
腿	TUǏ, leg, thigh 大腿 *dàtuǐ*, thigh	犭	QUǍN, DOG rad. (94)(H69) Compare 541, above. This form occurs only as a part of characters.
餓	È, hungry 饿	猜	CĀI, to guess 猜想 *cāixiǎng*, to suppose
掛	GUÀ, to hang 掛號 *guàhào*, to register (as, at a hospital; also, a letter)	倉	CĀNG, granary 倉房 *cāngfáng*, storehouse 仓
待	DÀI, to deal with; to wait for 待命 *dàimìng*, wait for orders	蒼	CĀNG, sky; be sky blue; be pale; be gray; lush vegetation 苍
玄	XUÁN, be dark; be abstruse; be absurd. DARK rad. (95)	槍	QIĀNG, spear; pistol, rifle 枪

248

搶	QIǍNG, to rob, to snatch 搶救 qiǎngjiù, to rescue <div align="right">抢</div>	碼	MǍ, to lay in neat piles; yard (of cloth); a counter or marker <div align="right">码</div>
瘡	CHUĀNG, sore, abcess, ulcer <div align="right">疮</div>	豈	QǏ, How can it be that…? 豈有此理 qǐ yǒu cǐ lǐ, outrageous! Bunkum! <div align="right">岂</div>
創	CHUÀNG, to begin; CHUĀNG, to wound <div align="right">创</div>	碗	WǍN, bowl 飯碗 fànwǎn, "rice bowl," livelhood
養	YǍNG, to support (one's dependents); to nourish <div align="right">养</div>	強	QIÁNG, be strong; might; QIǍNG, to force, to compel; JIÀNG, be stubborn
指	ZHǏ, to point; finger 指示 zhǐshì, to point out	盜	DÀO, to rob, robber 盜用 dàoyòng, to embezzle
脂	ZHĪ, animal fat, lard, ointment; cosmetics; wealth	狗	GǑU, dog 走狗 zǒugǒu, "running dog," stooge, toady
增	ZĒNG, to add to 增添 zēngtiān, to add	磅	BÀNG, a pound (weight; unit of English money); to weigh
贈	ZÈNG, to give a present, to present <div align="right">赠</div>	況	KUÀNG, even more so Also printed 况. 況且 kuàngqiě, furthermore
層	CÉNG, story (of a building) <div align="right">层</div>	村	CŪN, village 村長 cūnzhǎng, village chief
媽	MĀ, mama, "ma;" woman servant, nurse <div align="right">妈</div>	材	CÁI, material; ability, "genius"; coffin
罵	MÀ, to scold; to curse 罵名 màmíng, bad reputation <div align="right">骂</div>	財	CÁI, wealth 財產 cáichǎn, property <div align="right">财</div>

腦	NǍO, brain 頭腦, *tóunǎo*, brain 脑	輸	SHŪ, to lose (as in gambling) Printed 輸. 输
弄	NÒNG, to do, to handle; to make; to play with, fool with	猪	ZHŪ, pig (often written 豬) 母猪, *mǔzhū*, sow
獸	SHÒU, animal 野獸, *yěshòu*, wild animal 兽	煮	ZHǓ, to boil, to cook up
牀	CHUÁNG, bed (now often written 床) 牀位 *chuángwèi*, bunk	著	ZHÙ, to spread out, to display, be displayed; to author
店	DIÀN, store, inn 店鋪 *diànpù*, shop, store	暑	SHǓ, summer, summer heat
碎	SUÌ, be smashed, be in bits and pieces	緒	XÙ, end of a thread; clue; to tie together; succession; dynasty; profession 绪
醉	ZUÌ, be drunk 醉鬼 *zuìguǐ*, drunkard, wino	賭	DǓ, gamble, bet on 打賭 *dǎdǔ*, to make a bet 赌
虧	KUĪ, to lose, to fail; fortunately, happily 亏	屠	TÚ, to butcher 屠殺 *túshā*, to massacre
醒	XǏNG, to wake up 醒酒 *xǐngjiǔ*, to sober up	竟	JÌNG, to end; in the end, after all
腥	XĪNG, smell (of fish or raw meat)	境	JÌNG, a field's edge; borders; region; circumstances
牌	PÁI, placard 路牌 *lùpái*, signpost, road sign	鏡	JÌNG, mirror, lens 鏡頭 *jìngtóu*, lens 镜

250

物	WÙ, thing, object 動物 dòngwù, animal	筒	TŎNG, tube, large cylinder
討	TĂO, to ask for; to marry (be a groom); to discuss 讨	卤	LŬ, natural salt. SALT rad. (197) 卤
罰	FÁ, to punish 罰金 fájīn, a fine 罚	喊	HĂN, to yell 喊叫 hănjiào, to cry out
驚	JĪNG, to scare 驚人 jīngrén, be amazing 惊	感	GĂN, to feel (emotionally); to move (emotionally); to appreciate
濕	SHĪ, be wet 濕氣 shīqì, dampness 湿	鹹	XIÁN, be salty 鹹菜 xiáncài, salted vegetables 咸
顯	XIĂN, be visible; to show; be note worthy 显	关	JUĂN, roll; rolled rice dumpling (H.rad.158)
暗	ÀN, be dark 暗淡 àndàn, be dim, gloomy	卷	JUÀN, roll, scroll; section or chapter
窗	CHUĀNG, window 窗戶 chuānghu, a window	捲	JUĂN, to roll up 捲入 juănrù, to get involved in 卷
泥	NÍ, mud; NÌ, to daub with mud or plaster	倦	JUÀN, be tired, be weak 疲倦 píjuàn, be tired, be weak
毀	HUĬ, to break apart; to destroy	圈	QUĀN, circle; to encircle; JUĀN, to imprison; JUÀN, pen, fold (e.g., of sheep)
洞	DÒNG, cave, hole; incisively	券	QUÀN, bond, deed, contract, diploma

251

拳	QUÁN, fist; to tuck in; a measure for punches (with the fist)
勝	SHÈNG, victory 勝利 shènglì, victory 胜
騰	TÉNG, to make room for; to ride up on; TĒNG, to steam 腾
滕	TÉNG, a family name
籐	TÉNG, climbing plant, vine; rattan, cane
膝	XĪ, knee
漆	QĪ, to paint, to varnish; paint
夢	MÈNG, dream 夢想 mèngxiǎng, to dream of 梦
賀	HÈ, send a present with congratulations; to congratulate 贺
晴	QÍNG, clear sky 晴空 qíngkōng, blue sky
睛	JĪNG, pupil of the eye 眼睛 yǎnjing, eye

傘	SǍN, umbrella 雨傘 yǔsǎn, umbrella 伞
詩	SHĪ, poem, a shi poem, poetry 诗
持	CHÍ, to support; to grasp, to hold; to manage; to restrain
拔	BÁ, to pull up, to pull out 拔除 báchú, to remove
髮	FÀ, hair 頭髮 tóufa, (human-head) hair 发
監	JIĀN, to supervise; prison 监
鹽	YÁN, salt 鹽水 yánshuǐ, brine 盐
藍	LÁN, be blue (color); family name 蓝
籃	LÁN, basket (usually with a curved handle); "basket" in basketball 篮
覽	LǍN, to look at 览
播	BŌ, to spread, to scatter 播音 bōyīn, to broadcast

翻	FĀN, to flip; translate; search through; change one's attitude; to reprint; go over (a hill)
擇 择	ZÉ, ZHÁI, to pick out
澤 泽	ZÉ, marsh; to dampen; to enrich; to favor
譯 译	YÌ, to explain, to interpret, to translate
釋 释	SHÌ, to loosen up, to explain
漸 渐	JIÀN, gradually 漸顯 jiànxiǎn, fade in (movie term)
符	FÚ, symbol; written charm or incantation
附	FÙ, to attach 附近 fùjìn, be near to
腐	FÚ, to decay 腐化 fǔhuà, to turn rotten
它	TĀ, it
引	YǏN, to lead, to draw out 引起 yǐnqǐ, to give rise to

途	TÚ, road; trip; career 途中 túzhōng, en route
農 农	NÓNG, farming 農業 nóngyè, agriculture
濃 浓	NÓNG, be heavy, be thick, be strong in flavor; be intense (as one's interest can be)
扁	BIĂN, door-plaque; signboard; be flat
遍	BIÀN, to go around; be ubiquitous; a turn, a time
編 编	BIĀN, to weave, to braid; to classify; to compile
偏	PIĀN, to lean to one side; be partial; on the side; secondary
篇	PIĀN, article, essay; a measure for articles, essays
騙 骗	PIÀN, to fool, to cheat 騙人 piànrén, B.S! Nonsense!
旗	QÍ, flag 國旗 guóqí, national flag
揮 挥	HUĪ, to wave; to sprinkle; to wipe away

253

勞	LÁO, hard work 疲勞 pílǎo, be weary 劳	儉	JIǍN, be thrifty, be frugal 儉省 jiǎnshěng, be thrifty 俭
撈	LĀO, to drag for, to fish for; to make money improperly 捞	簽	QIĀN, to sign (formally); lots (as in "draw lots"); label 签
榮	RÓNG, to flourish, be glorious 荣	驗	YÀN, to try out, to examine 驗證 yànzhèng, to verify 验
營	YÍNG, camp; battalion; to manage 营	麗	LÌ, be beautiful 丽
弱	RUÒ, be weak 弱點 ruòdiǎn, weakness, weak point	福	FÚ, good luck 福利 fúlì, prosperity; material benefits
妻	QĪ, wife	副	FÙ, assistant 副手 fùshǒu, assistant
贊	ZÀN, to approve 贊成 zànchéng, to approve of 赞	富	FÙ, be rich, abundant; family name
讚	ZÀN, to praise, to eulogize 赞	朝	ZHĀO, morning; CHÁO, dynasty; imperial; reign; to face; visit a superior
鑽	ZUĀN, to worm into; to drill; to study hard; ZUÀN, to bore into; a drill 钻	潮	CHÁO, tide; be damp 低潮 dīcháo, low tide
潛	QIÁN, to lie under water; to ford; be hidden Usually written 潜.	廟	MIÀO, temple 庙
蠶	CÁN, silkworm; sericulture 蚕	碰	PÈNG, to touch; to run into 碰頭 pèngtóu, to talk over

舞	WǓ, dance 舞動 wǔdòng, to brandish	恭	GŌNG, be respectful 恭喜 gōngxǐ, Congratulations!
桃	TÁO, peach 桃红 táohóng, be pink, pink	烘	HŌNG, to warm or dry something over a fire
逃	TÁO, to run away 逃跑 táopǎo, to run away	巷	XIÀNG, crooked side street, lane
挑	TIĀO, carrying pole (with bucket or basket on each end); to carry; TIǍO, to probe	港	GǍNG, small stream; port, lagoon 香港 Xiānggǎng, Hong Kong
壁	BÌ, wall, screen 壁虎 bìhǔ, gecko	哄	HǑNG, to coax, to deceive; HŌNG, to make a noise
避	BÌ, to flee from 逃避 táobì, to dodge	居	JŪ, to reside; family name 居然 jūrán, unexpectedly
劈	PǏ, to split; PǏ, to pull apart with the hands; to divide	鋸	JÙ, saw, to saw 手鋸 shǒujù, hand saw 锯
招	ZHĀO, to beckon to; to invite; to recruit; to tease; to pass a disease to; to confess	雇	GÙ, to hire, be hired Often seen with the "side-man:" 僱. 雇農 gùnóng, farmhand
超	CHĀO, to catch up to; to surpass	顧	GÙ, to look after, to take care of; to take into consideration 顾
針	ZHĒN, needle, pin 針對 zhēnduì, be aimed at 针	娘	NIÁNG, mother; young woman 新娘 xīnniáng, bride
供	GŌNG, to supply; GÒNG, to offer in worship, offering; to testify, testimony	議	YÌ, to discuss 提議 tíyì, to propose 议

255

渴	KĚ, be thirsty 渴望 kěwàng, to yearn for	搬	BĀN, to lift (a heavy object) palms up (not above the head); to transport
季	JÌ, season (of the year); family name	盤	PÁN, plate, tub, dish; to coil up; to move; to sell; price; a measure for games 盘
委	WĚI, to appoint; to abandon; really	職	ZHÍ, to oversee; job, duty 职
秀	XIÙ, grain in the ear; to flourish; be elegant; be accomplished	態	TÀI, attitude, manner 態度 tàidu, attitude, manner 态
繡	XIÙ, to embroider Sometimes written 繍 繡花 xiùhuā, to embroider 绣	環	HUÁN, to encircle; ring, bracelet 环
誘	YÒU, to lead on, to mislead 誘奸 yòujiān, to seduce 诱	質	ZHÌ, disposition; substance; to question; (bookish) to pawn, pledge 质
透	TÒU, to go through 濕透 shītòu, get drenched	之	ZHĪ; a particle similar to 的: (noun/pronoun)'s; him, her, it, them
陣	ZHÈN; a measure for windstorms or rainstorms 阵	乏	FÁ, be exhausted; be feeble in ability; low (said of a fire)
雲	YÚN, cloud; family name 雲集 yúnjí, to congregate 云	群	QÚN, herd, crowd (君 and 羊 may appear in the form 羣.) 人群 rénqún, a crowd
料	LIÀO, material, grain; to expect (Distinguish 科, 1010, above). 料想 liàoxiǎng, to expect	盡	JÌN, to exhaust; JǏN, as much as possible; to put first 尽
般	BĀN, to transport; to distribute, to classify, classification, category	達	DÁ, to reach 達到 dádào, to reach, arrive at 达

遊	YŌU, to travel around This character is often replaced by 游 (= the next character, below)	歐	ŌU, to vomit; used in writing foreign words; Europe 欧
游	YÓU, to swim; to travel; to saunter; section of a river	倡	CHÀNG, to get something started; to advocate
競	JÌNG, to quarrel 競爭 jìngzhēng, to compete 竞	擔	DĀN, to carry with a pole on your shoulder (between two persons) 担
育	YÙ, to give birth to; to bring up; to nourish	膽	DĂN, gall bladder; courage; inside of a thermos bottle 胆
依	YĪ, to agree with; to forgive; according to	缶	FǑU, crock. CROCK rad. (121)(H175)
益	YÌ, profit. Printed 益 益處 yìchu, beneficial feature	灌	GUÀN, to sprinkle; to irrigate; to record (on tape or disc); to assemble
衆	ZHÒNG, crowd Variant: 眾 群眾 qúnzhòng, the masses 众	罐	GUÀN, jar, can 罐頭 guàntou, tin can
品	PǏN, good; quality; rank; personality; to judge the quality; to sample	權	QUÁN, (political) power 权
區	QŪ, be small; to distinguish between; region, district 区	尾	WĚI, tail 尾巴 wěiba, tail
驅	QŪ, to rush, to chase, to urge 驱	皇	HUÁNG, emperor; be imperial
嘔	ǑU, to vomit; OU; a sentence-final particle of warning or caution 呕	蝗	HUÁNG, locust

257

帝	DÌ, emperor; supreme ruler 皇帝 *huángdì*, emperor		勇	YǑNG, be brave 勇敢 *yǒnggǎn*, be brave
蹄	TÍ, hoof		守	SHǑU, to guard 守備 *shǒubèi*, do guard duty
評	PÍNG, to judge, to umpire, to criticize; review <div align="right">评</div>		抗	KÀNG, to resist, oppose 抗爭 *kàngzhēng*, to resist
響	XIǍNG, sound, to sound 響應 *xiǎngyìng*, to respond <div align="right">响</div>		骯	ÁNG, be dirty <div align="right">肮</div>
批	PĪ, to comment on, comment, annotation; to mark (an exam); batch; wholesale		坑	KĒNG, pit, shallow hole; to cheat somebody
屁	PÌ, gas (in the bowels); fart; (figuratively, of speech) be stupid		擊	JĪ, to hit (Distinguish 繫, next.) 攻擊 *gōngjī*, to attack <div align="right">击</div>
敵	DÍ, enemy 敵人 *dírén*, enemy <div align="right">敌</div>		繫	XÌ, to tie together; to haul up or let down on a rope; remember <div align="right">系</div>
滴	DĪ, drop, to drip 滴答 *dīdā*, tick-tock		獨	DÚ, alone 獨立 *dúlì*, be independent <div align="right">独</div>
摘	ZHĀI, to pick (flowers, fruit); to criticize		燭	ZHÚ, candle; to illumine 燭心 *zhúxīn*, candle wick <div align="right">烛</div>
厭	YÀN, to detest; be fed up with <div align="right">厌</div>		偉	WĚI, be great 偉大 *wěidà*, be mighty <div align="right">伟</div>
壓	YĀ, to push down 壓力 *yālì*, pressure <div align="right">压</div>		違	WÉI, to go against, to disobey <div align="right">违</div>

却	QUÈ, but, however; step back, drive back Sometimes seen as 卻.	週	ZHŌU, circle, revolution; a week, a year; be ubiquitous (often replaced by character above, 周)
流	LIÚ, to flow; go astray; be prevalent; a current; a measure for (a person's social) class; class, ilk	綢	CHÓU, to bind; to plan; thin silk 绸
荒	HUĀNG, be deserted, be desolate; be reckless; excessive; famine	綱	GĀNG, a leading line of a net; general principle; to regulate 纲
慌	HUĀNG, be nervous 驚慌 jīnghuāng, be scared	崗	GĂNG, ridge; sentry In the sense of "ridge" sometimes has only one mountain: 岡. 岗
謊	HUĂNG, a lie; to overcharge 谎	網	WĂNG, net, to net 網球 wăngqiú, tennis 网
緣	YUÁN, along; be bound to (do something) 缘	調	TIÁO, to harmonize; to incite; DIÀO, tune; to transfer 调
則	ZÉ, and then… 则	族	ZÚ, race, tribe 族長 zúzhăng, clan head
側	CÈ, side; to lean aside; to side with someone; secondary 侧	胃	WÈI, stomach 胃口 wèikŏu, appetite
測	CÈ, to estimate, to guess 測量 cèliáng, to survey 测	謂	WÈI, to talk about; to call; to say 谓
廁	CÈ, toilet 廁所 cèsuŏ, toilet 厕	資	ZĪ, fee, capital, resources; talent; to aid 资
周	ZHŌU, circle, revolution, to go around, be ubiquitous, everywhere; all; a week; family name	姿	ZĪ, posture, carriage 姿勢 zīshì, posture

259

格	GÉ, ruled line or space (on paper); category; compartment	榨	ZHÀ, to press out (as oil or sugar), press for extracting oil, sugar
錐	ZHUĪ, awl; to make holes with an awl 锥	始	SHǏ, to begin 開始 *kāishǐ*, to begin
堆	DUĪ, to pile; pile; crowd 堆積 *duījī*, to pile up	頓	DÙN, to pause; to prepare; suddenly; a measure for actions 顿
維	WÉI, to maintain, to hold together 维	純	CHÚN, be pure (said of objects) 纯
某	MǑU, a certain…	領	LǏNG, to lead; neck, collar; main point 领
煤	MÉI, coal 煤油 *méiyóu*, coal oil, kerosene	鈴	LÍNG, small bell 門鈴 *ménlíng*, doorbell 铃
謀	MÓU, to find (a job); to plot, a plot 谋	導	DǍO, to lead 領導 *lǐngdǎo*, to lead, leader 导
礦	KUÀNG, mine (for minerals) 矿	份	FÈN, share, portion; a measure for portions
炸	ZHÀ, to set off, blast 炸藥 *zhàyào*, explosives	貧	PÍN, be poor, insufficient (divide the cowries = "be poor") 貧乏 *pínfá*, to lack 贫
詐	ZHÀ, to pretend, to swindle, to deceive; to get information by pretending to know 诈	盆	PÉN, basin, bowl 臉盆 *liǎnpén*, wash-basin (literally, "face-basin")
窄	ZHǍI, be narrow 寬窄 *kuānzhǎi*, width, breadth	盼	PÀN, to gaze at, to long for 盼望 *pànwàng*, to hope for

鼓	GǓ, drum, to drum. DRUM rad. (207)(H224) 鼓舞 *gǔwǔ*, to inspire
製	ZHÌ, to make, to manufacture 製造 *zhìzào*, to manufacture 制
損	SǓN, be cruel, be sarcastic; to damage; loss 損害 *sǔnhài*, to harm 损
效	XIÀO, effect; to imitate; to devote 效能 *xiàonéng*, efficacy
咬	YǍO, to bite; to incriminate an innocent person with false testimony; to bark
准	ZHǓN, to permit (now often seen as short form of 準, 630, above) 准許 *zhǔnxǔ*, to permit
隊	DUÌ, squadron; team; file (of people); a measure for formations 队
敗	BÀI, defeat 腐敗 *fǔbài*, be putrid 败
匪	FĚI, bandit or rebel; to act or talk in a way suggestive of moral irresponsibility
悲	BĒI, be sad, be grieved 悲觀 *bēiguān*, be pessimistic
排	PÁI, to arrange; a row; to shove, get rid of 排除 *páichú*, get rid of
輩	BÈI, a generation; kind or class; lifetime 辈
糧	LIÁNG, provisions (food) 糧食 *liángshí*, grain 粮
揚	YÁNG, to lift up; to throw into the air; to winnow; to display; to publish; to praise 扬
楊	YÁNG, poplar; family name 楊樹 *yángshù*, poplar tree 杨
腸	CHÁNG, intestine; sausage 腸兒 *chángr*, sausage 肠
傷	SHĀNG, wound, to wound 悲傷 *bēishāng*, be sorrowful 伤
湯	TĀNG, soup; hot water; a family name 清湯 *qīngtāng*, consommé 汤
燙	TÀNG, be scalding hot, to scald, to heat up; to iron; to get a permanent 烫
丈	ZHÀNG, ten Chinese feet (=144 inches); wife's parents; husband
仗	ZHÀNG, war, battle 打仗 *dǎzhàng*, to wage war
悔	HUǏ, to repent; to turn away from 後悔 *hòuhuǐ*, to regret; to feel remorse

匀	YÚN, be evenly distributed; to spare (space, time, money)	兵	BĪNG, soldier; weapons 兵法 *bīngfǎ*, art of war
均	JŪN, be equal, be fair 平均 *píngjūn*, average; on average, equally	際	JÌ, boundary; occasion; at the time that… 际
律	LÜ, law 法律 *fǎlǜ*, law	彈	DÀN, a bullet; TÁN, to hurl; to pluck (a musical instrument); to flick 弹
技	JÌ, skill 技工 *jìgōng*, skilled worker; mechanic	戰	ZHÀN, war; family name 游擊戰 *yóujīzhàn*, "rove-and-strike" (=guerrilla) war 战
術	SHÙ, craft, art, profession; device 技術 *jìshù*, technique, technology 术	僅	JĬN, barely 僅僅 *jǐnjǐn*, barely, merely 仅
述	SHÙ, to tell a story; to transmit 述職 *shùzhí*, to report on your work	勤	QÍN, be hardworking, diligent; be frequent 勤儉 *qínjiǎn*, be hardworking and thrifty
序	XÙ, introduction (to a book); order, sequence 序文 *xùwén*, preface, foreword	擴	KUÒ, to expand 擴大 *kuòdà*, to enlarge 扩
朿	CÌ, thorn (H rad. 167). Distinguish *cì* from "bundle" 束 (657, above).	州	ZHŌU, administrative region; state (of the U.S.)
刺	CÌ, thorn; splinter; fishbone; to stab, to pierce; to murder; be "thorny," unpleasant	洲	ZHŌU, continent (large land mass)
策	CÈ, plan, policy; whip 策動 *cèdòng*, to foment	酬	CHÓU, to repay; (bookish) to pledge with wine 酬金 *chóujīn*, remuneration
棗	ZǍO, jujube; date (fruit tree) 枣	亞	YÀ, be inferior; used to write foreign words (the short form = H rad. 168) 亚

哑	YǍ, be hoarse; be dumb or mute 哑	掃	SÀO, broom; SǍO, to sweep 掃除 sǎochú, to wipe out; clean-up 扫
惡	È, be evil; be fierce; WÙ, to consider evil, hateful 好惡 hàowù, likes and dislikes 恶	略	LÜÈ, to omit; be simple, be rough; sketch, plan 侵略 qīnlüè, aggression, invasion
壺	HÚ, kettle, jug 茶壺 cháhú, teapot 壶	阻	ZǓ, to block 阻止 zǔzhǐ, to prevent
妨	FÁNG, to hinder 妨害 fánghài, to impair	粗	CŪ, be coarse (not fine) 粗野 cūyě, (be coarse and wild:) be uncouth
紡	FǍNG, to spin, to reel; silk 紡織娘 fǎngzhīniáng, katydid 纺	失	SHĪ, to lose 失敗 shībài, be defeated
訪	FǍNG, to look for; to dig up (the news); to visit 訪查 fǎngchá, to investigate 访	缺	QUĒ, to lack 缺課 quēkè, to cut class
防	FÁNG, to guard against 防備 fángbèi, to guard against	孫	SŪN, grandson; a family name 子孫 zǐsūn, descendants 孙
侵	QĪN, to move in on, to encroach 侵害 qīnhài, to encroach on	宣	XUĀN, proclaim; family name 宣傳 xuānchuán, to propagandize (for)
浸	JÌN, to soak, to immerse 浸透 jìntòu, to saturate	涉	SHÈ, to ford; to pass through; be connected with
帚	ZHǑU, broom	終	ZHŌNG, end; to the end of. 終究 zhōngjiū, after all 终
婦	FÙ, (woman with broom:) wife; woman 夫婦 fūfù, husband and wife 妇	混	HÙN, to mix up; to fool around: HÚN, be muddy; be foolish; whole

263

棍	GÙN, stick, club; bad guy 惡棍 *ègùn*, tough guy
階	JIĒ, step (on a stairway); rank, class 階段 *jiēduàn*, phase 阶
揩	KĀI, to rub 揩油 *kāiyóu*, to scrounge
及	JÍ, to reach, together with; and; a verb-ending: "be able to"
級	JÍ, level, class, grade; a measure for levels, classes, or grades 级
吸	XĪ, to inhale, to soak up 吸煙 *xīyān*, to smoke (tobacco)
伯	BÓ, father's elder brother; earl, count
迫	PÒ, to oppress, to persecute, be in difficulties 迫使 *pòshǐ*, to compel
拍	PĀI, to pat, to clap; to bounce; take (a picture); send (a telegram); to fawn on; a beat (in music)
恨	HÈN, to hate, to regret 恨不得 *hènbude*, to want badly to
乘	CHÉNG, to ride; to take advantage of, make use of (e.g., an opportunity)

剩	SHÈNG, to have left, be left over; remnant 剩餘 *shèngyú*, remainder
互	HÙ, mutually; each other 互相 *hùxiāng*, on each other
陳	CHÉN, be properly aged (wine); be stale; to display; to state; a family name 陈
標	BIĀO, target; to quote a price; to bid (commercially); sign 标
飄	PIĀO, to float (in the air or on the water) 飘
寅	YÍN, to respect; the third "earthly branch" 寅時 *yínshí*, 3-5 a.m.
演	YǍN, to act in (a play); to put on a show 演出 *yǎnchū*, to perform
阜	FÙ, mound. MOUND rad. (170). This is the independent form; compare 76, above.
轟	HŌNG, to drive off; to bombard; boom! boom! 轰
欺	QĪ, to cheat 欺騙 *qīpiàn*, to dupe
廠	CHǍNG, factory (the short form is H rad. 13) 工廠 *gōngchǎng*, factory 厂

滅	MIÈ, to extinguish, to go out (a fire, lights); to wipe out 灭
獲	HUÒ, to grab 獲得 huòdé, to obtain 获
祝	ZHÙ, to wish; to pray; family name 祝賀 zhùhè, congratulate
源	YUÁN, spring (of water), source 源泉 yuánquán, source
秩	ZHÌ, order, arrangement 秩序 zhìxù, order, sequence
節	JIÉ, joint; tempo; festival; section; to restrain, restraint; to economize 节
漢	HÀN, the Han (Chinese) race; man 好漢 hǎohàn, brave man 汉
抄	CHĀO, to copy; to confiscate; to parboil 抄寫 chāoxiě, to copy
吵	CHĂO, to quarrel; to make noise, disturb with noise 吵鬧 chǎonào, to wrangle
炒	CHĂO, to fry (in oil, stirring all the time) 炒冷飯 chǎo lěngfàn, to rehash
沙	SHĀ, sand, gravel; to sound gravelly, be hoarse; a family name
紗	SHĀ, gauze, sheer cloth 紡紗 fǎngshā, spinning (i.e., making thread) 纱
妙	MIÀO, be slender, be graceful, be beautiful; be marvelous, be clever
秒	MIĂO, beard of grain; smallest part; a measure for seconds (of time or angles)
佈	BÙ, to lay out; to inform Often written 布 (see 958, above).
災	ZĀI, disaster (often written 灾) 旱災 hànzāi, drought
肥	FÉI, be fat; be fertile (soil); be loose, be baggy; fertilizer
井	JĬNG, well, mineshaft 打井 dǎjǐng, to dig a well
耕	GĒNG, to plow, to till 耕作 gēngzuò, farming
朱	ZHŪ, bright red; a family name 朱紅 zhūhóng, be vermillion
珠	ZHŪ, pearl, bead 算盤珠 suànpán zhū, abacus beads
域	YÙ, boundary; to keep within bounds; region 異域 yìyù, foreign lands

265

括	KUŌ, to embrace, include
蒙	MĚNG, Mongolia; MÉNG, be stupid; to cover; MĒNG, to cheat; to guess wildly; to get knocked out
藏	ZÀNG, stash, treasure; Tibet; CÁNG, to hide, to store
臟	ZÀNG, viscera, entrails; ZĀNG, be dirty 心臟 xīnzàng, the heart <div align="right">脏</div>
森	SĒN, forest; be forest-like (dark; close-set) 森林 sēnlín, forest
梁	LIÁNG, horizontal beam, bridge, top-handle, ridge; a family name
粱	LIÁNG, (bookish) millet; birdseed; good food
畜	XÙ, to store up; to breed or raise animals; CHÙ, domestic animal
蓄	XÙ, to store up; to breed or raise; to harbor (idea) 蓄意 xùyì, be premeditated
抽	CHŌU, to draw out; to smoke (tobacco); to levy; to whip; to shrink; to conscript
袖	XIÙ, sleeve 袖口 xiùkǒu, cuff (of sleeve)

罒	WǍNG, net. NET rad. (122) Compare 446 and 637, above. This form is used as part of characters.
深	SHĒN, be deep 深入 shēnrù, to penetrate; be thoroughgoing
探	TÀN, to lean out; to search out 探聽 tàntīng, ask around
罩	ZHÀO, cover; bamboo basket used to catch fish
掉	DIÀO, to fall, to let fall; to lose; to fade; to remove (a stain); verb-suffix: "away, out"
島	DǍO, island 半島 bàndǎo, peninsula <div align="right">岛</div>
彎	WĀN, to bend, a bend 彎曲 wānqū, be meandering <div align="right">弯</div>
灣	WĀN, curving shore, bay; to moor 河灣 héwān, river bend <div align="right">湾</div>
蠻	MÁN, barbarians to the south of China; be barbarous <div align="right">蛮</div>
斧	FǓ, axe, hatchet 斧頭 fǔtou, axe, hatchet
孔	KǑNG, small hole; Confucius; a family name

恢	HUĪ, to extend, be great 恢復 *huīfù*, to restore
盛	SHÈNG, be abundant, vigorous; be widely known; be impressive; be completely…; family name
斯	SĪ, this (bookish); used to write foreign words; a family name
撕	SĪ, to tear up 撕毀 *sīhuǐ*, rip to shreds
佛	FÓ, Buddha 佛法 *Fófǎ*, dharma
犯	FÀN, to commit an offense; have a recurrence of or revert to; a criminal
刷	SHUĀ, brush, to brush; to give someone the brush-off; to cut class
做	ZUÒ, to make; to be; to act as 做夢 *zuòmèng*, to dream
搖	YÁO, to shake, to rock, to swing to and fro 搖動 *yáodòng*, to shake
謠	YÁO, folk song, ballad; rumor 民謠 *mínyáo*, folksong <div align="right">谣</div>
遙	YÁO, be far off; be long 遙遠 *yáoyuǎn*, be distant

尊	ZŪN, respect; "your" (polite); measure for Buddhist statues and for cannons (artillery)
遵	ZŪN, to obey, to comply with 遵從 *zūncóng*, comply with
採	CǍI, to pick, to pick out, to gather; to extract, to mine <div align="right">采</div>
衝	CHŌNG, to crash through; thoroughfare; CHÒNG, to face; be strong, be tactless <div align="right">冲</div>
腫	ZHǑNG, to swell up <div align="right">肿</div>
納	NÀ, to pay in; to accept 納入 *nàrù*, to bring in <div align="right">纳</div>
抵	DǏ, to take the place of; to push against, to resist 抵制 *dǐzhì*, to boycott
忠	ZHŌNG, be loyal 忠誠 *zhōngchéng*, be loyal
串	CHUÀN, a string of things (such as cash), to string together; to thread your way through
患	HUÀN, to suffer; calamity 患病 *huànbìng*, to get sick
配	PÈI, to match up, go well with, to mate (said of animals)

267

帚	LĬ, cauldron. CAULDRON rad. (193)(H219).	矩	JǓ, carpenter's square; standard, rule, custom 矩形 *jǔxíng*, rectangle
獻	XIÀN, to give 獻計 *xiànjì*, to give advice 献	拒	JÙ, to refuse, resist 拒絕 *jùjué*, to reject
軌	GUĬ, rut; orbit; rule; law; axle 軌道 *guǐdào*, track 轨	距	JÙ, be separated from, be distant from; distance 距離 *jùlí*, be distant from
韭	JIǓ, leeks. LEEKS rad. (179). Distinguish from the "wrong" rad. 非 (654, above)	繁	FÁN, be complicated, be numerous 繁榮 *fánróng*, to flourish
耐	NÀI, to endure, to bear 耐心 *nàixīn*, to be patient	兼	JIĀN, to put together 兼職 *jiānzhí*, to moonlight, hold two jobs
克	KÈ, to conquer; gram 攻克 *gōngkè*, to capture; to overcome	歉	QIÀN, apology; crop failure, bad harvest 歉收 *qiànshōu*, bad harvest
寧	NÍNG, be peaceful; to prefer to; Nanjing (Nanking) 宁	嫌	XIÁN, to dislike; to suspect 嫌惡 *xiánwù*, to loathe
奪	DUÓ, to take by force, to fight over 奪取 *duóqǔ*, seize 夺	賺	ZHUÀN, to make money; profit To put cowries together: profit 赚
征	ZHĒNG, to attack, to travel; to draft (troops); to solicit; evidence	繳	JIǍO, to make a payment; to capture 缴
症	ZHÈNG, ZHĒNG, disease	鞭	BIĀN, whip; string of firecrackers 鞭策 *biāncè*, to spur on
嚴	YÁN, be airtight, be strict; family name 嚴格 *yángé*, be strict 严	具	JÙ, tool; to write out; (bookish) a measure for dead bodies and machines

俱 JÙ, be complete; every
俱全 *jùquán*, be complete in all respects

珍 ZHĒN, precious object; be precious
珍重 *zhēnzhòng*, to value

疹 ZHĚN, a rash
疹子 *zhěnzi*, (colloquial) measles

診 ZHĚN, examine medically
診斷 *zhěnduàn*, to diagnose
诊

趁 CHÈN, to chase; to turn to one's own use; according to

衰 SHUĀI, to get weak
衰弱 *shuāiruò*, to get feeble

畝 MǓ, Chinese acre (*mou*): 733-1/2 square yards
亩

款 KUĂN, sum of money; article (in treaty, contract); inscription; to entertain

誤 WÙ, be late, be too late for; mistake, by mistake; lead astray
误

庭 TÍNG, hall, courtyard; the imperial court; family

挺 TǏNG, be straight and stiff; to hold on to; fairly; a measure for machine guns

廳 TĪNG, hall, room; department of a provincial government
厅

栽 ZĀI, to plant; to insert; to fall down; to impose
栽跟頭 *zāi gēntou*, to fall

載 ZÀI, to carry, to contain a load; ZǍI, a year; to record (in writing)
载

裁 CÁI, to cut out (a pattern); to reduce, to lay off employees; to decide

截 JIÉ, to cut in two; to intercept; a measure for segments

承 CHÉNG, to inherit; to manage; to admit
承認 *chéngrèn*, to recognize, acknowledge

姻 YĪN, bride; marriage connections

托 TUŌ, to carry on the palm; to ask a favor; to rely on

託 TUŌ, to entrust, to ask someone to do a job for you (often replaced by 托)
托

歸 GUĪ, to go or come back (to where the person belongs)
归

疑 YÍ, to mistrust
疑心 *yíxīn*, suspicion

269

礙	ÀI, to get in the way 妨礙 *fǎng'ài*, to obstruct 碍	繩	SHÉNG, string 绳
詞	CÍ, word, term; statement; a *ci* (old style "*tz'u*") poem 词	蠅	YÍNG, fly (insect) 蠅拍 *yíngpāi*, fly-swatter 蝇
捕	BǓ, to seize, to arrest 捕獲 *bǔhuò*, to capture	甲	JIǍ, armor, shell (as, a turtle's); first; the first "heavenly stem"
補	BǓ, to patch up, to fill in 添補 *tiānbǔ*, to replenish 补	匣	XIÁ, small box
簿	BÙ, notebook, ledger 簿紀 *bùjì*, bookkeeping	藝	YÌ, craft, art 藝術 *yìshù*, art 艺
薄	BÓ, BÁO, be thin, be weak 薄弱 *bóruò*, be weak	販	FÀN, to peddle, to deal in 小販 *xiǎofàn*, pedlar 贩
博	BÓ, be broad or comprehensive (in knowledge); of all kinds; to win, to gain	板	BǍN, board; printing plate; a measure for editions; be "wooden" (lifeless)
移	YÍ, to shift 移動 *yídòng*, to shift	版	BǍN, printing block; edition 版權 *bǎnquán*, copyright
鼠	SHǓ, mouse, rat. MOUSE rad. (208)(H225) 鼠輩 *shǔbèi*, bad guys	隶	DÀI, to grab, to catch hold of. GRAB rad. (171) Now used as the short form for 隸 *lì* (p.298a).
龜	GUĪ, tortoise. TORTOISE rad. (213) 龟	康	KĀNG, good health; family name 健康 *jiànkāng*, health(y)
黽	MǏN, toad. TOAD rad. (205) (the short form is H rad. 207) 黾	糠	KĀNG, be dry and pulpy; chaff

黹	ZHǏ, to embroider. EMBROIDER rad. (204)	擾	RǍO, to annoy 打擾 dǎrǎo, to annoy 扰
庚	GĒNG, the evening star; the seventh "heavenly stem"	豸	ZHÌ, (bookish) snake. SNAKE rad. (153)(H198)
莊	ZHUĀNG, be serene; hamlet; store; dealer (cards); family name 庄	苗	MIÁO, sprout; jet of flame; vein of ore; progeny; Miao people; vaccine; family name
智	ZHÌ, wisdom, learning 智力 zhìlì, intellect	描	MIÁO, to trace over 描畫 miáohuà, to depict
穩	WĚN, be steady; definitely, "You can depend on it." 稳	貓	MĀO, cat 貓叫 māojiào, purring 猫
隱	YǏN, to hide 隱藏 yǐncáng, to hide 隐	巧	QIǍO, be ingenious; be timely, opportune 巧妙 qiǎomiào, be clever
含	HÁN, to hold something in your mouth; to contain 含義 hányì, implication	墨	MÒ, ink, be inky; family name 墨水 mòshuǐ, ink
錄	LÙ, to record; to employ 抄錄 chāolù, to copy 录	遷	QIĀN, to shift 遷就 qiānjiù, to adjust to 迁
肅	SÙ, to command respect, to respect 肃	寶	BǍO, be precious; "your" (polite) 寶貝 bǎobèi, a treasure 宝
憂	YŌU, be grieved, be worried 憂患 yōuhuàn, misery 忧	瓦	WǍ, tile, earthenware; WÀ, to roof, to tile. TILE rad. (98)(H98)
優	YŌU, to excel; actor 優秀 yōuxiù, be outstanding 优	餅	BǏNG, cakes; round, flat pastries with or without filling 饼

271

併	BÌNG, to combine; to annex; go side by side with. Often replaced with 并.	視	SHÌ, to look, to look at 電視 diànshì, television 视
拼	PĪN, to put together; to fight or work furiously 拼音 pīnyīn, to spell	飽	BǍO, be full, to have had enough to eat 饱
瓶	PÍNG, bottle, vase 瓶裝 píngzhuāng, be bottled	抱	BÀO, to wrap in one's arms, to embrace; to hold; to carry; to adopt (a point of view, a child)
梅	MÉI, plum; family name 梅花鹿 méihuālù, sika deer	袍	PÁO, long gown or robe 旗袍 qípáo, "ch'i-p'ao:" long woman's dress
卯	MǍO, the fourth "earthly branch" 卯時 mǎoshí, 5-7 a.m.	泡	PÀO, to soak; to pester; be together; bubble; blister; light bulb; PĀO, be fluffy
柳	LIǓ, willow; family name 柳條 liǔtiáo, wicker	砲	PÀO, cannon, artillery; a shot from a gun Now often seen in the form 炮.
哈	HĀ, ha! ha!; to blow 哈欠 hāqiàn, a yawn	暴	BÀO, be violent, be fierce; stick out, lay out 暴力 bàolì, violence
恰	QIÀ, be exact, be appropriate 恰當 qiàdàng, be suitable	爆	BÀO, to explode; to boil, to fry quickly in hot oil 爆炸 bàozhà, to explode
屈	QŪ, to bend; be wronged; to submit unwillingly; injustice; family name	丰	FĒNG, be pretty, be graceful, elegant Fēng is a picture of a blossoming flower.
帥	SHUÀI, leader, commander; be beautiful, stylish; family name 帅	豐	FĒNG, be abundant, fruitful, luxuriant 丰
師	SHĪ, specialist, teacher; (army) division 师	逢	FÉNG, to meet with; to happen; whenever 逢迎 féngyíng, to toady to

272

縫	FÉNG, to sew, to mend (usually by hand); FÈNG, seam; crack 缝	爬	PÁ, to crawl, to creep; to climb 爬行 páxíng, to crawl
鋒	FÉNG, sharp point; the tip of a bayonet or lance 锋	陪	PÉI, to keep someone company; with 陪同 péitóng, accompany
蜂	FÉNG, bees, hornets, wasps 蜜蜂 mìfēng, honeybee	賠	PÉI, to pay damages; to lose money (in business) 賠罪 péizuì, apologize 赔
邦	BĀNG, nation 邦交 bāngjiāo, diplomatic relations	伴	BÀN, to keep someone company, companion 陪伴 péibàn, to keep company
綁	BǍNG, to bind, to tie; to kidnap 绑	胖	PÀNG, be fat 胖子 pàngzi, fatso
捧	PĚNG, to hold something in your cupped two hands; measure for two handfuls; praise; support (as patron)	幣	BÌ, currency, coin; silk; gifts 外幣 wàibì, foreign money 币
棒	BÀNG, bat, nightstick; be terrific (Beijing slang)	撇	PIĒ, to abandon; to skim something off the surface of a liquid; PIĚ, to throw
罷	BÀ, to cease, to quit; BA, a sentence-final particle (= 吧, 277, above) 罢	撥	BŌ, to move (as with a fingertip); to set, adjust, transfer; subtotal, part 拨
擺	BǍI, to swing; pendulum; to display; to put in order; to put 摆	潑	PŌ, to throw liquid out of a container; to spill; be shrewish 泼
爪	ZHǍO, claws. CLAWS rad. (87)(H116). Compare 338, above. This is the independent form.	廢	FÈI, to abolish, to discard; crippled, useless 废
爸	BÀ, papa, father 爸爸 bàba, papa	摩	MĀ, to smooth out with the hand; MÓ; used to write foreign words

磨	MÓ, to rub; to grind, to sharpen; to dawdle; to pester; MÒ, to mill, to grind; millstone	搭	DĀ, to lay across; to build (for temporary use); to travel by; to add, "plus"
魔	MÓ, evil spirit, demon 魔鬼 móguǐ, demon	塔	TǍ, pagoda, tower 燈塔 dēngtǎ, lighthouse
墓	MÙ, tomb 墓地 mùdì, cemetery	端	DUĀN, to raise up, to hold level in front of you; be upright; tip
幕	MÙ, stage curtain; a measure for acts of a play; screen	喘	CHUǍN 喘氣 chuǎnqì, to pant
摸	MŌ, to feel with the hand; to grope for; to sneak in or out	抬	TÁI, to carry (between two or more people); to raise the price
鼎	DǏNG, tripod, sacrificial vessel, a "ting". TRIPOD RAD. (206)	胎	TĀI, the pregnant womb; foetus; stuffing; tire 胎兒 tāiér, foetus
噴	PĒN, to spurt, to puff, to spray; PÈN, puff 噴射 pēnshè, to spurt 喷	痰	TÁN, phlegm, spit
墳	FÉN, grave, tomb 墳墓 fénmù, tomb 坟	毯	TǍN, rug 地毯 dìtǎn, carpet
憤	FÈN, zeal, ardor; be exasperated with; be very angry 愤	倘	TǍNG, if 倘若 tǎngruò, if
浮	FÚ, to float; be flighty; be insubstantial; excess FÙ, to swim	躺	TǍNG, to lie down 躺到 tǎngdào, to lie down
俘	FÚ, to take prisoner; to capture military hardware 俘獲 fúhuò, to capture	趟	TÀNG; a measure for trips or visits; column, row

274

梯	TĪ, ladder, stairs 電梯 *diàntī*, elevator	驢	LǗ, donkey 驴
剃	TÌ, to shave 剃刀 *tìdāo*, razor	慮	LǛ, be anxious; to plan 疑慮 *yílǜ*, be worried, worry (noun) 虑
吐	TǓ, TÙ, to spit out, to vomit 吐痰 *tǔtán*, to spit	攔	LÁN, to stop someone from doing something; to enclose; to separate 拦
肚	DÙ, belly; DǓ, tripe 一肚氣 *yì dù qì*, be very angry, "pissed off"	欄	LÁN, railing; (newspaper) column or section 栏
狼	LÁNG, wolf 狼狗 *lánggǒu*, wolf-hound	爛	LÀN, be tender (from cooking); be soggy; be rotten or infected; to glisten 烂
浪	LÀNG, breakers, waves; be undisciplined, be reckless 浪花 *lànghuā*, seaspray	鐮	LIÁN, scythe, sickle 鐮刀 *liándāo*, sickle 镰
龍	LÓNG, dragon. DRAGON rad. (212) (the short form is H rad. 137) 龙	簾	LIÁN, hanging screen; curtain, drape 帘
聾	LÓNG, be deaf 聾子 *lóngzi*, deaf person 聋	溝	GŌU, gutter, ditch; to connect 沟
臘	LÀ, winter sacrifice (in the twelfth month) 腊	購	GÒU, to buy 購買 *gòumǎi*, to buy 购
獵	LIÈ, hunt, to hunt 獵取 *lièqǔ*, to hunt 猎	搞	GǍO, to do, to make; to manage; to get; to purge 搞鬼 *gǎoguǐ*, make mischief
爐	LÚ, fire pan, stove; brazier; censer 爐條 *lútiáo*, grate 炉	稿	GǍO, draft of a speech or article; manuscript; (bookish) grainstalk

膏	GĀO, ointment; fat; grease; be oily, rich, sleek 牙膏 *yágāo*, toothpaste	跨	KUÀ, a step; to straddle; to extend through; to carry something hanging at your side
估	GŪ, to appraise, to estimate 估計 *gūjì*, to estimate	墾	KĚN, to open new land to cultivation 垦
姑	GŪ, unmarried girl; father's or husband's sister; temporarily; be lenient	懇	KĚN, to beseech; earnestly 懇求 *kěnqiú*, to implore 恳
枯	KŪ, dried wood; be withered, be dried out	喉	HÓU, throat 喉結 *hóujié*, Adam's apple
攴	PŬ, to knock. KNOCK rad. (66). Compare 384, above.	猴	HÓU, monkey
敲	QIĀO, to rap on; to blackmail; to gyp 敲詐 *qiāozhà*, to extort	漿	JIĀNG, to starch; thick fluid, starch 浆
鍋	GUŌ, pot, pan; bowl (of a pipe) 锅	獎	JIĂNG, prize; to reward 獎許 *jiǎngxǔ*, to praise, encourage 奖
禍	HUÒ, calamity 禍害 *huòhài*, disaster 祸	醬	JIÀNG, sauce, (food) paste 醬油 *jiàngyóu*, soy sauce 酱
窩	WŌ, small hole; nest or burrow; to harbor; to bend 窝	嫁	JIÀ, get married (be a bride); give (a daughter) in marriage
誇	KUĀ, to praise; to boast 誇張 *kuāzhāng*, to exaggerate 夸	稼	JIÀ, husbandry; grain; to sow 耕稼 *gēngjià*, farm work
垮	KUĂ, to collapse 累垮了 *lèikuǎ le*, be exhausted from overwork	頸	JĬNG, neck 頸項 *jǐngxiàng*, neck 颈

276

勁	JÌN, strength, energy, spirit; JÌNG, strong 用勁 yòngjìn, to work hard 劲	盾	DÙN, shield Also pronounced shǔn 矛盾 máodùn, contradiction
煎	JIĀN, to fry; to simmer in water	澆	JIĀO, to sprinkle; to wet down; to trickle; to insinuate yourself 浇
剪	JIǍN, scissors; to cut with scissors 剪裁 jiǎncái, to cut out	饒	RÁO, to let somebody get away with something; to give away 饶
箭	JIÀN, arrow 箭頭 jiàntóu, arrowhead; arrow (sign)	繞	RÀO, to wind one thing around another; to go around; detour; sometimes RĂO 绕
夾	JIĀ, to press (between two things, like chopsticks, tongs), to squeeze 夹	橋	QIÁO, bridge 旱橋 hànqiáo, overpass 桥
狹	XIÁ, be narrow 狹窄 xiázhǎi, be cramped 狭	驕	JIĀO, high-spirited horse; "get on your high horse," be arrogant 骄
挾	XIÉ, to press, to pinch; to carry under the arm 要挾 yàoxié, to coerce 挟	娶	QǓ, to marry (be a groom) 娶親 qǔqīn, (of a man) to get married
戒	JIÈ, to guard against; to warn against; be cautious 戒備 jièbèi, be on guard	聚	JÙ, to get together, to assemble 聚積 jùjí, to accumulate
械	XIÈ, tool; weapon; (bookish) shackles or fetters 機械 jīxiè, machine, mechanism	削	XIĀO, to shave off, to peel (with a knife). Printed 削.
焦	JIĀO, to burn, scorch; to be anxious; family name 焦急 jiāojí, be anxious	銷	XIĀO, to melt (metal); to destroy; spend; sell 销
瞧	QIÁO, (colloquial) to look at 瞧得起 qiáodeqǐ, (colloquial) to esteem	捎	SHĀO, to take or bring (for someone) 捎帶 shāodài, in passing

277

稍	SHĀO, soldier's ration; a little bit 稍許 shāoxǔ, a tiny bit	註	ZHÙ, to annotate (often replaced by 注, 801, in modern texts)
鎖	SUǑ, to lock, to chain up, lock; to do a lock-stitch 锁	植	ZHÍ, plant, to plant. To establish.
欣	XĪN, be happy 歡欣 huānxīn, be happy	置	ZHÌ, buy. 添置 tiānzhì, to acquire
掀	XIĀN, to lift to one side; to raise up; to open; to whisk away	振	ZHÈN, to shake, shake up 振作 zhènzuò, to jump to (a task), do with spirit
刑	XÍNG, law, to punish, punishment 死刑 sǐxíng, death penalty	震	ZHÈN, thunderclap; to shake; get very excited 地震 dìzhèn, earthquake
型	XÍNG, earthen mold for casting; model, pattern 血型 xuèxíng, blood type	晨	CHÉN, dawn; morning 清晨 qīngchén, dawn
媳	XÍ, daughter-in-law	唇	CHÚN, lips 唇膏 chúngāo, lipstick
熄	XĪ, to put out (a fire) 熄滅 xīmiè, to die out	帳	ZHÀNG, canopy; account, account book; debt 帳單 zhàngdān, check, bill 帐
箱	XIĀNG, box, case 皮箱 píxiāng, leather suitcase	脹	ZHÀNG, to swell up, distend 腫脹 zhǒngzhàng, swelling 胀
霜	SHUĀNG, frost 霜害 shuānghài, frostbite	徵	ZHĒNG, evidence; to examine evidence; to summon to court; to recruit or levy
柱	ZHÙ, pillar; to prop up, to support 柱子 zhùzi, pillar, post	懲	CHÉNG, to punish; to repress, to restrain 懲辦 chéngbàn, to punish 惩

微	WĒI, be tiny, be small, be slight. Distinguish from *zhēng* 徵 (p.278b).	帖	TIĚ, to submit; be smooth; TIĚ, card, note; TIĒ, model calligraphy book
掌	ZHǍNG, palm of the hand; paw; to handle; to take in the hand	貼	TIĒ, to paste something on; be close to; to pay; allowance 貼
賞	SHǍNG, to reward; to enjoy 賞識 *shǎngshí*, to appreciate 賞	徹	CHÈ, to penetrate; be thorough 徹底 *chèdǐ*, be thorough 彻
棧	ZHÀN, gallery, covered passage; shed; shop 貨棧 *huòzhàn*, warehouse 栈	撤	CHÈ, to take away Distinguish *sǎ* 撒, below. 徹除 *chèchú*, to remove
殘	CÁN, to cut to pieces, to murder, murderer, bandit 残	撒	SǍ, scatter; SĀ, to release. Distinguish from 撤 (just above).
鎮	ZHÈN, rural market town; to press down; to be calm; to cool 镇	臭	CHÒU, to stink; be conceited
慎	SHÈN, be attentive, be careful.	嗅	XIÙ, to sniff, to smell 嗅覺 *xiùjué*, sense of smell
顛	DIĀN, top of the head; top; to take a header, to tumble 颠	壽	SHÒU, long life 長壽 *chángshòu*, long life 寿
填	TIÁN, to fill, to stuff full 填寫 *tiánxiě*, to fill in	籌	CHÓU, tally, ticket; plan, to plan 籌備 *chóubèi*, to prepare 筹
沾	ZHĀN, to moisten; to receive benefits; be infected by	鑄	ZHÙ, to cast metal; to model 鑄幣 *zhùbì*, metal money 铸
粘	ZHĀN, to paste, to glue; NIÁN, be sticky	牲	SHĒNG, cattle; sacrifical animal

279

甥	SHĒNG, sister's son; nephew 甥女 *shēngnǚ*, niece	髒	ZĀNG, be dirty 骯髒 *āngzāng*, be filthy 脏
審	SHĚN, to investigate judicially; to try 審議 *shěnyì*, to consider 审	宿	SÙ, to lodge; old, in the past; XIŬ, measure for nights; night
嬸	SHĚN, wife of father's or husband's younger brother 婶	縮	SUŌ, to coil up, to bind fast; to draw in, to shorten; to shrink 缩
率	SHUÀI, to lead, be led; generally; LǛ; a suffix: "rate"	搜	SŌU, to investigate 搜集 *sōují*, to gather
摔	SHUĀI, to throw down; to lose your balance and fall; to plunge	瘦	SHÒU, be emaciated; be tight; be poor (as, soil) 枯瘦 *kūshòu*, be skinny
牽	QIĀN, to drag, to drag into 牽涉 *qiānshè*, to drag in 牵	嫂	SǍO, older brother's wife; polite address for a married woman about your own age
糟	ZĀO, be pickled; be rotten, ready to fall apart 糟心 *zāoxīn*, be vexed	唉	ĀI, Yes?, Right! (as a response); ÀI, ÀI, Alas! That's too bad!
遭	ZĀO, to revolve; turn or revolution; to meet with; chance	挨	ĀI, to crowd against; in sequence; ÁI, to delay; to suffer
澡	ZǍO, to bathe 洗澡 *xǐzǎo*, to bathe	呀	YĀ, a sentence-final particle of surprise or admiration
操	CĀO, to take hold of, to take charge of 操勞 *cāoláo*, to work hard (on)	鴉	YĀ, crow, raven 鴉片 *yāpiàn*, opium 鸦
葬	ZÀNG, to bury 葬禮 *zànglǐ*, funeral	芽	YÁ, bud, sprout 芽苗 *yámiáo*, rice shoot

280

秧	YĀNG, rice shoot, sprout; the young (of animals) 秧苗 *yāngmiáo*, rice shoot	勾	GŌU, hook; to involve another person in wrong-doing; to cancel (as, a debt); to remind
映	YÌNG, be bright; to reflect 映照 *yìngzhào*, shine on	什	SHÍ, ten; file of ten soldiers; SHÉ, first syllable in 什麼, what?
紋	WÉN, lines; veins; grain (of wood) 紋理 *wénlǐ*, veins, grain 纹	仇	CHÓU, enemy; enmity; QIÚ, family name 仇敵 *chóudí*, foe
蚊	WÉN, mosquito 蚊帳 *wénzhàng*, mosquito net	汁	ZHĪ, juice, gravy 牛肉汁 *niúròu zhī*, beef extract
枉	WǍNG, be crooked, be unjust; to treat unjustly; be in vain	扔	RĒNG, to throw; to throw away 扔下 *rēngxià*, to abandon
旺	WÀNG, be bright, be glorious 旺盛 *wàngshēng*, be exuberant, vigorous	冊	CÈ, booklet, album; a measure for copies (of a book) Also 册. 小冊子 *xiǎo cèzi*, booklet
筐	KUĀNG, basket (usually without a handle); a measure for basketfuls	仙	XIĀN, a Daoist ("Taoist") "immortal;" hermit 仙姑 *xiāngū*, female "immortal," witch
狂	KUÁNG, be reckless, be wild 發狂 *fākuáng*, go mad	瓜	GUĀ, melon. MELON rad. (97)(H151) 西瓜 *xīguā*, watermelon
乙	YǏ, twist; the second "heavenly stem;" TWIST rad. (5)(H7). Compare 5, above.	幼	YÒU, be immature 幼小 *yòuxiǎo*, be immature
叉	CHĀ, fork; CHÁ, block up; CHǍ, to spread (usually, one's legs)	奶	NǍI, breasts; milk; to suckle 奶頭 *nǎitóu*, (colloquial) nipple, tit
刁	DIĀO, be tricky, wicked; family name 刁難 *diāonán*, make difficulties	污	WŪ, filth; stagnant water; be foul; to befoul 污水 *wūshuǐ*, waste water

池	CHÍ, pool; space with raised sides; family name 電池 diànchí, battery	朵	DUǑ, flower; a measure for flowers and clouds 朵兒 duǒr, a flower
妄	WÀNG, be phony, be rash 狂妄 kuángwàng, be arrogant	伙	HUǑ, mess (food); partner, partnership; to join; a measure for groups, bands
冰	BĪNG, ice 冰箱 bīngxiāng, icebox	伍	WǓ, five (used in documents for 五); file of five men; company; a family name
扣	KÒU, to detain; to deduct; to invert (cup, bowl, etc.); to latch; a measure for a ten percent discount	伏	FÚ, to lie face down; to surrender; to admit; ten-day period in July-August Fú = "man" + "dog."
灰	HUĪ, ashes, dust; be ash-colored, gray 灰心 huīxīn, lose heart	沉	CHÉN, be heavy; to sink Sometimes seen as 沈. 沉醉 chénzuì, get 'high' (on experience or alcohol)
匠	JIÀNG, mechanic, workman 匠人 jiàngrén, craftsman	牢	LÁO, pen for cattle; prison; firmly, securely 坐牢 zuòláo, be in prison
尖	JIĀN, be sharp 尖利 jiānlì, be sharp	灶	ZÀO, kitchen stove 灶神 zàoshén, the kitchen god
劣	LIÈ, be vile 粗劣 cūliè, be shoddy	玖	JIǓ, nine (used in documents for 九)
帆	FĀN, sail 帆布 fānbù, canvas	址	ZHǏ, site 地址 dìzhǐ, address
兇	XIŌNG, be severe, be fierce, be stern; be strong (liquor or tobacco) 凶	赤	CHÌ, be bright red; loyal; bare. RED rad. (155)(H190) 赤貧 chìpín, be destitute
企	QǏ, to stand on tiptoe; to expect 企求 qǐqiú, to hanker for	抖	DǑU, to tremble, to shiver 抖動 dǒudòng, to vibrate

扶	FÚ, to support with your hand; straighten; to help 扶持 *fúchí*, to support	忌	JÌ, to abstain from; be taboo 忌煙 *jìyān*, quit smoking
丑	CHǑU, clown; the second "earthly branch."	尿	NIÀO, SUĪ, urine; NIÀO, to piss 尿盆 *niàopén*, urinal; pisspot
扭	NIǓ, to twist, to wring; to swing the hips when walking	吼	HǑU, roar (of animals)
投	TÓU, to drop; to move to; to surrender; to project; to fit in with	妥	TUǑ, be safe, be reliable 妥當 *tuǒdàng*, be appropriate
抛	PĀO, to throw away	吞	TŪN, to swallow; to embezzle 吞沒 *tūnmò*, to embezzle; to engulf
折	ZHÉ, to snap off; to fold; to pay as collateral; discount; SHÉ, be broken; to lose money; ZHĒ, to spill	肘	ZHǑU, elbow
抓	ZHUĀ, to scratch; to grab; to arrest; to draft someone	伸	SHĒN, to stretch out (a part of the body) 伸手 *shēnshǒu*, hold out the hand; ask for help
杏	XÌNG, apricot	佃	DIÀN, to rent land to farm 佃農 *diànnóng*, tenant farmer
邪	XIÉ, be evil, be unorthodox 邪路 *xiélù*, vice	皂	ZÀO, be black; soap; *yamen* runner 肥皂 *féizào*, soap
否	FǑU, not; to deny 否認 *fǒurèn*, to repudiate	妒	DÙ, be jealous 妒忌 *dùjì*, be jealous
即	JÍ, at once; very soon; precisely; even. Printed 卽	妖	YĀO, be weird, bewitching 妖魔鬼怪 *yāomó-guǐguài*, evil beings of all kinds

姊	ZǏ, older sister Also pronounced *jiě* 姊妹 *zǐmèi*, sisters
肩	JIĀN, shoulder 肩負 *jiānfù*, to shoulder
衫	SHĀN, shirt, garment for upper part of body 汗衫 *hànshān*, undershirt, T-shirt
炊	CHUĪ, to cook 炊具 *chuījù*, pots and pans, cooking gear
武	WǓ, military, martial 武器 *wǔqì*, weapons of war
坦	TǍN, be level, be candid 平坦 *píngtǎn*, be level
臥	WÒ, to crouch (animals); to lie, sleep. Printed 卧. 臥房 *wòfáng*, bedroom
協 协	XIÉ, be united in; to help 協作 *xiézuò*, to cooperate
抹	MǑ, to wipe clean, to wipe out; to wipe on, to smear on
拖	TUŌ, to drag 拖拉 *tuōlā*, be dilatory
拆	CHĀI, to take apart Dist. 析, next column, and 折, p. 283a. 拆除 *chāichú*, to demolish

枕	ZHĚN, to lay your head on; pillow 枕頭 *zhěntou*, pillow
杯	BĒI, cup, glass, goblet or other small vessel to drink from; a measure for these
松	SŌNG, pine tree; family name (now often seen as the short form for 鬆 (p. 299a))
析	XĪ, to split wood; to divide up; to analyze 析義 *xīyì*, analyze the meaning of
奈	NÀI, in 奈何 *nàihé*, Why do that? (see also below) 無可奈 *wúkěnài*, helpless
孤	GŪ, be fatherless, solitary 孤單 *gūdān*, be alone
叔	SHŪ, father's younger brother; husband's younger brother
呼	HŪ, to exhale; to call out; to snore 呼吸 *hūxī*, to breathe
刮	GUĀ, to scrape, to pare; take advantage of, exploit 刮臉 *guāliǎn*, to shave (your face)
股	GǓ; measure for puffs, whiffs, skeins, bands, gangs, surges, and shares of stock
兔	TÙ, rabbit (distinguish 免, 439 above) 野兔 *yětù*, wild rabbit

284

延	YÁN, to delay, protract; lengthen; to invite 延期 *yánqī*, to postpone	疫	YÌ, pestilence, epidemic 鼠疫 *shǔyì*, the plague
叁	SĀN, three (used in documents for 三)	毒	DÚ, be poisonous; be malicious; poison; bad drugs 吸毒 *xīdú*, to take drugs
糾	JIŪ, to collect; confederacy; to investigate; to correct 纠	挖	WĀ, to dig 挖根 *wāgēn*, to uproot, deracinate
柒	QĪ, seven (used in documents for 七)	拴	SHUĀN, to fasten one thing to another 拴住 *shuānzhù*, to tie up, make fast
染	RǍN, to dye; form bad habits; to catch (a disease) 污染 *wūrǎn*, to pollute, pollution	砍	KǍN, to chop, slash; hit with a thrown object 砍刀 *kǎndāo*, chopper
津	JĪN, ford, ferry; saliva, sweat, moisture; Tianjin 津贴 *jīntiē*, subsidy	耍	SHUǍ, to play with, to juggle 耍笑 *shuǎxiào*, to joke, fool around
室	SHÌ, a room 卧室 *wòshì*, bedroom	柔	RÓU, be soft, to soften; be gentle or mild 柔和 *róuhé*, be gentle
突	TŪ, to stick out; break through; offend; sudden 突出 *tūchū*, burst out; to highlight; be pushy	屎	SHǏ, shit, feces; secretion 拉屎 *lāshǐ*, to defecate
迹	JĪ, footprint; trace of; to search out or run down, to track	屍	SHĪ, corpse, carcass (now often in the form 尸) 屍體 *shītǐ*, corpse
迷	MÍ, to get lost; to get dirt in your eye; to develop an (unreasonable) passion for; fan, "bug"	眉	MÉI, eyebrow 眉頭 *méitóu*, brows
施	SHĪ, to spread, to spray; to give as charity; to put into effect (laws, etc.) (Dist. 旋, p. 288b.)	虐	NÜÈ, be cruel 虐政 *nüèzhèng*, tyranny

咱	ZÁN, I (dialect) 咱們 zánmen, we (you and I, the speaker and person spoken to)
炭	TÀN, charcoal 木炭 mùtàn, charcoal
卸	XIÈ, to unload; to unhitch; shirk; get rid of 卸車 xièchē, to unload
缸	GĀNG, cistern, vat, crock 缸子 gāngzi, mug, bowl
威	WĒI, to threaten, to inspire awe; by force 威權 wēiquán, power
怨	YUÀN, to hate; to criticize 怨恨 yuànhèn, to hate
肺	FÈI, lungs 肺炎 fèiyán, pneumonia
勉	MIĂN, to exert yourself; to urge
促	CÙ, to rush, be rushed; to urge 促進 cùjìn, push forward
侮	WŬ, insult, to insult, to demean 侮慢 wŭmàn, to disrespect
追	ZHUĪ, to chase; to investigate; to remember 追查 zhuīchá, to investigate

姨	YÍ, mother's sister; wife's sister
娃	WÁ, baby, child; pretty girl 娃娃 wáwa, baby, child
侄	ZHÍ, brother's son, nephew
怒	NÙ, anger, passion, rage 發怒 fānù, get angry
浴	YÙ, to bathe 浴盆 yùpén, bathtub
宮	GŌNG, palace, temple, college, dwelling 子宮 zǐgōng, womb
悟	WÙ, to wake up; to notice 悟性 wùxìng, ability to understand
凍	DÒNG, to freeze; be cold, be freezing; jelly 凍冰 dòngbīng, to freeze 冻
訊	XÙN, to admonish someone; to make a judicial investigation 讯
疾	JÍ, be sick; to consider "sick," to hate; be rushed 疾病 jíbìng, disease
疼	TÉNG, to ache; to dote on 疼痛 téngtòng, to ache

庫	KÙ, armory, granary, treasury 庫存 *kùcún*, stock, reserve 庫	栗	LÌ, chestnut; family name
座	ZUÒ, a measure for buildings, mountains, cities, clocks, tombs	捌	BĀ, eight (used in documents for 八)
扇	SHÀN, a fan; a measure for windows 電扇 *diànshàn*, electric fan	捉	ZHUŌ, to catch, to capture 捕捉 *bǔzhuō*, to catch (as, a bug; an opportunity)
祥	XIÁNG, auspicious, lucky	捐	JUĀN, to contribute; to solicit contributions 捐款 *juānkuǎn*, to contribute (money)
羞	XIŪ, be shy; feel ashamed; shame 害羞 *hàixiū*, feel bashful	挽	WǍN, to pull back; to restore 挽救 *wǎnjiù*, to rescue
素	SÙ, be white; be elemental, simple, plain; element 素食 *sùshí*, be a vegetarian	核	HÉ, pit, fruitstone; nucleus; to check up on 核心 *héxīn*, nucleus, core
索	SUǑ, rope; to tie up; to demand; rule 索引 *suǒyǐn*, index	桂	GUÌ, cassia, cinammon; Guangxi; family name
恥	CHǏ, to feel ashamed, shame (often = 耻) 羞恥 *xiūchǐ*, shame, sense of shame	鬯	CHÀNG, mixed wine, sacrificial wine. MIXED WINE rad. (192)
埋	MÁI, to bury 埋葬 *máizàng*, to bury	套	TÀO, to wrap in; to harness or hitch up; covering; measure for sets, suits of clothes
速	SÙ, speed 快速 *kuàisù*, be fast	辱	RǓ, to disgrace; disgrace; insult 恥辱 *chǐrǔ*, to humiliate; humiliation
逐	ZHÚ, to chase; one by one 逐步 *zhúbù*, step by step	桑	SĀNG, mulberry tree; family name

柴	CHÁI, firewood; family name 柴草 *cháicǎo*, firewood
閃	SHǍN, to flash, to dodge; to twist, sprain; lightning 閃光 *shǎnguāng*, flash of light, gleam 闪
哪	NǍ, NĚI, which one? whichever; NA; sentence-final particle: 啊, or 呢 + 啊
恩	ĒN, grace, mercy 恩德 *ēndé*, kindness
爹	DIĒ, (colloquial) papa, daddy 爹爹 *diēdie*, daddy
翁	WĒNG, old man; father; father-in-law; respectful address to older man
耗	HÀO, to waste; to keep deadlocked 耗子 *hàozi*, mouse, rat
秤	CHÈNG, steelyard; weight used with a steelyard 秤盤 *chèngpán*, balance pan
胸	XIŌNG, thorax, chest 胸部 *xiōngbù*, chest
脈	MÀI, blood vessel; vein (ore; in a leaf); pulse 脈息 *màixí*, pulse
烏	WŪ, crow; be black; family name 烏黑 *wūhēi*, be very black 乌

癸	GUǏ, the tenth "heavenly stem"
徒	TÚ, disciple; pupil; bum; in vain; be bare; on foot 佛教徒 *Fójiàotú*, a Buddhist
剝	BĀO, BŌ, to peel 剝奪 *bōduó*, to deprive
娛	YÚ, to amuse 娛樂 *yúlè*, amusement
液	YÈ, juices, sap 胃液 *wèiyè*, gastric juice
淚	LÈI, tears, to weep (now the form 泪 is much used) 淚液 *lèiyè*, a tear
淋	LÍN, to pour on, to drench; LÌN, to strain, to filter 淋浴 *línyù*, shower bath
淹	YĀN, to submerge, to flood 淹沒 *yānmò*, to inundate
毫	HÁO, a fine hair; one thousandth part; before 不, intensifies the negation
旋	XUÁN, to revolve; thereupon (dist. 施, p. 285a) 旋繞 *xuánrào*, to wind around
啟	QǏ, to begin; to announce 啟事 *qǐshì*, announcement 启

288

粒	LÌ, grain, tiny piece 每服五粒 *měi fú wǔ lì*, dose: 5 pills each time	晝	ZHÒU, daytime 晝夜 *zhòuyè*, day and night, around the clock 昼
執	ZHÍ, to take hold of; to manage, direct 執行 *zhíxíng*, to carry out, do 执	陷	XIÀN, to sink down (as into mud); trap; to entrap, to capture; a defect
軟	RUǍN, be soft, pliable 疲軟 *píruǎn*, be tired, be weak 软	虛	XŪ, be empty; be unreal; be poor (in health); be humble
堅	JIĀN, be firm, be strong 堅持 *jiānchí*, to persist in 坚	荷	HÉ, lotus 荷包 *hébāo*, pouch
掘	JUÉ, to dig 掘土機 *juétǔjī*, power shovel	閉	BÌ, to close, to stop up 閉合 *bìhé*, to close 闭
授	SHÒU, to give; to teach 授意 *shòuyì*, give somebody an idea, inspire	蛇	SHÉ, snake 畫蛇添足 *huà shé tiān zú*, overdo and spoil a job
捨	SHĚ, to give as charity; to part with 捨不得 *shěbudé*, to begrudge 舍	貪	TĀN, be greedy for, be avaricious 貪心 *tānxīn*, be avaricious 贪
梳	SHŪ, comb, to comb	彩	CǍI, be ornamented; be good luck; color(ful) 五彩 *wǔcǎi*, be multicolored
桶	TǑNG, a (six-pint) bucket; tub, cask	釣	DIÀO, to go fishing, to catch with hook and line 钓
麥	MÀI, wheat; family name. WHEAT rad. (199) (the short form is H. rad. 188) 麦	斜	XIÉ, to slant, to cause to slant 斜坡 *xiépō*, a slope
爽	SHUǍNG, be lively, agreeable; be bright; to deviate 爽利 *shuǎnglì*, be brisk and efficient	敍	XÙ, to chat, to chat about; rank, to rank 敍述 *xùshù*, to tell, narrate

289

笨	BÈN, be stupid, be clumsy 笨蛋 *bèndàn*, a fool	渡	DÙ, to ferry across; to spend (some time) 渡船 *dùchuán*, ferryboat
笛	DÍ, flute, whistle 汽笛 *qìdí*, steam whistle	湊	CÒU, to crowd, to form a crowd, to get together 湊集 *còují*, to get together
甜	TIÁN, be sweet 甜美 *tiánměi*, be delicious	渣	ZHĀ, sediment, refuse; fragment 猪油渣兒 *zhūyóu zhār*, cracklings
梨	LÍ, pear	湧	YǑNG, to bubble up, to flow rapidly 湧現 *yǒngxiàn*, to spring up (in large numbers)
脱	TUŌ, to take off clothes, shed skin; to escape from 脱離 *tuōlí*, separate from	寒	HÁN, be cold, be wintry 膽寒 *dǎnhán*, be terrified
腳	JIǍO, foot; kick; JUÉ, role (in a play) Often seen as 脚. 腳步 *jiǎobù*, pace, step	割	GĒ, to cut 割斷 *gēduàn*, to sever
售	SHÒU, to sell 售賣 *shòumài*, to sell	冤	YUĀN, an injustice; enmity; to cheat, get cheated. Often seen as 冤 (crown, not roof, over rabbit)
偽	WĚI, be fake. Usually printed 僞. 偽裝 *wěizhuāng*, to fake; disguise 伪	惰	DUÒ, be lazy 惰性 *duòxìng*, inertia
健	JIÀN, to strengthen, be strong; be regular 健康 *jiànkāng*, health, physique; be healthy	愉	YÚ, be happy 愉快 *yúkuài*, be happy
偵	ZHĒN, a spy, to spy 偵探 *zhēntàn*, do detective work 侦	惱	NǍO, be angry, be mad at 惱火 *nǎohuǒ*, be annoyed 恼
猛	MĚNG, be fierce, be violent; be potent (as medicine); suddenly	棄	QÌ, to throw away (now sometimes = 弃) 抛棄 *pāoqì*, throw away

290

裕 YÙ, be abundant, be generous; to enrich
富裕 *fùyù*, be abundant; be affluent

善 SHÀN, be good; be good at
善心 *shànxīn*, benevolence

貳 ÈR, be double; two (used for 二 in documents)
贰

琴 QÍN, an ancient musical instrument, like the zither; a "ch'in"

壹 YĪ, one (used for 一 in documents)

逼 BĪ, to press, to crowd; to annoy
逼迫 *bīpò*, to compel

堤 DĪ, dike, dam
堤岸 *dī'àn*, dyke, embankment

惑 HUÒ, to mislead, to doubt
誘惑 *yòuhuò*, to entice

粟 SÙ, millet; a family name

喪 SĀNG, funeral, mourning; SÀNG, to lose
丧

揀 JIĂN, to choose
揀選 *jiănxuăn*, to choose
拣

握 WÒ, to hold fast
握拳 *wòquán*, make a fist

插 CHĀ, to stick in, to insert
插手 *chāshŏu*, lend a hand; to butt into

捏 NIĒ, to hold tight (between the thumb and fingers), to pinch; to mold with the fingers

椒 JIĀO, pepper
胡椒 *hújiāo*, pepper

棉 MIÁN, cotton-padded; cotton, kapok
棉花 *miánhuā*, cotton

硬 YÌNG, be hard, be stiff; be stubborn; be capable
硬挺 *yìngtĭng*, to resist stubbornly

雄 XIÓNG, male (animals); be imposing, powerful
雄貓 *xióngmāo*, tomcat

尋 XÚN, to look for
尋常 *xúncháng*, be common
寻

粥 ZHŌU, congee (rice gruel, millet gruel)

紫 ZĬ, be purple, purple color
紫藤 *zĭténg*, Chinese wistaria

菌 JÙN, mushroom; JŪN, mildew; bacteria
菌苗 *jūnmiáo*, vaccine

291

喂	WĒI, to feed (child or animal); "hello" (on the phone); Hi!	黍	SHǓ, glutinous millet. MILLET rad. (202)
悶	MÈN, be stuffy; be bored; MĒN, be stuffy; be muffled; to steep 闷	腔	QIĀNG, hollow space, cavity; tune; accent; speech 腔调 qiāngdiào, tune; accent
晶	JĪNG, be clear 晶體 jīngtǐ, crystal	傲	ÀO, be arrogant 傲慢 àomàn, be haughty
跌	DIĒ, to stumble and fall; to drop (in price) 跌倒 diēdǎo, to fall, tumble	貸	DÀI, to lend at interest; to borrow; to forgive 贷款 dàikuǎn, to lend; loan 贷
嵌	QIÀN, to inlay, be inlaid with	堡	BǍO, walled village; stronghold; -burg
飲	YǏN, to drink; YÌN, to water animals 飲食店 yǐnshídiàn, eatery 饮	貿	MÀO, to barter 贸易 màoyì, trade, commerce 贸
筋	JĪN, tendon, muscle; prominent vein; plant fibre 筋肉 jīnròu, muscles	猶	YÓU, (bookish) to be like; and, yet, still 猶疑 yóuyí, (to hesitate) 犹
筍	SǓN, bamboo shoot (now often 笋) 筍雞 sǔnjī, broiler (chicken)	絨	RÓNG, wool, floss, down, sponge, velvet; fine hair 絨衣 róngyī, sweat shirt 绒
程	CHÉNG, a regulation: procedure; journey, stage of a journey; distance; a family name	絡	LUÒ, net-like thing; to hold in a net; to wind 络
稀	XĪ, be sparse, thin, infrequent 稀爛 xīlàn, be mashed up good; be overcooked	滑	HUÁ, be slippery; be cunning, slippery; to slide 滑行 huáxíng, to slide
犁	LÍ, plow, to plow	塗	TÚ, to daub; to erase; make a mess of; family name 塗層 túcéng, coating 涂

292

溜	LIŪ, to slide; be smooth; to sneak off; LIÙ, current; a row (as, of houses); neighborhood	隔	GÉ, partition, to partition; be separated from; every other
塞	SĀI (SÈ in some compounds), to stop up; stopper, cork; SÀI, strategic pass	虜	LǓ, to capture; captive 虜獲 lǔhuò, to capture; booty　虏
煉	LIÀN, to boil down; to refine, to purify 煉鐵 liàntiě, iron-smelting　炼	暈	YŪN, YÙN, feel dizzy, be faint; YÙN, halo 暈車 yùnchē, be car-sick　晕
匯	HUÌ, to remit; to come together, to bring together　汇	睜	ZHĒNG, to open your eyes
雷	LÉI, thunder; mine (military weapon); family name 雷達 léidá, radar	盟	MÉNG, solemn declaration before the gods; oath; covenant; Mongol prefecture; MÍNG, swear an oath
頑	WÁN, be stupid; be stubborn; be mischievous 頑固 wángù, be obstinate　顽	歇	XIĒ, to rest, to stop 歇工 xiēgōng, stop work
塘	TÁNG, pond, tank, embankment 河塘 hétáng, river bank	爺	YÉ, grandfather; father; "sir" 爺爺 yéye, paternal grandfather; "sir"　爷
肆	SÌ, four (used for 四 in documents)	飾	SHÌ, ornament, to ornament 飾物 shìwù, jewelry　饰
禁	JÌN, to prohibit; JĪN, to endure; to control oneself 紫禁城 Zǐjìnchéng, the Forbidden City in Beijing	筷	KUÀI, chopsticks 筷子 kuàizi, chopsticks
碑	BĒI, a memorial tablet, monument, gravestone	愁	CHÓU, be worried; be depressed; to worry about 愁苦 chóukǔ, anxiety
疊	DIÉ, to pile up; to repeat Often seen as 叠. 疊次 diécì, repeatedly　迭	腰	YĀO, waist; small of the back; kidney; pocket 彎腰 wānyāo, to stoop

293

催	CUĪ, to urge, to press 催促 *cuīcù*, to urge	豪	HÁO, outstanding person; be bold; be despotic 豪富 *háofù*, the rich and powerful
舅	JIÙ, maternal uncle; wife's brother 舅母 *jiùmǔ*, wife of mother's brother	慘	CǍN, be tragic; be cruel; be "bad news" (students' slang) 惨
躲	DUǑ, to dodge; to hide from, to hide 躲避 *duǒbì*, to dodge, hide yourself	瘟	WĒN, epidemic 瘟疫 *wēnyì*, pestilence
龠	YUÈ, flute. FLUTE rad. (214)	瘋	FĒNG, be insane; to act wild 瘋狂 *fēngkuáng*, be insane
剿	JIǍO, to attack; CHĀO (bookish) to plagiarize 剿滅 *jiǎomiè*, to exterminate	塵	CHÉN, dust, dirt; the non-spiritual world 尘
滾	GǓN, to roll; to roil, to boil 滾蛋 *gǔndàn*, (rude) Get lost!	魂	HÚN, soul 神魂不定 *shénhún búdìng*, be stressed out
漲	ZHǍNG, to rise (a river, a price); ZHÀNG, to swell, to rise 涨	墊	DIÀN, to fill up; to shim 墊款 *diànkuǎn*, cash advance 垫
漏	LÒU, to leak 漏洞 *lòudòng*, a leak, to leak	酸	SUĀN, acid; to taste sour; be pedantic; be grieved 酸甜苦辣 *suān-tián-kǔ-là*, joys and sorrows
寡	GUǍ, be few, be alone; to lessen	誓	SHÌ, oath; to vow 發誓 *fāshì*, to take an oath
辣	LÀ, be hot, be peppery; be harsh; to get burned by peppery food	磁	CÍ, be magnetic; porcelain, china 磁鐵 *cítiě*, magnet
遮	ZHĒ, to cover, to shade 遮藏 *zhēcáng*, to conceal	凳	DÈNG, stool 長凳 *chángdèng*, bench

屢	LǓ, repeatedly, time after time 屢次 *lǚcì*, repeatedly 屡	潔	JIÉ, be clean, be pure, be clear 潔淨 *jiéjìng*, be spotless 洁
蒜	SUÀN, garlic 大蒜 *dàsuàn*, garlic	潤	RÙN, to wet; be sleek; to enrich; to adorn 潤滑 *rùnhuá*, to lubricate 润
蓋	GÀI, lid; bug's or turtle's shell; put a lid on; to build; to mark with a "chop;" family name 盖	諒	LIÀNG, to suppose; to forgive; to sympathize with 谅
蒸	ZHĒNG, to steam something 蒸發 *zhēngfā*, to evaporate	廚	CHÚ, kitchen 廚房 *chúfáng*, kitchen
嗽	SÒU, to cough	慶	QÌNG, to congratulate; celebration; family name 慶祝 *qìngzhù*, to celebrate 庆
夥	HUǑ, to collaborate; be partners; band, partnership 伙	褲	KÙ, trousers 褲子 *kùzi*, trousers 裤
蝕	SHÍ, to nibble; eclipse 蝕本 *shíběn*, lose your capital 蚀	穀	GǓ, grain, corn 穀蒼 *gǔcāng*, granary 谷
熏	XŪN, to smoke; to fumigate 熏染 *xūnrǎn*, slowly to corrupt	輛	LIÀNG, a measure for vehicles 辆
鼻	BÍ, nose. BIG NOSE rad. (209) (H226). Called "big nose" to distinguish it from 515, above.	輪	LÚN, wheel; revolve; take turns; a round thing 輪班 *lúnbān*, in shifts 轮
銜	XIÁN, hold in the mouth; to harbor; rank, title 衔	豎	SHÙ, to set upright; be vertical; vertical stroke (in calligraphy) 竖
嫩	NÈN, be tender, inexperienced; be light (in color) 嫩手 *nènshǒu*, greenhorn	賢	XIÁN, be virtuous; to esteem 賢明 *xiánmíng*, be sagacious 贤

295

遲	CHÍ, be late 遲早 chízǎo, sooner or later 迟	膚	FŪ, skin 肤
醋	CÙ, vinegar 吃醋 chīcù, be jealous	齒	CHǏ, teeth. TEETH rad. (211) (the short form is H. rad. 206) 齿
歎	TÀN, to sigh 歎氣 tànqì, to sigh 叹	瞎	XIĀ, be blind; blindly, foolishly, be tangled up 说瞎話 shuō xiāhuà, to lie
撞	ZHUÀNG, to hit, to collide with; meet by chance 撞擊 zhuàngjī, to ram	閱	YUÈ, to examine; to read carefully; to pass through 阅
概	GÀI, in general 概念 gàiniàn, concept	蝦	XIĀ, shrimp 龍蝦 lóngxiā, lobster 虾
撲	PŪ, to pounce on; to flap 撲打 pūdǎ, to swat, to pat 扑	蹤	ZŌNG, footprint, trace Often seen as 踪. 蹤跡 zōngjī, trace
樁	ZHUĀNG, stake or post; a measure for affairs 桩	踢	TĪ, to kick 踢皮球 tī píqiú, kick a ball; pass the buck
橫	HÉNG, be horizontal; to set horizontally; horizontal stroke (writing); HÈNG, rude; unexpected	踏	TÀ, to step on; to pedal; to step out, to stroll 踏板 tàbǎn, peddle, treadle
厲	LÌ, be severe, harsh; family name 厲禁 lìjìn, strictly forbid 厉	遺	YÍ, to leave behind 遺迹 yíjī, vestiges 遗
履	LǓ, to carry out; shoe; to walk on; footstep	銳	RUÌ, be sharp 尖銳 jiānruì, be penetrating 锐
慰	WÈI, to console, to soothe 慰問 wèiwèn, to console	鋤	CHÚ, hoe, to hoe 鋤頭 chútou, hoe 锄

296

稻	DÀO, rice plant; paddy 稻田 *dàotián*, rice paddy
膠	JIĀO, be sticky; glue; sticky stuff; rubber, plastic 胶
皺	ZHÒU, be wrinkled; to wrinkle 皺紋 *zhòuwén*, wrinkles 皱
激	JĪ, to force out under pressure (as water); to spray; to stir up
憑	PÍNG, to lean on; due to the fact that; basis; What! (exclamation of surprise) 凭
辨	BIÀN, to tell apart 辨別 *biànbié*, to tell apart
謎	MÍ, riddle 謎語 *míyǔ*, riddle 谜
諜	DIÉ, to spy 諜報員 *diébàoyuán*, a spy 谍
糕	GĀO, cake 糕點 *gāodiǎn*, cake
燃	RÁN, to burn, set on fire 燃燒 *ránshāo*, to burn, to set on fire
融	RÓNG, to smelt 融合 *rónghé*, to fuse

擁	YŌNG, to hug; to crowd; to rally to the support of; support 拥
擋	DǍNG, to block 阻擋 *zǔdǎng*, to resist 挡
奮	FÈN, to rouse; be aroused 奮鬥 *fèndòu*, to struggle 奋
磚	ZHUĀN, brick, tile 磚廠 *zhuānchǎng*, brickyard 砖
蔬	SHŪ, pulse, legumes 蔬菜 *shūcài*, vegetables
瞞	MÁN, to blind, to deceive 瞞哄 *mánhǒng*, to deceive 瞒
鴨	YĀ, duck (the fowl) 公鴨 *gōngyā*, drake 鸭
嘴	ZUǏ, mouth, bill, spout 閉嘴 *bìzuǐ*, Shut up!
錫	XĪ, tin, copper 錫匠 *xījiàng*, tinsmith 锡
錘	CHUÍ, hammer, to hammer; weight on a steelyard 锤
築	ZHÙ, to ram down, build 建築 *jiànzhù*, build, building 筑

澀	SÈ, to taste tart; to feel rough (to the touch) 涩	薑	JIĀNG, ginger; family name 姜
賽	SÀI, to compete, to rival 賽馬 *sàimǎ*, horse race 赛	瞭	LIǍO, to finish, to conclude; to understand; LIÀO, to look into the distance 了
糞	FÈN, manure, shit 糞土 *fèntǔ*, dung and dirt 粪	顆	KĒ, a measure for seeds, grains, bullets, stars, jewels 颗
臨	LÍN, be near; to copy (a painting or calligraphy) 临	闊	KUÒ, be wealthy; be broad 闊老 *kuòlǎo*, rich guy 阔
醜	CHǑU, be ugly 醜惡 *chǒu'è*, be hideous 丑	嚇	XIÀ, to scare; HÈ, to threaten 嚇壞了 *xiàhuàile*, be scared silly 吓
擦	CĀ, to rub, wipe, brush, scrape 擦澡 *cāzǎo*, take a sponge bath	鮮	XIĀN, be fresh; to taste delicious; XIǍN, be rare 鲜
擠	JǏ, to crowd, be crowded; to squeeze (e.g., a pimple) 挤	儲	CHǓ, to collect; family name 儲蓄 *chǔxù*, save; deposit (bank) 储
隸	LÌ, be attached to; be controlled by 隸屬 *lìshǔ*, be subordinate to 隶	縱	ZÒNG, to let something go uncontrolled; vertical; even though 纵
翼	YÌ, wing 翼手動物 *yìshǒu dòngwù*, a bat (the animal)	瀉	XIÈ, to flow swiftly; to have diarrhea 瀉藥 *xièyào*, laxative 泻
薪	XĪN, firewood; salary 薪金 *xīnjīn*, salary	灑	SǍ, to sprinkle, to spill 灑淚 *sǎlèi*, to weep 洒
薦	JIÀN, to recommend someone 薦舉 *jiànjǔ*, to recommend 荐	額	É, forehead; fixed number, quota 額外 *éwài*, extra 额

戀	LIÀN, to love 戀愛 *liànài*, to love <div align="right">恋</div>	鬚	XŪ, whiskers, beard 留鬚 *liúxū*, grow a beard <div align="right">须</div>
懷	HUÁI, bosom; to embosom; to carry next to the bosom; be pregnant; to harbor; have in mind <div align="right">怀</div>	覆	FÙ, to overturn, defeat; to cover; to reply; to repeat (short form for latter two only) <div align="right">复</div>
癢	YĂNG, to itch, tickle 怕癢 *pàyǎng*, be ticklish <div align="right">痒</div>	攤	TĀN, to spread out, to display; vendor's stand; to spread around <div align="right">摊</div>
襪	WÀ, stocking, sock 襪子 *wàzi*, stockings, socks <div align="right">袜</div>	櫃	GUÌ, counter (in a store), showcase, cupboard, cabinet, wardrobe; store <div align="right">柜</div>
襖	ĂO, coat, jacket 棉襖 *miánǎo*, cotton padded jacket <div align="right">袄</div>	麵	MIÀN, flour; noodle 麵包 *miànbāo*, bread <div align="right">面</div>
霸	BÀ, bully, tyrant, to bully, to tyrannize 霸道 *bàdao*, be overbearing; strong (liquor)	戳	CHUŌ, to jab; to stand a thing up; stamp, seal 戳穿 *chuōchuān*, to puncture, to expose
露	LÙ, dew, juice; to expose to view 露天 *lùtiān*, be outdoors	曬	SHÀI, to sun a thing; be sunny and hot 曬被子 *shài bèizi*, to sun a quilt <div align="right">晒</div>
靈	LÍNG, be effective; be alert; spirit, soul; remains (of the dead) <div align="right">灵</div>	蟲	CHÓNG, bug; worm 蟲害 *chónghài*, insect pest <div align="right">虫</div>
騎	QÍ, to sit astride; to ride (e.g., an animal or bicycle) <div align="right">骑</div>	壘	LĔI, to heap up; ramparts 壁壘 *bìlěi*, ramparts <div align="right">垒</div>
騾	LUÓ, mule <div align="right">骡</div>	饑	JĪ, famine; to go hungry 饑荒 *jīhuāng*, famine <div align="right">饥</div>
鬆	SŌNG, be loose, to loosen up; be easy-going; be light (said of cakes) <div align="right">松</div>	鑲	XIĀNG, to inlay, set (as, jewels); trim with 鑲嵌 *xiāngqiàn*, to inlay with <div align="right">镶</div>

299

鑼	LUÓ, gong 锣	沿	YÁN, border, edge; to follow, to fringe; along 沿海 *yánhǎi*, along the coast
鑰	YÀO, key 钥	牧	MÙ, to herd, tend 牧童 *mùtóng*, shepherd boy, buffalo boy
籍	JÍ, population record, register; membership 國籍 *guójí*, nationality	紛	FĒN, tangled, confusing; profuse 紛擾 *fēnrǎo*, be in turmoil 纷
仍	RÉNG, as before, still 仍然 *réngrán*, still, yet	衛	WÈI, to defend; guard; a family name 衛兵 *wèibīng*, a guard 卫
判	PÀN, to separate, to judge Printed 判.	亦	YÌ, (bookish) and, also; both... and... (H rad. 162) 亦即 *yìjí*, namely, *viz.*
狀	ZHUÀNG, shape, appearance; condition; document. Not = 壯 (1048), 莊 (p.271a) 状	乛	No pronunciation, H. rad. 5 "Back-turned stroke"
席	XÍ, mat; banquet; measure for banquets; family name 一席酒 *yì xí jiǔ*, a banquet	丁	No pronunciation. H rad. 6 "Top of 刁 *diáo*"
淺	QIĂN, be shallow, superficial; be mild 膚淺 *fūqiǎn*, be superficial 浅	𠂇	No pronunciation. H rad. 14 "Top of 左 *zuǒ*"
犧	XĪ; used mainly in 犧牲 *xīshēng*, sacrifice 牺	𠂉	No pronunciation. H rad. 20 "Top of 每 *měi*"
譽	YÙ, fame; praise, to praise 誉	厂	No pronunciation. H rad. 22 "Top of 盾 *dùn*"
纏	CHÁN, to wrap around, to roll up; to keep bothering someone 缠	乂	No pronunciation. H rad. 25 "Bottom of 义 *yì*" (see 935, above, short form)

300

几	No pronunciation. With 几 *jī* "table" (r. 16; 645, above) this top of 風 *fēng* and 朵 *duǒ* = H. rad. 30.	○	LÍNG, zero 五〇九號, *wǔlíngjiǔ hào*, No. 509
マ	No pronunciation. H rad. 31 "Top of 予 *yú*"	屯	TÚN, to collect; to station (troops); village 屯糧 *túnliáng*, to store grain
主	No pronunciation. H rad. 89 "Top of 青 *qīng*"	凸	TŪ, to protrude, stick up 凸面 *tūmiàn*, be convex
耂	No pronunciation. H rad. 92 "Top of 老 *lǎo*"	凹	ĀO, be concave, sunken in 凹凸不平 *āotū bùpíng*, be full of holes and bumps, uneven
聿	No pronunciation. H. rad. 124. "Top of 書 *yù*"	卵	LUǍN, egg, ovum; spawn 卵黃 *luǎnhuáng*, egg yolk
夫	No pronunciation. H rad. 130. "Top of 春 *chūn*"	叛	PÀN, to rebel against 叛變 *pànbiàn*, to turn traitor
艹	No pronunciation. H rad. 134. "Top of 労" (= short form of 勞 *láo*, p. 254a)		Also in the H. category of 餘類 *yúlèi*, "leftovers," are five characters which the student has learned; the short form, 东, of 東 *dōng*, "east" (165, above); 巴 *bā* "the open hand," (276, above); the short form 乡 of 鄉 *xiāng*, "country" (350, above); 民 *mín*, "folk" (624, above); and the short form 举 of 舉 *jǔ*, "to lift" (934, above).
尚	No pronunciation. H rad. 139. "Top of 常 *cháng*"		
𢆶	No pronunciation. H rad. 165. "Top of 栽 *zāi*"		
卓	No pronunciation. H rad. 203. "Side of 朝 *zhāo*"	末	MÒ, last part; end; dust 末尾 *mòwěi*, the end
	餘類 *yúlèi*, the 227th category in H, "leftovers," for these eleven "leftovers," see the column on right.		

301

INDEXES

ALPHABETICAL INDEX

The alphabetical index includes all the characters presented in this book. The characters are alphabetized according to their pronunciation in the *Hanyu Pinyin* system of romanization. A character with two or more pronunciations will appear under each pronunciation. All characters with the same *Hanyu Pinyin* spellings are listed in order of ascending tone. Exceptions to this arise in the case of phonetic-series listings; here, the character that provides the key to the phonetic series appears first, followed by characters sharing that element and having the same reading. Since the tone of the key character may sometimes be numerically higher than that of a character in its group, the student should make sure, when using this index, to scan up and down a group of characters sharing the same spelling. This kind of index arrangement reflects the nature of the Chinese writing system and therefore provides a convenient visual review aid.

If a character is in the first character group, that character's series number (1–1062) is given in roman type. If a character is also a traditional radical, its number in the sequence of 214 radicals is given in superscript. Characters in the second group are referenced by the page number (pp. 245–301) set in italic type and followed by the letter *a* or *b* to indicate whether the character appears on the left (*a*) or right (*b*) side of the page.

307

pinyin	char	ref
fū	膚	p.296b
fú	俘	p.274a
fú, fù	浮	p.274a
fú	伏	p.282b
fú	弗	869
fú	扶	p.283a
fú	复	908
fù	復	909
fù	複	911
fù	覆	p.299b
fú	福	p.254b
fù	副	p.254b
fù	富	p.254b
fú, fù	服	839
fǔ	甫	404
fù	付	815
fú	符	p.253a
fǔ	府	816
fǔ	腐	p.253a
fù	附	p.253a
fù	婦	p.263a
fù	父	211[88]
fǔ	斧	p.266b
fù	負	1030
fù	傅	638
fù	阜	p.264b[170]
fù	卜	76[170]

—G—

pinyin	char	ref
gāi	該	926
gǎi	改	734
gài	概	p.296a
gài	蓋	p.295a
gān	乾	617
gān	甘	144[99]
gān	干	87[51]
gān	肝	p.247a
gān, gǎn	桿	p.247a
gǎn	稈	p.247a
gǎn	趕	p.247a
gàn	幹	p.247a
gǎn	感	p.251b
gǎn	敢	652
gāng	岡	96
gāng	剛	759
gāng	崗	p.259b
gāng	綱	p.259b
gāng	鋼	97
gāng	缸	p.286a
gǎng	港	p.255b
gāo	高	75[189]
gāo	膏	p.276a
gǎo	搞	p.275b
gǎo	稿	p.275b
gāo	糕	p.297a
gǎo	杲	161
gào	告	261
gē	割	p.290b
gē	哥	217
gē	歌	318
gē	戈	43[62]
gé	革	369[177]
gè	個	170
gè	各	320
gé	格	p.260a
gè	高	p.268a[193]
gé	隔	p.293a
gěi	給	177
gěn	艮	31[138]
gēn	根	827
gēn	跟	197
gēng	庚	p.271a
gēng	耕	p.249a
gèng	更	125
gōng	公	862
gōng	工	443[43]
gōng	功	p.246b
gōng	攻	p.246b
gòng	貢	p.246b
gōng	弓	218[57]
gōng	躬	988
gōng	宮	p.286b
gǒng	廾	141[55]
gòng	共	297
gōng, gòng	供	p.255a
gōng	恭	p.255b
gōu	勾	p.281b
gǒu	狗	p.249b
gǒu	苟	978
gòu	夠	290
gòu	冓	634
gōu	溝	p.275b
gòu	購	p.275b
gǔ	古	168
gū	估	p.276a
gū	姑	p.276a
gù	固	169
gù	故	441
gū	孤	p.284b
gǔ	穀	p.295b
gǔ	股	p.284b
gǔ	谷	373[150]
gǔ	賈	817
gǔ	骨	511[188]
gǔ	鼓	p.261a[207]
gù	雇	p.255b
gù	顧	p.255b
guā	刮	p.284b
guā	瓜	p.281b[97]
guǎ	寡	p.294a
guà	掛	p.246a
guài	夬	469
guài	怪	592
guàn	丱	504
guān	絲	505
guān	關	506
guān	官	407
guǎn	管	742
guǎn	館	408

310

hūn	昏	779	jì, jǐ	忌	p.283b	jiǎn	簡	771
hūn	婚	780	jì	記	738	jiǎn	儉	p.254b
hún	魂	p.294b	jǐ	幾	419	jiǎn	檢	1015
hùn	混	p.263b	jī	機	420	jiǎn	剪	p.277a
huó	活	663	jī	饑	p.299b	jiàn	箭	p.277a
huǒ	火	414⁸⁶	jǐ	擠	p.298a	jiàn	煎	p.277a
huǒ	⺍	34⁸⁶	jì	濟	1046	jiǎn	柬	1002
huǒ	伙	p.282b	jǐ	給	177	jiǎn	揀	p.291a
huǒ	夥	p.295a	jì	季	p.256a	jiǎn	減	885
huò, huo	和	p.245a	jì	寄	956	jiàn	件	477
huò	或	113	jì	与	997⁵⁸	jiàn	建	848
huò	惑	p.281a	jì	子	80⁵⁸	jiàn	健	p.290a
huò	禍	p.276a	jì	技	p.262a	jiàn	漸	p.253a
huò	蒦	851	jì	既	765	jiàn	薦	p.298a
huò	獲	p.265a	jì	繼	p.246b	jiàn	見	214¹⁴⁷
huò	貨	883	jì	計	1035	jiāng, jiàng	將	947
			jì	際	p.262b	jiǎng	獎	p.276b
	—J—		jiā	加	783	jiǎng	漿	p.276b
jī, jǐ	几	645¹⁶	jiā	架	1053	jiàng	醬	p.276b
jī	基	1054	jiā	夾	p.277a	jiāng	江	615
jī	擊	p.258b	jiā	家	390	jiāng	薑	p.298b
jī	激	p.297a	jià	嫁	p.277b	jiǎng	講	635
jī	績	p.246a	jià	稼	p.277b	jiàng	降	890
jī	積	p.246a	jiǎ	段	931	jiàng	強	p.249b
jī	迹	p.285a	jiǎ, jià	假	932	jiàng	匠	p.282a
jī	鶏	1034	jiǎ	甲	p.270b	jiāo	交	401
jí	人	175	jià	賈	817	jiāo	校	402
jí	即	p.283a	jià	價	818	jiào	較	1047
jí	吉	189	jiān	尖	p.282a	jiāo, jiào	教	386
jí	結	778	jiān	兼	p.268b	jiāo	椒	p.291b
jí	亟	568	jiān	堅	p.289a	jiāo	澆	p.277b
jí	極	569	jiān	莫	370	jiāo	焦	p.277a
jí	急	955	jiān	艱	371	jiāo	繳	p.268b
jí	疾	p.286b	jiān	奸	p.247b	jiāo	膠	p.297a
jí	籍	p.300b	jiān	开	502	jiāo	驕	p.277b
jí	及	p.264a	jiān	戔	166	jiāo	剿	p.294a
jí	級	p.264a	jiàn	賤	758	jiāo	腳	p.290a
jí	集	1025	jiān	監	p.252b	jiǎo	角	904¹⁴⁸
jǐ	己	273⁴⁹	jiān	肩	p.284a	jiào	叫	259
jì	紀	660	jiān	間	204			

kěn	肯	917	lài	賴	1031	lì	立	105[117]
kěn	墾	p.276b	lán	籃	p.252b	lì	粒	p.289a
kěn	懇	p.276b	lán	藍	p.252b	lì	秝	1004
kēng	坑	p.258b	lǎn	覽	p.252b	lì	麻	1005
kōng	空	900	lán	攔	p.275b	lì	曆	1006
kǒng	孔	p.266b	lán	欄	p.275b	lì	歷	1007
kǒng	恐	683	làn	爛	p.275b	lì	隸	p.298a
kǒu	口	33[30]	lǎn	懶	1032	lì	麗	p.254b
kòu	扣	p.282a	láng	狼	p.275a	lì	鬲	p.268a
kū	圣	591	làng	浪	p.275a	lián	憐	p.248b
kū	枯	p.276a	lāo	撈	p.254a	lián	簾	p.275b
kǔ	苦	985	láo	勞	p.254a	lián	鐮	p.275b
kū	哭	542	láo	牢	p.282b	lián	聯	1059
kù	褲	p.295b	lǎo	老	138[125]	lián	連	606
kuā	誇	p.276a	lào	絡	p.292a	liǎn	臉	585
kuǎ	垮	p.276a	le	了	17	liàn	戀	p.299a
kuà	跨	p.276b	lè	樂	894	liàn	煉	p.293a
kuāi	咼	513	lè	雷	p.293a	liàn	練	1003
kuài	塊	292	lěi	壘	p.299b	liáng	良	305
kuài	快	470	lěi	耒	1029[127]	liáng,	量	756
kuài	筷	p.293b	lèi	淚	p.288b	liàng		
kuài	會	330	lèi	累	29	liáng	糧	p.261b
kuān	寬	859	lèi	類	708	liáng	涼	731
kuǎn	款	p.269a	lěng	冷	920	liàng	諒	p.295b
kuāng	筐	p.281a	lí	犁	p.292a	liáng	梁	p.266a
kuáng	狂	p.281a	lí	离	582	liáng	梁	p.266a
kuàng	況	p.249b	lí	離	583	liǎng	兩	307
kuàng	礦	p.254a	lǐ	李	249	liàng	輛	p.295b
kuī	虧	p.250a	lǐ	里	106[166]	liàng	亮	647
kùn	困	902	lǐ	理	735	liǎo	了	17
kuò	括	p.266a	lǐ	裏	449	liǎo, liào	瞭	p.298b
kuò	擴	p.262b	lǐ	豊	479	liào	料	p.256a
kuò	闊	p.298b	lǐ	禮	481	liè	列	p.247b
			lì	例	p.247b	liè	烈	p.247b
			lì	利	937	liè	裂	p.248a
—L—			lì	梨	p.290a	liè	劣	p.282a
lā	拉	1021	lì	力	206[19]	liè	獵	p.275a
la	啦	p.246a	lì	吏	829	lín	林	156
là	臘	p.275a	lì	屬	p.296a	lín, lìn	淋	p.288b
là	辣	p.294a	lì	栗	p.287b	lín	臨	p.298a
lái	來	431						

313

mǒ	抹	*p.284a*	ní	尼	409	pái	排	*p.261a*
mō	莫	853	ní	呢	410	pái	牌	*p.250a*
mō	摸	*p.274a*	ní	泥	*p.251a*	pài	辰	833
mō	模	854	nǐ	你	49	pài	派	834
mò	墨	*p.271b*	nǐ	广	531[104]	pán	盤	*p.256b*
mò	沒	184	nián	年	463	pàn	盼	*p.260b*
mǒu	某	*p.260a*	nián	粘	*p.279a*	pàn	判	*p.300a*
móu	謀	*p.260a*	niàn	廿	142	pàn	叛	*p.301b*
mǔ	母	216	niàn	念	383	páng	旁	785
mǔ	畝	*p.269a*	niáng	娘	*p.255b*	pàng	胖	*p.273b*
mù	木	64[75]	niǎo	鳥	994[196]	pāo	拋	*p.283a*
mù	牧	*p.300b*	niào	尿	*p.283a*	páo	袍	*p.272b*
mù	目	120[109]	niē	捏	*p.285b*	pǎo	跑	510
mù	罒	132[109]	nín	您	71	pào, pāo	泡	*p.272b*
mù	莫	853	níng	寧	*p.268a*	pào	砲	*p.272b*
mú	模	854	niú	牛	260[93]	péi	賠	*p.273b*
mù	墓	*p.274a*	niú	牛	15[93]	péi	陪	*p.273b*
mù	幕	*p.274a*	niǔ	扭	*p.283a*	pèi	配	*p.267b*
			nóng	農	*p.253b*	pēn, pèn	噴	*p.274a*
			nóng	濃	*p.253b*	pén	盆	*p.260a*
	—N—		nòng	弄	*p.250a*	péng	朋	209
ná	拿	483	nú	奴	843	pěng	捧	*p.273a*
nà	納	*p.267b*	nǔ	努	844	pèng	碰	*p.254b*
nà	那	173	nù	怒	*p.286b*	pī	批	*p.258a*
nǎ, na	哪	*p.288a*	nǚ	女	11[38]	pì	屁	*p.258a*
nǎi	奶	*p.281b*	nuǎn	暖	*p.245b*	pī, pǐ	劈	*p.255a*
nài	奈	*p.284b*	nüè	虐	*p.285b*	pí	皮	662[107]
nài	耐	*p.268a*	nùn	嫩	*p.295a*	pí	疲	*p.245a*
nán	男	254				pǐ	匹	146
nán	南	570				pǐ	疋	245[103]
nán	難	372		**—O—**		piān	偏	*p.253b*
nǎo	惱	*p.290b*	ōu	歐	*p.257b*	piān	篇	*p.253b*
nǎo	腦	*p.250a*	ǒu, ou	嘔	*p.257b*	piàn	騙	*p.253b*
nào	鬧	681	ǒu	偶	*p.247b*	piǎn	便	126
ne	呢	410				piàn, piān	片	927[91]
nè, nèi	那	173				piào	票	957
něi	哪	*p.288a*		**—P—**		piāo	飄	*p.264b*
nèi	內	532	pá	爬	*p.273b*	piē, piě	撇	*p.273b*
nèn	嫩	*p.295a*	pà	怕	547	piě	丿	1[4]
néng	能	327	pāi	拍	*p.264a*	pīn	拼	*p.272a*

Pinyin	Character	Ref
rèn	任	822
rèn	刃	522
rěn	忍	523
rèn	認	524
rēng	扔	p.300a
réng	仍	p.300a
rì	日	160[72]
róng	容	374
róng	榮	p.254a
róng	戎	976
róng	絨	p.292b
róng	融	p.297a
róu	柔	p.285b
rǒu	內	488[114]
ròu	肉	928[130]
ròu	月	326[130]
rú	如	787
rǔ	辱	p.287b
rù	入	152[11]
ruǎn	軟	p.289a
ruì	銳	p.296b
rùn	潤	p.295b
ruò	弱	p.254a
ruò	若	p.247b
—S—		
sā, sǎ	撒	p.279b
sǎ	灑	p.298b
sài, sāi	塞	p.293a
sài	賽	p.298a
sān	三	10
sān	參	p.285a
sǎn	傘	p.252b
sàn	散	p.246b
sāng, sàng	喪	p.291a
sāng	桑	p.287b
sǎo	嫂	p.280b
sǎo, sào	掃	p.263b
sè	澀	p.298a
sè	色	901[139]
sēn	森	p.266a
shā	殺	722
shā	沙	p.265a
shā	紗	p.265b
shǎi	色	901[139]
shài	曬	p.299b
shān	山	95[46]
shān	彡	819[59]
shān	衫	p.284a
shǎn	閃	p.288a
shàn	扇	p.287a
shàn	善	p.291a
shāng	傷	p.261b
shāng	商	622
shàng	上	346
shàng	尚	367
shǎng	賞	p.279a
shāo	捎	p.277b
shāo	稍	p.278a
shāo	燒	1013
sháo	勺	233
shǎo	少	288
shào	召	740
shào	紹	741
shé	什	p.281b
shé	折	p.283a
shé	蛇	p.289b
shé	舌	313[135]
shě	捨	p.289a
shè	舍	315
shè	涉	p.263b
shè	射	187
shè	社	797
shè	設	836
shéi	誰	40
shēn	參	945
shēn	深	p.266b
shēn	申	812
shēn	伸	p.283b
shén	神	813
shēn	身	185[158]
shén, shèn	甚	153
shěn	審	p.280a
shěn	嬸	p.280a
shèn	慎	p.279a
shēng	升	887
shēng	生	248[100]
shēng	甥	p.280a
shēng	牲	p.279b
shēng	聲	705
shéng	繩	p.270b
shěng	省	856
shèng	剩	p.264b
shèng	勝	p.252a
shèng	盛	p.267a
shī	失	p.263b
shī	師	p.272a
shī	尸	329[44]
shī	屍	p.285b
shī	施	p.285b
shī	濕	p.251a
shī	詩	p.252b
shí	十	22[24]
shí	什	p.281b
shí	實	770
shí	拾	951
shí	時	456
shí	石	664[112]
shí	識	526
shí	食	306[184]
shí	蝕	309[184]
shì	飾	p.295a
shì	飾	p.293b
shǐ	史	828
shǐ	使	830
shǐ	始	p.260b
shǐ	屎	p.285b
shǐ	矢	63[111]

—T—			tī	梯	p.275a	tú	凸	p.301a
tā	他	7	tì	剔	p.275a	tú	圖	996
tā	她	12	tī	蹄	p.258a	tú	塗	p.294b
tā	牠	16	tī	踢	p.296b	tú	屠	p.250b
tā	它	p.253a	tí	提	916	tú	徒	p.288b
tǎ	塔	p.274b	tí	題	729	tú	途	p.253b
tà	踏	p.296b	tǐ	體	806	tǔ	土	86[32]
tái	台	865	tì	替	803	tǔ, tù	吐	p.275a
tāi	胎	p.274b	tiān	天	52	tù	兔	p.284b
tái	抬	p.274b	tiān	添	p.248b	tuán	團	1039
tài	太	74	tián	填	p.279a	tuī	推	881
tài	態	p.256b	tián	甜	p.290a	tuì	退	p.248a
tān	攤	p.299b	tián	田	23[102]	tuǐ	腿	p.248a
tān	貪	p.289b	tiāo, tiǎo	挑	p.255a	tūn	吞	p.283b
tán	彈	p.262b	tiào	跳	721	tún	屯	p.301b
tán	痰	p.274b	tiáo	條	563	tuō	托	p.269b
tán	談	673	tiáo	調	p.259b	tuō	託	p.269b
tǎn	毯	p.274b	tiē	帖	p.279b	tuō	拖	p.284a
tǎn	坦	p.284a	tiē	貼	p.279b	tuō	脫	p.290a
tàn	探	p.266b	tiě	鐵	864	tuǒ	妥	p.283b
tàn	歎	p.296a	tīng	聽	381			
tàn	炭	p.286a	tīng	廳	p.269b	**—W—**		
tāng	湯	p.261b	tíng	庭	p.269a	wā	挖	p.285b
tàng	燙	p.261b	tǐng	挺	p.269a	wá	娃	p.286b
táng	唐	311	tíng	亭	752	wǎ	瓦	p.271b[98]
táng	塘	p.293a	tíng	停	753	wà	襪	p.299a
táng	糖	312	tōng	通	716	wài	外	119
táng	堂	987	tǒng	桶	p.289a	wān	彎	p.266b
tǎng	倘	p.274b	tòng	痛	1011	wān	灣	p.266b
tǎng	躺	p.274b	tóng	同	775	wán	丸	677
tàng	趟	p.274b	tǒng, tǒng	筒	p.251b	wán	完	548
táo	桃	p.254a	tóng	銅	984	wán	玩	93
táo	逃	p.254a	tóng	童	107	wán	頑	p.293a
tǎo	討	p.251a	tǒng	統	880	wǎn	挽	p.287b
tào	套	p.287b	tōu	偷	975	wǎn	晚	440
tè	特	608	tóu	一	37[8]	wǎn	碗	p.249b
téng	疼	p.286b	tóu	投	p.283a	wàn	萬	490
téng	滕	p.252a	tóu	頭	454	wāng	尢	59[43]
téng	藤	p.252a	tòu	透	p.256a	wáng	亡	68
téng, tēng	騰	p.252a	tū	突	p.285a	wǎng	網	p.259b

xiàn	限	915	xiè	卸	p.286a	xū	鬚	p.299b
xiāng	皂	349	xiè	械	p.277a	xǔ	許	595
xiāng	鄉	350	xiè	謝	188	xù	續	p.247a
xiǎng	響	p.258a	xīn	心	70[61]	xù	序	p.262a
xiāng, xiàng	相	294	xīn	忄	67[61]	xù	敘	p.289b
			xīn	小	p.248b[61]	xù	畜	p.266a
xiāng	箱	p.278a	xīn	新	355	xù	蓄	p.266a
xiǎng	想	295	xīn	薪	p.298a	xù	綉	p.256a
xiāng	襄	706	xīn	欣	p.278a	xù	緒	p.250b
xiāng	鑲	p.299b	xīn	辛	549[160]	xuān	宣	p.263b
xiāng	香	1044[186]	xìn	信	487	xuán	旋	p.288b
xiáng	祥	p.287a	xīng	星	929	xuán	玄	p.248a[95]
xiáng	詳	824	xīng	腥	p.250a	xuǎn	選	777
xiáng	降	890	xǐng	醒	p.250a	xué	學	253
xiǎng	享	1040	xíng	刑	p.278a	xué	穴	574[116]
xiàng	巷	p.255b	xíng	型	p.278a	xuě	血	922[143]
xiàng	向	793	xíng	形	886	xuě	雪	993
xiàng	象	643	xíng	行	421[144]	xūn	熏	p.295a
xiàng	像	644	xìng	杏	p.283a	xún	尋	p.291b
xiàng	項	p.246b	xìng, xīng	興	991	xùn	巽	776
xiǎo	小	27[42]				xùn	訊	p.286b
xiào	孝	385	xìng	幸	89	xùn	訓	p.245b
xiào	肖	939	xìng	姓	255			
xiào	削	p.277b	xìng	性	790		—Y—	
xiào	消	940	xiōng	兄	237			
xiào	銷	p.277b	xiōng	凶	581	yā	壓	p.258a
xiào	效	p.261a	xiōng	兇	p.282a	yā	鴨	p.297b
xiào	校	402	xiōng	胸	p.288a	yá	牙	576[92]
xiǎo	曉	1014	xióng	雄	p.291b	yā	呀	p.280b
xiào	笑	56	xiū	修	855	yā	鴉	p.280b
xiē	些	269	xiū	休	709	yá	芽	p.280b
xiē	歇	p.293b	xiū	羞	p.287a	yà, yǎ	亞	p.262b
xié	協	p.284a	xiǔ	宿	p.280b	yǎ	啞	p.263a
xié	挾	p.277a	xiù	嗅	p.279b	yān	淹	p.288b
xié	斜	p.289b	xiù	秀	p.256a	yān	烟	969
xié	邪	p.283a	xiù	袖	p.266a	yán	延	p.285a
xié	鞋	964	xū	戌	498	yán	嚴	p.268a
xiě	寫	347	xū	虛	p.289b	yán	炎	672
xiě	血	923[143]	xū	需	971	yán	鹽	p.252b
xiè	瀉	p.298b	xū	須	p.245b	yán	研	767
						yán	言	38[149]

zhǔn	準	630	zǒng	總	605	zuì	最	366
zhuō	捉	p.287b	zǒng	縱	p.298b	zuì	罪	p.246b
zhuō	桌	162	zǒu	走	434[156]	zuì	醉	p.250a
zī	姿	p.259b	zū	租	970	zūn	尊	p.267b
zī	資	p.259b	zǔ	祖	804	zūn	遵	p.267b
zǐ	姊	p.284a	zǔ	組	906	zuó	昨	436
zǐ	子	18[39]	zǔ	阻	p.263b	zuò	作	343
zì	字	257	zú	族	p.259b	zuǒ	广	179
zǐ	紫	p.291b	zú	足	196[157]	zuǒ	左	572
zì	自	515[132]	zuǎn,	鑽	p.254a	zuò	做	p.267a
zōng	宗	808	zuān, zuàn			zuò	坐	430
zōng	蹤	p.296b	zuǐ	嘴	p.297b	zuò	座	p.289a

STROKE COUNT-STROKE ORDER
INDEX

This second index of characters is arranged by stroke count and stroke order and therefore enables the student to find, for reference or review, any character in this book whose pronunciation he or she does not know or is unsure of. The index has been organized by the stroke count-stroke order system rather than the traditional radical system because mastery of the latter requires considerable time. Mastery of the radicals is one of the goals of this book, not a skill assumed of its users, whereas the stroke count-stroke order system can be used by a student almost immediately. It is also a system that, as George Kennedy says, "appears to be widely used in China today."

In order to use the index, you should first count the number of strokes in the character under consideration. As you learn new characters and how to write them from the diagrams, the ability to count correctly the number of strokes and learn the little tricks familiar to every first year student of Chinese will come naturally. (For example, the shape ㄱ is counted as one stroke rather than two.) Characters in this index are grouped according to the total number of strokes in the character, beginning with characters having the fewest strokes (1 to 3 strokes) and concluding with those having the most strokes (18 or more). Where a discrepancy exists, count the strokes that are actually made as you write the character by hand rather than use the "official" count traditionally used in Chinese dictionaries.

You must then determine into which of the following four categories the *first stroke* in the character falls: 1) a dot, including any stroke downward to the right; 2) a horizontal stroke, including any angle that begins with a left to right horizontal; 3) a vertical stroke, including angles that begin with a vertical; or 4) a left, downward-slanting stroke, including angles that begin this way. To summarize:

1.	Dot	`	or	╰
2.	Across	─	or	┐
3.	Down	│	or	└
4.	Left	)	or	<

All characters with the same number of strokes are subdivided into these four categories of "first strokes." Much like an alphabetical system, these categories are further ordered according to the category (dot, across, down, left) into which the *second stroke* of the character falls. For example, if one character has twelve strokes and its first and second strokes are "dots" (盜) , it will appear before a character of twelve strokes of which the first is a dot and the second a horizontal stroke (童), and so on. Note that characters whose first element is the common "grass radical" 艹 are classified in the stroke count-stroke order system as if the first stroke were a downstroke, though this differs from the writing diagrams in the text.

All of the characters appearing in *Reading and Writing Chinese* are given here, with the exception of characters that appear in modern texts only as parts of other characters. The index does, however, include all forms of traditional radicals. On pages 300–301 of the text itself are introduced all *Han-Ying Cidian* radicals which have not been introduced earlier. A complete chart of *Han-Ying Cidian* radicals appears as the back endpapers.

The system of reference to characters and page numbers is explained in the introduction to the Alphabetical Index on page 304.

5 strokes

7 strokes

8 strokes

牌	p.250a
眾	p.257a
順	p.245b
堡	p.292b
貿	p.292b
猶	p.292b
猴	p.276b
街	423
復	909
須	p.245b
嫂	p.280b
統	880
結	778
絨	p.292b
給	177
絡	p.292b
絕	p.245b
絲	665
幾	419

13 strokes

[丶]

溝	p.275b
源	p.265a
梁	p.266a
溫	925
滑	p.292b
減	p.265a
塗	p.292b
準	630
溜	p.293a
塞	p.293a
資	p.259b
新	355
意	336
該	926
詳	824
試	943
詩	p.252b

[丨]

掌	p.279a
悲	p.261a
紫	p.291b
華	789
著	p.260b
菌	p.291b
莧	858
菜	518
黑	280[203]
遇	p.247b
過	514
喝	388
喂	p.292a
喘	p.274b
喊	p.251b
喚	960
喉	p.276b
景	774
貼	p.279b
晴	p.252a
晚	440
暑	p.250b
量	756
最	366
悶	p.292a
開	503
間	204
閒	203
晶	p.292a
距	p.268b
跌	p.292a
跑	510
貴	124
單	772
帽	354
買	133
嵛	p.271a[204]
嵌	p.292a
與	933

[丿]

爲	459
飲	p.292a
飯	310
創	p.249a
舒	p.246b
傘	p.252b
筐	p.281a
等	467
策	p.262a
筆	91
筒	p.251b
答	882
筋	p.292a
筍	p.292a
甥	p.280a
毯	p.274b
短	566
智	p.271b
剩	p.264b
無	749
稅	239
稍	p.278a
稈	p.247a
程	p.292a
稀	p.292a
犁	p.292a
黍	p.292b[202]
然	593
腔	p.292b
勝	p.252a
脹	p.278b
象	643
焦	p.277a
集	1025
傲	p.292b
傅	638
備	694
偉	p.258b
貸	p.292b

347

348

漢英詞典

The Chart of Modern Radicals

— 1 —

1. 、 dot 61
2. 一 one 8
3. 丨 down 3
4. 丿 left 1
5. ㇖ "back-turned stroke" *p. 300*
6. 乛 "top of 刁 ," *p. 300*
7. 乙 twist *p. 281, 5*

— 2 —

8. 冫 ice 564
9. 宀 lid 37
10. 讠 (side-) words 38 (cp. H185)
11. 二 two 9
12. 十 ten 22
13. 厂 slope 154
14. ナ "top of 左" *p. 300*
15. 匚 basket 143
16. 卜 (⺊) divine 118
17. 刂 knife 205
18. 冖 crown 47
19. 冂 borders 20
20. ⺈ "top of 每" *p. 300*
21. 亻 (side-)man 4
22. ⺊ "top of 盾" *p. 300*
23. 人 (入) man (enter) 2 (152)
24. 八 (䒑) eight 98, 88
25. 乂 "bottom of 义" *p. 300*
26. 勹 wrap 232
27. 刀 (勹) knife (--) 102
28. 力 strength 206
29. 儿 legs 57
30. 几 (几) table 645 (*p. 301*)
31. 乛 "top of 予" *p. 301*
32. 卩 seal 84
33. 阝 (on the left of characters) mound ("left ear") 76
34. 阝 (on the right of characters) city ("right ear") 136
35. 又 right hand 85
36. 辶 march 847
37. 厶 cocoon 24
38. 凵 bowl 464
39. 匕 ladle 137

— 3 —

40. 氵 "three-dots water" 181
41. 忄 heart 67
42. 爿 bed 849
43. 亡 to die 68
44. 广 lean-to 155
45. 宀 roof 127
46. 门 gate 45
47. 辶 halt 171
48. 工 work 443
49. 土 (士) earth (knight) 86 (134)
50. 艹 grass 192
51. 廾 clasp 141
52. 大 big 50
53. 尢 lame 59
54. 寸 thumb 186
55. 扌 (side-) hand 14
56. 弋 dart 42
57. 巾 cloth 352
58. 口 mouth 33
59. 囗 surround 21
60. 山 mountain 95
61. 屮 sprout 465
62. 彳 step 30
63. 彡 streaks 819
64. 夕 dusk 117
65. 夂 follow, slow 319, 337
66. 丸 bullet 677
67. 尸 corpse 329
68. 饣 (side-) food 309 (cp. H217)
69. 犭 (side-) dog, *p. 251* (cp. H96)
70. 彐 (彑, 彐) pig's head 80, 997
71. 弓 bow 218
72. 己 (巳) self (--) 273, (275)
73. 女 woman 11
74. 子 (孑) child (--) 18
75. 马 horse 35
76. 幺 coil 25
77. 纟 (糸) silk 28, 174
78. 巛 river 442
79. 小 (⺌) small 27

— 4 —

80. 灬 "fire-dots" 34
81. 心 heart 70
82. 斗 peck 1009

— 5 —

83. 火 fire 414
84. 文 pattern 360
85. 方 square 392
86. 户 door 391
87. 礻 (side-) sign 480 (cp. H132)
88. 王 king 92
89. 土 "top of 青" *p. 301*
90. 天 (夭) heaven (tender) 52 (53)
91. 韦 walk off 875
92. 耂 "top of 老" *p. 301*
93. 廿 twenty 142
94. 木 tree 64
95. 不 not 73
96. 犬 dog 541
97. 歹 chip 727
98. 瓦 tile, *p. 271*
99. 牙 tooth 576
100. 车 car 412
101. 戈 lance 43
102. 止 toe 195
103. 日 sun 160
104. 曰 say 82
105. 中 middle 112
106. 贝 cowrie 123
107. 见 see 214
108. 父 father 211
109. 气 breath 324
110. 牛 cow 260, 15
111. 手 hand 41
112. 毛 fur 293
113. 攵 knock 384
114. 片 slice 927
115. 斤 axe 262
116. 爪 (⺥) claws *p. 273* (338)
117. 尺 foot (length) 857
118. 月 moon 178
119. 殳 club 183
120. 欠 yawn 191
121. 风 wind 725
122. 氏 clan 224
123. 比 compare 567
124. 聿 "top of 書" *p. 301*
125. 水 water 362

126. 立 stand 105
127. 疒 sick 531
128. 穴 cave 574